Hark the Sound
of Tar Heel Voices

ALSO BY DANIEL W. BAREFOOT

Let Us Die Like Brave Men
General Robert F. Hoke: Lee's Modest Warrior
Haunted Halls of Ivy
North Carolina's Haunted Hundred: Haints of the Hills
North Carolina's Haunted Hundred: Piedmont Phantoms
North Carolina's Haunted Hundred: Seaside Spectres
Touring South Carolina's Revolutionary War Sites
Touring North Carolina's Revolutionary War Sites
Touring the Backroads of North Carolina's Lower Coast
Touring the Backroads of North Carolina's Upper Coast

EDITED BY DANIEL W. BAREFOOT

Hark the Sound of Tar Heel Voices

220 YEARS OF UNC HISTORY

JOHN F. BLAIR
PUBLISHER
Winston-Salem, North Carolina

JOHN F. BLAIR
PUBLISHER
1406 Plaza Drive
Winston-Salem, North Carolina 27103

First John F. Blair Publisher trade paperback edition September 2008

Manufactured in the United States of America

Cover design by Angela Harwood and Debra Long Hampton

COVER PHOTOGRAPHS
Courtesy of The North Carolina Collection, University of North Carolina at Chapel Hill

TOP LEFT TO RIGHT
Charles Bishop Kuralt (1934–1997) and William Clyde Friday made during University Day 1972
Andrew "Andy" Samuel Griffith in WUNC-TV television studio, 1957
Coach Dean E. Smith signaling for the "4 corners" during a game, ca. 1997
Portrait of Doris Betts (1932–) dated April 13, 1973
Thomas Clayton Wolfe in The Return of Buck Gavin, *1919*

BOTTOM
Old East, South Building and the Old Well, ca. 1963

Library of Congress Cataloging-in-Publication Data
Hark the sound of Tar Heel voices : 220 years of UNC history / edited by Daniel W. Barefoot.
     p.   cm.
  Includes bibliographical references and index.
  ISBN-13: 978-0-89587-365-1 (alk. paper)
  ISBN-10: 0-89587-365-6 (alk. paper)
  1. University of North Carolina at Chapel Hill—History—Sources. 2. University of North Carolina at Chapel Hill—Faculty—Anecdotes. 3. University of North Carolina at Chapel Hill—Students—Anecdotes. I. Barefoot, Daniel W., 1951–
  LD3943.H37 2008
  378.756'565—dc22   2008020749

www.blairpub.com

*To my two special
"Carolina girls," Kay and Kristie*

Contents

Preface

As the birthplace of publicly supported higher education in the New World, the University of North Carolina at Chapel Hill holds an unparalleled place in the history of the American republic. After it opened its doors in the last decade of the eighteenth century, the university cut the path, blazed the trail, and paved the road for all of the other great state universities in America. As the only state university to operate under the administration of every American president, the historic institution in Chapel Hill has countless stories to tell. In the pages that follow, you will read a cross-section of those stories as told in the firsthand accounts of the very people who lived and made the history of the University of North Carolina.

This volume offers a unique glimpse at life and times on the campus of the nation's oldest public university during the four centuries it has spanned. Never before has a book offered a sample of letters, diary and journal entries, speeches, narratives, interviews, and other first-person accounts about the university from every decade of its history. These writings represent the words of American presidents, university administrators, professors, students, coaches, journalists, and friends and supporters of the venerable institution. This book is not intended to be a complete narrative history of the university; rather, it is meant to offer a view of the lives and events that shaped the university through the words and memories of the men and women who came to Chapel Hill over the years to teach, learn, and partake of the academic excellence and freedom so long synonymous with the University of North Carolina at Chapel Hill.

Over the long history of the university, generations of students, professors, journalists, and others have exhibited a wide variety of writing styles and abilities. In an attempt to present their firsthand narratives as they were written, I have made limited editorial changes in this volume. Only where necessary for clarity have I effected corrections as to spelling, punctuation, syntax, etc.

About his alma mater, Thomas Wolfe, the celebrated novelist, once wrote to a former classmate at Chapel Hill, "So far from forgetting this blessed place, I think my picture of it grows clearer and clearer every year: it was as close to magic as I've ever been." No doubt, many of the students who preceded Tom Wolfe at the university held the sentiments he so eloquently expressed, and those of us who followed the famed author to "the Hill" have firsthand knowledge of the very magic of which he wrote.

My blood turned Carolina blue in the late summer of 1969, when my parents took me to Chapel Hill as an eighteen-year-old freshman. Before unloading all of my stuff at Teague Residence Hall, the three of us decided to have lunch on Franklin Street in the heart of Chapel Hill. My father, unfamiliar with the eateries along the famous street that borders the campus, happened upon Harry's, a now-defunct tavern located near the old post office building. Lunch in the legendary hangout of the longhaired hippies of that time was a difficult and alarming experience for my folks. My mother later told me that she, amid her tears on the long drive back to Catawba County, cried out to my father, "What have we taken our son into?"

Despite my mother's heartfelt misgivings, my parents took me to the magical place where I received a world-class education in the General College, the College of Arts and Sciences, and the School of Law; they took me to the place where I received excellent preparation for my career in law, writing, public speaking, and politics; they took me to the place where my skills in thinking critically and reasoning clearly were developed; they took me to the place where I began my serious study of history in the largest collections of materials related to North Carolina and the South in the entire world; they took me to the place where I broadened my horizons and gained an appreciation for the great diversity in our world; and they took me to the place where I found the love of my life.

It was almost two years from the day I first set foot on the Chapel Hill campus that Kay Townsend, a seventeen-year-old freshman from Winston-Salem, enrolled as a member of the first relatively large class of female students. Less than two weeks after her arrival, we met by chance at an ice-cream social on the lawn in front of her dormitory, Kenan Hall. For me, at least, it was love at first sight. In but a short time, we were college sweethearts, and for the last thirty-four years, that beautiful Carolina coed has been my wife.

Our daughter, Kristie, was born with Carolina blue blood coursing in her veins. Thirty years after my parents departed Chapel Hill in tears, the circle was complete as Kay and I left Kristie behind at Granville Towers as a freshman member of the class of 2003.

Throughout the chapters of this book, which are arranged chronologically, you will find selections that range from special moments on the campus to the mundane days of college life, from humor and mischief to the serious challenges that faced both students and school. Included are first-hand descriptions of how Carolina acquired some of its most famous icons and heroes—how the Old Well gained its world-famous appearance, how Rameses came to be the mascot of the athletic teams, how Dean Smith was hired by the university. You will read the words of far-famed Tar Heels such as Andy Griffith and Charles Kuralt and Frank Porter Graham, as well as the words of Tar Heels who made their mark in their own little corners of the world. Through them, you will relive the birth, growth, struggles, setbacks, problems, challenges, and triumphs of the University of North Carolina at Chapel Hill, which today stands as one of the premier seats of higher learning, public or private, in all the world.

As the nineteenth century drew to a close, William Starr Myers, class of 1897, penned the words to the song that became the official alma mater of the university. Since that time, the opening words to Myers's "Hail to the Brightest Star" have been slightly modified, and generations of Carolina faithful the world over have proudly proclaimed, "Hark the sound of Tar Heel voices, ringing clear and true."

Acknowledgments

This documentary history of the University of North Carolina at Chapel Hill would not have been possible without the magnificent historical research and preservation of documents provided over the years by eminent historians of the university such as Stephen B. Weeks, Kemp Plummer Battle, R. D. W. Connor, Archibald Henderson, J. G. De Roulhac Hamilton, Louis Round Wilson, Hugh T. Lefler, William D. Snider, William S. Powell, and H. G. Jones. Their names stand front rank among the greatest historians produced by North Carolina.

Unlike the previous ten books I have written, research for this volume, by its very nature, was confined to one institution—the University of North Carolina at Chapel Hill. On my numerous research visits, the staffs at the North Carolina Collection and the Southern Historical Collection were always helpful, cheerful, and knowledgeable. Bob Anthony, the very able curator of the North Carolina Collection, made it a point to offer his assistance to me on many of my visits to Wilson Library.

Friends and acquaintances often ask about the current project upon which I am working. And so it was when Sam Southern, a fellow attorney and my colleague on the USS *North Carolina* Battleship Commission, inquired about this project at a commission meeting. He gladly and generously provided me a copy of a previously unpublished letter written by his great-grandfather while a student at the university in the 1880s.

A deep debt of gratitude is owed to my publisher, John F. Blair. Carolyn Sakowski, the president of Blair, has long been quite familiar with my unabashed affection for the university, and as a consequence, she proposed this project to me. In doing so, she had me at the words, "University of North Carolina."

I am greatly appreciative that Carolyn and the acquisitions committee at Blair have over the years allowed me to write on the subjects that are near and dear to me—the North Carolina coast, the Civil War, the Revolutionary War, haunted history, and now the University of North Carolina at Chapel Hill.

From the time we first worked together in 1994, Steve Kirk, my editor at Blair, has played a major role in improving each manuscript that I have delivered for publication. His keen eye, his patience, his insightful suggestions and good advice, his hard work, his respect, and his friendship continue to be greatly valued by this author.

Debbie Hampton, Kim Byerly, Ed Southern, and the remainder of the Blair staff, past and present, with whom I have worked these many years are due much credit for the book you hold in your hands.

Most of all, my family is owed my praise, gratitude, and affection. It was my good fortune to have the best parents in the world—parents who were willing to entrust me to the University of North Carolina at Chapel Hill.

My daughter, Kristie, who in her teens typed a number of my handwritten manuscripts, has grown into a beautiful English teacher at the largest high school in North Carolina. On this project, her wise suggestions and thoughtful critique of the text have made for a better book.

Finally, one person above all deserves more praise than I can ever bestow upon her. From the outset of my career as an author, my dear wife, Kay, has stood at my side as a boundless source of support, encouragement, and love. Often laboring out of the limelight, she has willingly and cheerfully read and reread every single word of my work (at times in the wee hours of the morning), has offered timely suggestions for improvement, has traveled thousands upon thousands of miles with me for research and on book tours, has listened with a sympathetic ear and loving heart to the frustrations, doubts, and disappointments of her author husband, and has celebrated and applauded my triumphs and successes, whether they be large or small.

Ultimately, I have the University of North Carolina at Chapel Hill to thank for providing the venue at which I met my soul mate. Indeed, on that hot, sunny afternoon of Saturday, September 4, 1971, I found my thrill on "the Hill." And oh, what a thrill Kay has made my life every day since.

*W*hat is it that binds us to this place as to no other? It is not the well or the bell or the stone walls. Or the crisp October nights or the memory of dogwoods blooming. Our loyalty is not only to William Richardson Davie, though we are proud of what he did 200 years ago today. Nor even to Dean Smith, though we are proud of what he did last March. No, our love for this place is based on the fact that it is, as it was meant to be, *the University of the people.*

Charles Kuralt

*I*n Chapel Hill among a friendly folk, this old University, the first state University to open its doors, stands on a hill set in the midst of beautiful forests under the skies that gave their color and their charm to the life of youth gathered here. Tradition grows here with the ivy on the historic buildings and the moss on the ancient oaks. Friendships form here for the human pilgrimage. There is music in the air of the place. To the artist's touch flowers grow beautifully from the soil and plays come simply from the life of the people. Above the traffic of the hour, church spires reach toward the life of the spirit. Into this life, with its ideals, failures, and high courage, comes youth with his body and his mind, his hopes and his dreams. Scholars muster here the intellectual and spiritual resources of the race for the development of the whole personality of the poorest boy, and would make the University of North Carolina a stronghold of liberal learning with outposts of research along all the frontiers of the world. Great teachers on this hill kindle the fires that burn for him and light up the heavens of the commonwealth with the hopes of light and liberty for all mankind.

Frank Porter Graham

Introduction

*I*n the twilight of the eighteenth century, public-supported higher education was born in the Western Hemisphere at a place in central North Carolina called New Hope Chapel Hill. Now, after more than twenty decades of service as a seat of higher learning, the University of North Carolina at Chapel Hill is widely recognized as one of the most distinguished universities, public or private, in the United States of America.

When North Carolina declared independence from Great Britain in 1776, its statesmen envisioned the University of North Carolina when they inserted Article 41 in the first state constitution. That article authorized the establishment of "one or more universities" supported by the state. Nonetheless, no initial legislative appropriation was made for the construction or operation of such universities, and the exigencies of the Revolutionary War robbed the fledgling state of its financial resources.

Not until 1789, the year in which George Washington became president of the United States, was the University of North Carolina chartered. On December 11, during a session of the North Carolina General Assembly in Fayetteville, William Richardson Davie—a Revolutionary War hero and a North Carolina delegate to the Constitutional Convention of 1787 who in time would become known as "the father of the university"—spearheaded the successful effort to obtain a charter for the University of North Carolina. Ten days later, the same legislative body adopted "An Act for the Endowment of the University," whereby all property escheated to the state would devolve to the university. Unfortunately, the new university was devoid of cash, so in 1791, Davie prevailed upon a reluctant legislature to authorize a loan of ten thousand dollars.

A year later, the trustees of the university scoured the North Carolina countryside to select a suitable site for the campus of the first state university in the New World. Ultimately, they agreed upon a location in Orange County at the intersection of major east-west and north-south roads, marked only by a small Anglican chapel known as New Hope Chapel Hill. This site, set upon a promontory in a spectacular oak forest, was considered ideal. The site selection committee promptly obtained pledges of 1,386 acres of land and $1,600 from public-spirited donors.

Plans were prepared for the construction of the first campus building. On October 12, 1793, the cornerstone was laid for the two-story brick structure that would be known as Old East. Samuel E. McCorkle, a renowned Presbyterian minister and educator for whom one of the two historic campus plazas is named, was selected to provide the keynote address at the cornerstone-laying ceremony. His words annunciated the hopes and dreams of Davie and the others in attendance that day:

> Knowledge is liberty and law. When the clouds of ignorance are dispelled by the radiance of knowledge, power trembles, but the authority of the laws remains inviolable. And how this knowledge, productive of so many advantages to mankind, can be acquired without public places of education, I know not. . . .
> . . . The seat of the University was next sought for, and the public eye selected Chappel-Hill—a lovely situation—in the center of the state—at a convenient distance from the capital—in a healthy and fertile neighbourhood. May this hill be for religion as the ancient hill of Zion; and for literature and the muses, may it surpass the ancient Parnassus! We this day enjoy the pleasure of seeing the corner-stone of the University, its foundations, its materials, and the architects of the building; and hope ere long to see its stately walls and spire ascending to their summit—ere long we hope to see it adorned with an elegant village, accommodated with all the necessaries and conveniences of society.[1]

On January 15, 1795, by all accounts a bitter, dismal winter day, the University of North Carolina officially opened under inauspicious circumstances.

Attending the opening were Governor Richard Dobbs Spaight, numerous other dignitaries, and the lone faculty member, the Reverend David Ker. After inspecting the recently completed Old East building—which stood with the unpainted wooden house of the Reverend Ker as the only buildings on the campus—they declared the university open and promptly went home.

More than a month passed before Hinton James arrived on foot from coastal North Carolina to enroll as the first student at the university. Word quickly spread throughout the state, and a month later, forty-one students and two professors were at work in Chapel Hill. By the time the university embarked upon its first full academic year, the student body had increased to seventy-four.

Before the eighteenth century drew to a close, overcrowding at Old East compelled the trustees to initiate the construction of two additional campus buildings, which survive with Old East as the three oldest state university buildings in America. Person Hall, designed as a chapel, was begun in 1796, and the cornerstone of South (Main) Building was laid in 1798.

By the dawn of the nineteenth century, the University of North Carolina had graduated four classes and remained the only state university in operation in the country. By the time the University of Georgia, the second state university to open its doors, graduated its first class, the university in Chapel Hill had issued degrees to seven classes of graduates.

Chartered on January 27, 1785 (almost four years before the University of North Carolina), the University of Georgia has long challenged the claim of the Chapel Hill institution as the nation's first state university. About the controversy, William S. Powell, the highly respected North Carolina historian and beloved professor on the Chapel Hill campus, has opined, "I don't think there's any doubt that UNC is the first state university. What good is a charter if you do not do anything with it? I think it's rather vain of the people of Georgia to make any pretense of being the first state university."

In 1804, Joseph Caldwell, a Princeton-educated Presbyterian minister and professor of mathematics in Chapel Hill, was named first president of the University of North Carolina. Blessed with a keen intellect and great vision for the future, Caldwell served as the chief administrative officer of the university for all but four of the next thirty-one years. During his very able administration, the Chapel Hill campus grew in stature not only as a place of classical learning but one of scientific research as well. Eminent scientists such as Elisha Mitchell and Denison Olmstead were recruited to teach. Their work, which included the first geological survey in the United States, brought prominence to the university. In 1831, through the efforts of President Caldwell, the first astronomical observatory on a state university campus was constructed in Chapel Hill.

After the death of Joseph Caldwell on January 27, 1835, the mourning community was surprised to learn that David Lowry Swain, North Carolina's thirty-four-year-old governor, wanted to be the new president of the university. On December 5, the trustees acceded to Swain's wishes and appointed the man from the North Carolina mountains to the position. His tenure spanned thirty-three years, during which he guided the school to a place of national prominence on the eve of the War Between the States, kept the campus open throughout the ensuing four-year conflict, and waged a spirited battle to keep the university alive in the dark days following the war.

The university drew national attention in 1847 when the eleventh president of the United States came to Chapel Hill on a four-day visit to attend commencement exercises at his alma mater. James Knox Polk, an 1818 graduate, was accompanied by his secretary of the navy, John Mason Young, a member of the class of 1816. In his diary, President Polk—for whom the second of the historic campus plazas is named—noted of his visit, "Tuesday 1st June 1847 ... As soon as I arose this morning I found a large crowd at the hotel desiring to see me. After breakfast I visited the college buildings. They have been greatly enlarged and improved since my days at college. . . . The old chapel [Person Hall] I found had been converted into recitation rooms, and for the use of Trustees when they attended the University. . . . After night I attended the Chapel and heard several members of the sophomore and freshman classes recite speeches which they had committed to memory."[2]

During the antebellum period, enrollment fluctuated from a low of 76 to a high of 456. Students came not only from North Carolina but from many other states, and accordingly, the university produced many noted statesmen, scientists, jurists, and other men of distinction during the first half of the nineteenth century.

All the while, the faculty and the physical plant grew, and the university began to enjoy a reputation as an institution of national importance. By 1860, it employed nine professors and five tutors to serve a student body that was surpassed in size only by Yale College in New Haven, Connecticut. Forces were at work, however, that would soon usher the university into the darkest period of its history.

After North Carolina seceded from the Union on May 20, 1861, it proceeded over the next four years to provide the Confederate war effort with more soldiers than any other Southern state. As days melted into months and months into years, the conflict depleted the university of both students and resources. More than 270 of its students and graduates died fighting for the South. For the duration of the conflict, the university struggled but managed to keep its doors open, thus becoming one of the very few Southern institutions of higher learning to operate continuously during the war.

When a cavalry detail under the command of General S. D. Atkins rode into Chapel Hill on Easter afternoon in 1865, the Federal forces spared the university from the torch, thanks to the efforts of Governor Zebulon B. Vance (a former university student), President David Swain, and William A. Graham (a former North Carolina governor and a graduate of the university). Less than three weeks later, the university held its commencement exercises with Federal troops in attendance. Only four students were on hand to receive their diplomas.

Though the university had survived the war, the grim spectre of Reconstruction cast a pall over the Chapel Hill campus. Poverty wrought by the long, costly war and the radical politics of Governor William W. Holden combined to leave North Carolina and its state university in misery and turmoil. Faced with unpaid faculty salaries and indebtedness of more than one hundred thousand dollars, President Swain mounted a valiant but futile effort to keep the school afloat. Small classes graduated in 1866, 1867, and 1868—three, eleven, and twenty, respectively. But after North Carolina adopted its new constitution in March 1868 and reentered the Union during the summer that followed, a large majority of the university's trustees was replaced by political appointees, most of whom knew or cared little about the school. With great dispatch, these newly appointed trustees accepted the resignations of President Swain and every member of the faculty. Cornelia Phillips Spencer, the daughter of a long-serving professor, closed a diary entry during those dark summer days with somber words: "Holden's Gov. has announced that the University shall not be re-opened on the 17th of July as Governor Swain had advertised. All is at an end."[3]

Despite Spencer's dire words, the university was not yet dead, but its pulse was weak. Under the administration of Solomon Pool, a member of the class of 1853 and a close political ally of Governor Holden, the doors remained open on a campus virtually devoid of life. Only one student graduated in 1869, and no degrees were awarded in 1870. Recognizing the collapse that was before them, the trustees voted in November 1870 to end all faculty salaries on February 1, 1871. On the eve of that fateful date, only two students were enrolled.

Without faculty or students, America's first state university was shuttered, albeit temporarily, in 1871. In one of its darkened classrooms, an unidentified person scrawled a melancholy message in chalk: "February 1, 1871. This old University has busted and gone to hell today."

Notwithstanding the doleful atmosphere pervading Chapel Hill, the rapidly changing political climate in North Carolina offered a glimmer of hope. Democrats wrested control of the state legislature from the Radical Republicans in 1870; in March 1871, Holden became the first governor in American history to be impeached and removed from office; in 1873, voters amended the onerous portions of the constitution of 1868 that had resulted in the upheaval on the board of trustees; and a new group of trustees comprised of competent, qualified men was selected by the legislature in 1874. In the meantime, public support led by Cornelia Phillips Spencer helped to change the question concerning the reopening of the university from *if* to *when*.

As prescribed by the new trustees, the University of North Carolina resumed regular operation on the first Monday of September 1875 amid great excitement and pomp. Lucy Phillips Russell, the niece of Cornelia Phillips Spencer, described the revelry in the Chapel Hill home of her aunt that day:

> My aunt, Mrs. Spencer, was in the seventh heaven of happiness. Her home was open to every trustee who could get in; every alumnus was her brother; every student was her son; her welcome was like the sunrise after a night of storm and bitter wind. Every newcomer had to hear the story of how she climbed the belfry of Old South Building on her fiftieth birthday, March 20, 1875, accompanied by Mr. Andrew Mickle and several young girls, and made the old bell fairly shout the tidings of the rebuilding of the University. Her fine, dark eyes glowed with joy and triumph and hope. After long, bleak years of loneliness here was companionship; after silence here was the sound of friendly voices, laughter and converse, badinage and repartee. She had every right to be happy and proud, and she drained the cup of appreciative flattery down to the lees. A deaf middle-aged woman in an isolated village, with no wealth and no weapon but her pen, had stirred a whole state from its lethargy until the penurious legislature responded to her proddings and reopened the University.[4]

Professor Charles Phillips, the father of Lucy Phillips Russell, agreed to serve as president of the university during the first year of its new beginning. He was succeeded by Kemp Plummer Battle, a member of the class of 1849. Battle, who had traveled the length and breadth of the state to persuade citizens to contribute the funds needed to enable the university to reopen, would provide strong, effective leadership during his fifteen-year tenure as president.

At the outset of his administration, Battle initiated programs designed to restore the university to its place of national prominence. In 1876, graduate study with advanced degrees was introduced in Chapel Hill. A year later, the university opened the first summer school for teachers in the United States.

Instruction in medicine was implemented as a regular course offering in 1879, and on September 23, 1880, the School of Pharmacy opened. In 1885, the precursor to the School of Education was initiated.

To strengthen the academic standing of the university, President Battle strived to assemble an outstanding cadre of preeminent professors. His greatest success occurred when Dr. Francis P. Venable, a highly regarded chemist, joined the faculty in 1880 as the only member to hold a Ph.D.

A decade later, Dr. Venable and one of his students, William Rand Kenan, Jr., conducted experiments in a campus laboratory that led to their discovery of calcium carbide and the development of the formula for producing acetylene gas. Their inventions attracted the attention of one of Venable's former prized students, John Motley Morehead, class of 1891. Kenan and Morehead parlayed the scientific discoveries made on the Chapel Hill campus to form the core business of Union Carbide Corporation. The subsequent success and fortunes of Kenan and Morehead, and particularly their generosity to their alma mater, have inexorably linked their names to the university.

Two other notable achievements of the Battle administration should be noted.

Cognizant of the continuing financial distress of the university, President Battle, with the assistance of Professor George T. Winston, made a convincing appeal to the state legislature in 1881 for an annual, recurring appropriation. Prior to that time, the Chapel Hill campus had survived solely on escheats, student tuition and fees, gifts, loan proceeds, and other miscellaneous income. As a result of the efforts of Battle, Winston, and other stalwart supporters of the university, the general assembly made its very first annual appropriation for the school that year in the amount of five thousand dollars.

Not only was Kemp Battle a strong advocate for academics, he also understood the importance of extracurricular activities on the growing campus. During his administration, he championed the cause of college sports. Accordingly, the university fielded its first intercollegiate athletic squads in football, baseball, and track, the forerunners of the teams that would be a source of inestimable pride for students and friends alike in the decades to follow.

With athletics came school colors and a nickname. Light, or "Carolina," blue was the color of the Dialectic Society, and white was the color of the competing Philanthropic Society. These two debating societies had evolved early in the history of the university, and their combined colors were selected as those to be worn by all school athletic teams. As to a nickname, residents of North Carolina had long been known as Tar Heels, so it was only natural that the athletes at the state university would be known by the same name.

As the nineteenth century neared its end, the institution in Chapel Hill had all the trappings of a major university. Its law school opened in 1894 amid a campus that offered myriad student activities—sports, fraternities, a glee club, a magazine, a yearbook (the forerunner of the current *Yackety Yack*), and a student newspaper, the *Tar Heel*. The recovery from the War Between the States had been slow but steady, as evidenced by the size of the student body (512) and the faculty (35) at the close of the century.

Under the brief but effective four-year presidency of Edwin Alderman (class of 1882), the university admitted its first female student in 1897. President Alderman departed Chapel Hill to accept a similar post at Tulane University after making the commencement address in 1900. In his speech, he proudly applauded the university and its core values anchored in democracy, tolerance, and freedom: "It is the child of civic virtue and democratic necessity and it has been forever true to its parentage. . . . All sects, parties, and conditions meet and mingle here on an equal footing and love the place with an equal love. I have seen men fight in unity of purpose for this place who did not agree with each other on any other public question in heaven or on earth beneath, and some of them could not agree with themselves for long. North Carolina owes much of the dignity and freedom in its public life to the manly spirit of respect for motives engendered here."[5]

In Alderman's stead, the trustees appointed Dr. Francis Venable, who skillfully guided the school into the new century with determination and a clear view toward the future. Throughout his thirteen-year presidency, the native Virginian headed a massive building plan that would serve as the foundation of the modern campus. Among the landmarks erected during the Venable administration were Bynum Hall (as a gymnasium), the YMCA building, Howell Hall (as the chemistry building), Abernethy Hall (as the infirmary), the president's house, Hill Hall (as the Carnegie library), Davie Hall, Caldwell Hall (as the medical school), the Battle-Vance-Pettigrew building (as a dormitory), Peabody Hall, Smith Hall, and the Confederate Memorial Statue (affectionately known to generations as "Silent Sam").

Like his predecessors, Venable realized that an outstanding faculty was a vital component of a university. His efforts to recruit superb professors brought to Chapel Hill men who were or would be recognized as some of the nation's foremost scholars, among them William Coker, Edwin Greenlaw, William M. Dey, J. G. De Roulhac Hamilton, and Edward Kidder Graham, all of whom now have campus buildings dedicated to their memory. Venable's efforts to strengthen the national academic reputation of the university were further rewarded in 1905 with the establishment of the state's Alpha Chapter of Phi Beta Kappa.

Hark the Sound of Tar Heel Voices

When Venable stepped down as president eight years later, one of his young protégés was selected as his replacement. At age thirty-seven, Edward Kidder Graham was a brilliant, very personable native North Carolinian who had served his alma mater as an English professor and dean of the College of Liberal Arts under Venable. Graham's boundless enthusiasm for the future of the university and his winning personality were infectious. In 1915, when student enrollment exceeded one thousand for the first time, he embarked upon a successful campaign to garner significant increases in the annual legislative appropriation for the university. Similarly, graduates were encouraged to bestow gifts upon their alma mater. Accordingly, in 1915, Captain Isaac Emerson, "the Bromo-Seltzer King" of Baltimore and a member of the class of 1874, donated funds to construct the school's first modern athletic stadium, known as Emerson Field.

But no gift in the history of the university could match the bequest of Mary Lily Kenan Flagler Bingham on July 17, 1917. The heiress to the fortune of Florida business tycoon Henry Flagler, Mrs. Bingham bequeathed to the university—as a memorial to her father and her uncles, all graduates—an endowment to pay at least seventy-five thousand dollars annually in perpetuity for professorships. The sheer size of the endowment, one of the largest ever made to a public university to that time, required an initial principal investment of two million dollars.

Edward Kidder Graham was extremely popular with the student body. During his tenure, the president's home on Franklin Street—the famed main street of Chapel Hill—was often filled with groups of students who enjoyed the hospitality of the energetic university leader and his wife. Graham was a proponent of expanded educational opportunities for female students. His campaign was attended with success in 1917 when the university relaxed its requirement that women must graduate from other colleges before enrolling at Chapel Hill.

When he welcomed students at the opening of the fall session in 1916, Graham offered a stirring speech entitled "The Spirit of the University." In it, he eloquently reaffirmed the principles of academic freedom and student responsibility that have been the hallmarks of the university throughout its history:

> You may think that you have come to ask it [the university] how to get into medicine, or how to make money, or how to make an N.C. sweater or a Phi Beta Kappa key, or how to be an engineer, or how to get into society or any other of the one thousand things that men work and die for. These are understandable motives for coming to college, and the college incidentally can respond to them all; but it could not answer them successfully if there

were no deeper motive behind them. The great question that you bring to the University to-day has a deeper center than a desire for either physical satisfaction or success in the world. It is the question that the young man came to the Master with—"What shall I do to inherit life"—the larger, abundant life that will satisfy all of the finer passions of life.

... What the University stands for is this natural loyalty to truth, to work, to life at its fullest and best that comes through the intellectual way of life. Its faith is that through that way it may lead men into the richest and most abundant expression of their best selves. Its mission, therefore, is to lead them to come to themselves in the highest degree, and so through whatever travail of spirit to be "born again." In this way, the University is truly our alma mater— mother of the best in men.[6]

The infectious enthusiasm of Graham and growing optimism about the university's steadily improving financial condition were tempered by the onset of World War I. As campus buildings and grounds were converted to military training facilities, President Graham rallied the faculty, students, and university community to aid the nation and its allies in the fight to save democracy.

On October 26, 1918, the university was robbed of one of its most gifted and talented sons when Graham fell prey to the influenza epidemic that ravaged Chapel Hill. On June 16, 1919, anxious to continue the successes of the Graham administration, the trustees tapped the chairman of the faculty, Henry Woodburn Chase, as the tenth president of the university. Upon his appointment, Chase was about the same age as his predecessor, yet he was unlike Graham and all of the other presidents who had served since the War Between the States. Born in Massachusetts and educated at Dartmouth, Chase was not a Southerner by birth or education. Nonetheless, he assumed the presidency with a great respect and admiration for the university, having served it since 1910.

Increases in state funding allowed Chase to launch a massive construction program during his eleven-year tenure. An impressive assemblage of buildings was added to the campus during that time: Phillips Hall; Steele Hall (as a dormitory); Grimes, Mangum, Aycock, Graham, and Lewis dormitories; Saunders Hall; Murphey Hall; Spencer Hall (as a dormitory for women); the Carolina Inn; Venable Hall; and Wilson Library. Because Emerson Field could no longer accommodate the growing throngs of spectators who came to Chapel Hill to watch intercollegiate football, a new stadium was erected at what was then the extreme southern portion of the campus. On November 24, 1927, the university accepted Kenan Memorial Stadium, a gift from William Rand Kenan, Jr., in memory of his parents.

Just four years earlier, two events had given a hint of the increasing importance of athletics at Chapel Hill. The 1924 basketball team went undefeated in twenty-six games and was subsequently declared the national champion. During the football season that followed, "Rameses the Ram" made his first appearance as the school's official mascot.

President Chase sought to enhance the national academic standing of the university through excellence in its classrooms and laboratories, luring outstanding faculty members to the campus. Paul Green, class of 1921, won the Pulitzer Prize in drama in 1927, just four years after accepting an assistant professorship at his alma mater. Howard Odum, who came to Chapel Hill in 1920 to begin the School of Public Welfare (later Social Work), quickly made the university a center in the study of Southern society. Robert D. W. Conner, class of 1899, was named Kenan Professor of History and Government in 1921. He stayed at the university until 1934, when he was selected as the first national archivist of the United States.

One of the highest academic honors achieved by the university came in 1922, when it was invited to join the exclusive Association of American Universities. At the time of its admission, it joined only one other Southern school in the twenty-two-member group, comprised of the preeminent research universities in North America. Almost a century later, just forty other institutions have been granted admission to the elite group.

When Chase departed Chapel Hill in 1930 to accept the presidency of the University of Illinois, he left behind a student body that had almost tripled in size in just fifteen years. The faculty had mushroomed to 222 full-time and 85 part-time positions. To manage the enormous growth and to lead the school out of the economic misery of the Great Depression, the trustees turned once again to a son of North Carolina and its state university, a man who was to become one of the most beloved in the history of the school. Frank Porter Graham, class of 1909, promptly rolled up his sleeves and mounted a vigorous statewide campaign to restore legislative funding, which had been significantly cut as a result of the national economic calamity. Though Graham was only moderately successful in the short run, he marshaled the resources to further extend the influence of the university far beyond the borders of North Carolina.

In the midst of its financial woes, the university managed to open the School of Library Science in 1931. Also that year, the Institute of Government, a national pioneer in the field of state and local government administration, opened in Chapel Hill. At the same time, the general assembly, desperate to cut costs and to eliminate duplication on state-supported campuses, voted to consolidate the university in Chapel Hill with North Carolina State College in Raleigh and Woman's College in Greensboro. Under the consolidation plan, female students were expected to attend Woman's College before enrolling in Chapel Hill. Frank Porter Graham was named the first president of the consolidated university.

Although his tenure as chief executive of the Chapel Hill campus lasted but one year, Graham did not move his office from South Building, and he maintained his residence at the president's house on Franklin Street. During his distinguished service as head of the consolidated university from 1931 to 1949, the tireless spokesman for campus freedom and social causes cultivated a deep affection for his alma mater and lent to it his passion for academic excellence, justice, and service to the outside world. When he delivered the commencement speech in Chapel Hill in 1943, President Graham espoused the ideas that would forever be his legacy:

> Most of you have come from small towns and farms. . . . Whether you come with the advantages of the greatest city or from the remotest mountain cove, we trust that Chapel Hill will always remain for you a home and community which gives deeper meaning to the old home of your family and neighborhood and nobler meaning to the new world of your dreams. While struggling to make fairer and more decent the neighborhood, state, section and nation, you will also widen your neighborhood beyond the horizons of America to include all peoples of the earth regardless of race, color, nationality, religious faith, or economic creed, beyond the poison of hate or the damage of fear in the world neighborhood of human brotherhood.
>
> . . . In deep remembrance we muster here this morning for our University and all the precious things of the human spirit for which she stands, the spiritual worth of every human personality, a humane and liberal learning, the freedom of the mind and the future of freedom in the world.[7]

When Frank Porter Graham assumed the helm of the consolidated university, the titular head of the campus in Chapel Hill was known as the dean of administration until the office of chancellor was created in 1945. Robert Burton House, class of 1916, rendered exemplary service under each title from 1934 until 1957.

As the university emerged from its Depression-era financial hardships, it developed new avenues of public service. In 1936, the School of Public Health opened. And once the United States entered World War II, several officer training programs, including Naval Pre-flight School and Naval ROTC, had a conspicuous presence on the campus.

Postwar prosperity led to another period of campus growth. An onslaught of soldiers-turned-students created an enormous housing shortage that required the construction of several makeshift villages for veterans and their families. Campus landmarks including the Morehead Planetarium (erected in 1949) continued to spring up. Public television came to North Carolina on January 8, 1955, when WUNC-TV went on the air from Swain Hall.

In the meantime, the university established the Division of Health Sciences, which included the Schools of Medicine, Public Health, Pharmacy, Nursing, and Dentistry, thereby making the institution one of very few in the nation to offer degrees in each of the health professions. In 1952, North Carolina Memorial Hospital opened on the campus as a great teaching tool for the schools allied in the Division of Health Sciences.

Not until the 1950s were the first black students admitted to the university. A federal court ruling in March 1951 resulted in the admission of four black law students later that same year. Further litigation made it possible for three students from Durham, North Carolina, to enroll as the first black undergraduates in 1954.

When Chancellor House retired in 1957, he placed the burgeoning campus of more than seven thousand students in the capable hands of William Brantley Aycock, a native North Carolinian who had earned his master's and law degrees at Chapel Hill. Aycock assumed the chancellorship at an exciting time when the university was celebrating its recent NCAA national championship in men's basketball. But clouds on the horizon portended stormy weather for the university.

Much like his close friends Frank Porter Graham and William C. Friday (who had become president of the consolidated university in 1956), Aycock expressed serious concern about the dominant role that college athletics had begun to assume on major university campuses. Their worst fears were realized in January 1960, when the NCAA placed the men's basketball program on a one-year probation for recruiting violations. The athletic program at the university recovered in short order. Over the decades that followed, its basketball teams won an additional four NCAA championships (three by the men's team and one by the women's), while school teams in other sports won some thirty national titles, the ninth-highest total in the NCAA. Nonetheless, debate over the prominence of intercollegiate athletics on the campus has continued to rage.

In the early 1960s, Chancellor Aycock and the university community came face to face with one of the most significant and alarming threats to the academic freedom long treasured and fiercely protected on the Chapel Hill campus. In June 1963, the North Carolina General Assembly passed legislation known as the Speaker Ban Law. Under the provisions of the statute, it became unlawful for communists or persons "known to advocate the overthrow of the Constitution of the United States" to speak on any state-supported campus in North Carolina. Despite extensive lobbying efforts and the protestations of university administration, faculty, students, and friends, the legislature refused to repeal the law, which appeared on its face to be vague, difficult to enforce, and unconstitutionally restrictive of speech. Ultimately, a panel of three federal judges declared the law unconstitutional on February 20, 1968.

Each of the chancellors who followed Aycock—Paul F. Sharp, J. Carlyle Sitterson, N. Ferebee Taylor, Christopher C. Fordham, Paul Hardin, Michael Hooker, and James Moeser—was faced with controversies, protests, and challenges concerning the university's stand on matters related to academic, faculty, and student freedoms, racial and social justice, and the environment. Each guided the university through the assaults on its academic integrity and managed growth on the 729-acre central campus, which was designated in 1999 as one of the most beautifully landscaped spots in the United States by the American Society of Landscape Architects.

During the final four decades of the twentieth century, an assortment of buildings was constructed in the few gaps that remained on the old campus proper: Dey Hall, Coker Hall, Hamilton Hall, Greenlaw Hall, the Frank Porter Graham Student Union, the Josephus Daniels Student Stores, the Kenan Laboratories, the new law school complex, the House Undergraduate Library, the Walter R. Davis Library, and Carmichael Auditorium (which supplanted Woollen Gymnasium, circa 1938, and served as the venue for men's basketball until 1986).

South of the old campus, growth exploded in the last third of the century. Numerous dormitories including high-rise facilities, the George Watts Hill Alumni Center, Boshamer Baseball Stadium, the Dean E. Smith Student Activities Center, and the sprawling medical complex now punctuate that portion of campus long dominated by pine forests.

On October 12, 1993, the university celebrated the bicentennial of public-supported higher education in America with grand ceremonies in Kenan Stadium. William J. Clinton, the president of the United States, offered the keynote address. In his remarks, he noted the singular importance of the events that had transpired in Chapel Hill two hundred years earlier, and he intimated the importance of the university in the future of the nation:

> Tonight we celebrate the day this University began—the laying of the cornerstone marks a milestone in the entire American journey. . . . Historians

Hark the Sound of Tar Heel Voices

tell us now that there was then a joyous ceremony—that the "maple leaves flamed red in the eager air." Great joy there was, but remember now, it was in the face of great uncertainty. The ruins of the Revolutionary War had yet to heal. The debts had yet to be repaid. And a new democracy seemed still untested and unstable. Yet, in spite of all these problems, the Americans of that time had the courage to build what had never before existed—a great new republic and a public university.

. . . We honor today the men and women who had the courage to create a new university in a new nation. We must, like them, be builders and believers, the architects of a new security to empower and embolden America and the University of North Carolina on the eve of a new century. The only difference between America two centuries ago and America today is the difference between dawn and high noon of a beautiful day.

In the words of your great alumnus, Thomas Wolfe, the true discovery of America is still before us. The true fulfillment of our spirit of our people, of our mighty and immortal land is yet to come. Let us believe in those words and let us act on them, so that 200 years from now our children, 12 generations removed, will still celebrate this glorious day.[8]

In late September 2007, James Moeser announced that he would step down as chancellor in June 2008 after almost eight years of service. Holden Thorp, a native of Fayetteville, North Carolina, a graduate of the University, and a member of its faculty since 1993, was subsequently selected by the Board of Governors as the new chancellor and charged to build upon the outstanding record of bold, innovatiave leadership established by his predecessors.

Since its humble beginnings as the parent of all state universities, the University of North Carolina has educated nearly eight hundred thousand men and women spanning parts of four centuries. Almost a quarter-million of its graduates now live throughout the world. A partial roll of illustrious sons and daughters reads like a veritable who's who in American history: United States president James K. Polk; United States vice president William R. King; United States senators Sam Ervin and John Edwards; Erskine Bowles, chief of staff for President Clinton; Josephus Daniels and William Alexander Graham, secretaries of the United States Navy; Walker Percy, Clyde Edgerton, Thomas Wolfe, Shelby Foote, Robert Ruark, and Paul Green, literary giants; Tom Wicker, Vermont Royster, Charles Kuralt, Roger Mudd, Jeff MacNelly, and David Brinkley, celebrated journalists; Andy Griffith, Rick Dees, Louise Fletcher, Oliver Swofford, Whit Bissell, John Forsythe, Kay Kyser, Jay Thomas, Jim Lampley, Jack Palance, and Randolph Scott, entertainment stars; Michael Jordan, Mia Hamm, Jim Beatty, Lawrence Taylor, and Davis Love III, world-class athletes; Hugh McColl, Ken Thompson, and Richard "Dick" Jenrette, noted American business leaders; and Caleb Bradham, the pharmacist who invented Pepsi-Cola.

From an enrollment of one in 1795, the modern student body, drawn from every state and over 100 foreign countries, has grown to more than 27,000 men and women enrolled in 71 bachelor's, 107 master's, and 74 doctoral degree programs. More than 2,200 full-time faculty members serve on the campus, which now contains in excess of 250 permanent buildings. Recent national surveys have consistently ranked the school as one of the top five public universities in the country, one of the best research universities in the world, and the best value of all public universities in the United States.

In the pages that follow are the words of men and women who have worked and studied in Chapel Hill at the school built by its state to be—and to remain—the university of the people.

1792
–
1799

The Infant University

One of the most beloved landmarks on the ancient campus at Chapel Hill towered above the pristine landscape when the site-selection committee paid its visit to the wilderness crossroads in the summer of 1792. The Davie Poplar, nurtured through storm, drought, and disease by the school administration for over two hundred years, has graced the campus at the center of McCorkle Place through every day of the long history of the university. A story attributed to William Richardson Davie concerning the role of the venerable tree in the selection of Chapel Hill as the site of the university may be only legend, but it ranks among the most famous of all campus traditions.

As the story goes, the trustees charged with the mission of finding a suitable site for the campus decided to rest under the canopy of the expansive poplar after an exhausting morning's work in the heat of August. There, they enjoyed liquid refreshment of the "exhilarating" kind, a picnic lunch, and a nap. Davie, who was not a member of the site-selection committee, supposedly convinced its members that they should end their search then and there.[1]

Beyond the realm of fable, Davie, the heroic commander of General Nathanael Greene's cavalry and one of the great champions of the United States Constitution, was enamored with the site at New Hope Chapel Hill.

He left invaluable documentation related to the earliest history of the university, including his description of the place.

Actual construction on the campus commenced on an October day in 1793 when "the sweetgums and dogwoods and maples were relieving with their russet and golden hues the general green of the forest." Davie's pen also chronicled the laying of the cornerstone of Old East. His firsthand account of the event was published in the *North-Carolina Journal* on October 30, 1793, and in the *North Carolina Gazette* on November 18, 1793.

The weather on its opening day did not portend the bright future the university was to enjoy. Those who came to Chapel Hill on January 15, 1795, were unceremoniously greeted by a drizzling rain and bone-penetrating cold. An account of the events of that day was published in the *North-Carolina Journal* on February 23, 1795. Several months later, the same newspaper offered praise for the young institution.

Though the story of the university's first student hints of fable, it is indeed fact that Hinton James traversed the miles from his home in Wilmington, North Carolina, to Chapel Hill on foot to enroll on February 12, 1795. A letter written by James some forty years after his graduation yields insight into the early days of the fully functioning university.

> When this University was first created by the Legislature in 1789 it was intended to be a special place.
>
> Vermont Royster

Among the first students to join Hinton James at the university were two brothers from Tyrrell County in the North Carolina coastal plain. John and Ebenezer Pettigrew, the sons of one of the original trustees of the university, wrote their father a letter on February 25, 1795, wherein they described their journey to Chapel Hill, their living conditions, and their studies. Their missive is the earliest letter yet discovered by a student at the university.

Two subsequent letters penned by John Pettigrew to his father in 1796 and 1797 offer a glimpse of the misbehavior that was apparently commonplace on the campus in the late eighteenth century. When student naughtiness continued to manifest itself in the succeeding decades, detractors of the university bestowed upon Chapel Hill a less-than-favorable soubriquet, "Sin City."

ooooo

Description of the Campus Site

BY WILLIAM RICHARDSON DAVIE, SEPTEMBER 25, 1793

The seat of the University is on the summit of a very high ridge. There is a gentle declivity of 300 yards to the village, which is situated on a handsome plain, considerably lower than the site of the public buildings, but so greatly elevated above the neighboring country as to furnish an extensive and beautiful landscape, composed of the heights in the vicinity of Eno, Little and Flat Rivers. . . .

There is nothing more remarkable in this extraordinary place than the abundance of springs of purest and finest water, which burst from the side of the ridge, and which have been the subject of admiration both to hunters and travelers ever since the discovery and settlement of that part of the country.

The University is situated about 25 miles from the city of Raleigh and 12 miles from the town of Hillsboro, and is said to be the best direction for that road. The great road from Chatham, and the country in the neighborhood of that country, to Petersburg [Virginia], passes at present directly through the village . . . being the newest and best direction.

This town being the only seat of learning immediately under the patronage of the public, possessing the advantages of a central situation, on some of the most public roads in the state, in a plentiful country and excelled by few places in the world, either for beauty of situation or salubrity of air, promises, with all moral certainty, to be a place of growing and permanent importance.[2]

ooooo

Davie's Description of the Laying of the Cornerstone of Old East

ON OCTOBER 12, 1793

Halifax, October 30 [1793]

On the 12th inst. the Commissioners appointed by the Board of Trustees of the University of this state, met at Chappel-Hill for the purpose of laying the corner-stone of the present building and disposing of the lots in the village. A large number of the brethren of the Masonic order from Hillsborough, Chatham, Granville and Warren, attended to assist at the ceremony of placing the corner-stone; and the procession for this purpose moved from Mr. Patterson's at 12 o'clock, in the following order: The Masonic Brethren in their usual order of procession, the Commissioners, the Trustees not Commissioners, the Hon. Judge Macay and other public officers, then followed the gentlemen of the vicinity. On approaching the south end of the building, the Masons opened to the right and left, and the Commissioners, etc. passed through and took their place. The Masonic procession then moved on round the foundation of the building and halted with their usual ceremonies opposite to the south-east corner, where *William Richardson Davie*, Grand-Master of the fraternity, etc. in this state, assisted by the two Masters of lodges and four other officers, laid the corner-stone, enclosing a plate to commemorate the transaction.

The Rev. Dr. McCorkle then addressed the Trustees and spectators in an excellent discourse suitable to the occasion. . . .

This discourse was followed by a short but animated prayer, closed with the united *amen* of an immense concourse of people.

The Commissioners then proceeded to sell the lots in the village, and we have the pleasure to assure the public, that although there were but twenty-nine lots, they sold for upwards of one thousand five hundred pounds, which shews the high idea the public entertain of this agreeable and healthful situation.[3]

ooooo

Account of Opening Day Exercises
ON JANUARY 15, 1795
AS RECORDED IN THE *NORTH-CAROLINA JOURNAL*

Pursuant to the request of the Board of Trustees of the University of North-Carolina, his Excellency Richard Dobbs Spaight, Esq. Governor of the state, and President of the Board, accompanied by several Members of the Corporation, and many other gentlemen, Members of the General Assembly, made a visit on the 15th day of January last, to the seat of the University of this state, in order to be present at the beginning of the exercises in that institution. The unfavourable state of the weather disappointed many of our fellow-citizens who wished to be present on that much desired occasion. The Governor, however, with the Trustees who accompanied him, viewed the buildings, and made report to the Board, by which they are enabled to inform the public that the buildings prepared for the reception and accommodation of Students, are in part finished: That the exercises of the institution have begun, and that youths disposed to enter at the University may come forward with an assurance of being received.

Students are to pay fifteen pounds per annum, North-Carolina currency, for their board. Five dollars per annum for room rent, to be paid half yearly in advance. They are to be furnished with tables and bed-steads, but they are to provide their own beds, etc. They are also to provide wood and candles for their chambers, and pay for their washing.[4]

ooooo

The University at the Close of Its First Term
JUNE 22, 1795
AS NOTED IN THE *NORTH-CAROLINA JOURNAL*

It is only four months since this national school was opened, and there are already forty-one students. These young gentlemen collected from private schools and academies, where regular application and habits of order can never be duly enforced[,] have submitted with a degree of cheerfulness and promptitude to the regulations of the University, which does them the

In the winter and spring of 1795 at Chapel Hill were assembled three buildings, a faculty, and a student body of an organic, living, working, going University of North Carolina. Not for six years in any American state was there a building, a faculty, a student body or even a piece of land set aside for another state university.

Frank Porter Graham

greatest honour. Their time, which is properly apportioned to the objects of study, recreation and refreshment, appears to pass off agreeably. The rooms of the building now finished, are calculated for study and lodging, and accommodate four persons very conveniently. The commons have exceeded the expectations of both the students and strangers. No combination of circumstances in this country could exhibit a more delightful spectacle than the spirit of improvement, order and harmony which reigns in this little community, emulously engaged in the noble work of cultivating the human mind.

An examination will take place on the 13th of July, under a visitation of the Board. This period completes the half year, and is attended with a vacation or holiday of one week. As the classes will then undergo some arrangement, it becomes a proper time for the entry of students.

We have also the pleasure to announce to the public that the academy at Thyatira, erected and conducted by Dr. M'Corkle, the Warrenton academy, under the management of the Rev. Mr. George, and the Chatham and Newbern academies, are all in a very flourishing state. The high reputation and great experience of the gentlemen who have the direction of these seminaries, will ensure their establishment and success, prepared to enter at once the University upon the higher branches of science.

"The desert shall rejoice and the wilderness shall blossom as a rose."[5]

ooooo

Hinton James's Letter to William H. Owen Recollecting His Days at the University

Wilmington NC
October 20 1838

Mr. Owen
Chapel Hill

Dear Sir

I received your favor some few days ago, expressing a wish that I would communicate to you some facts relative to the commencement of our College. This letter would have been answered at an earlier date, but at the time I was just recovering from a severe attack of Typhos fever. In the last few days I have examined some old papers with a view of revising my recollection, but I found them so much injured from the mice and other causes that I could make nothing of them. My memory does not serve to save but very little.

Board the first year, was fifteen dollars per cession, thirty dollars per year, with the steward who was then a Mr. Taylor. The first President of the institution, was a Mr. [David] Kerr an Irish, Presbyterian preacher who on leaving Chapel Hill commenced the practice of law. The first assistant that Parson Kerr had was a Mr. Charles Harris, who remained until Mr. Joseph Caldwell was engaged by the trustees. Mr. Harris shortly after Mr. Caldwells arrival left the College and commenced the practice of law. Maurice and Alfred Moore sons of Judge A Moore of Brunswick County NC and Richard Eagle a connection of . . . Mr. Moores were the students that entered College next to me[,] and at or about the same time John Taylor son of the then steward, and who was and perhaps is now, clerk of the Court of Orange County[. E]ntered next to him were sons of Colo. Burton of Granville County, viz Hutchins Burton, Frank and Robert Burton, also at the same time William M. Sneede, son of Williamsborough, Granville.

The first semiannual examination was attended by Governor Richard D. Speight and lady from Newbern, John Haywood publick treasurer, General Davie from Halifax County, Mr. James Hogg from near Hillsborough, Judge A Moore from Brunswick County NC. I do not recollect any others. Mr. James Hogg, Genl. Davie and John Haywood were very active and attentive to the institution, and others might have been equally so but my memory does not innable me to designate them. I am not able to state with any precision any number of students in College during my stay

> Judging from the past of the future, I flatter myself that the rays of knowledge, with virtue attendant, diverging from Chapel Hill, shall likewise illumine not only the state of North-Carolina, but the utmost limits of the United States.
>
> Willie Jones,
> speaker at the first graduation
> exercises at UNC, 1798

at the Institution. The first semiannual examination appeared to excite but little interest. Mrs. Speight was the only lady that attended the examination and I do not think their were more than a dozen Gentlemen included that attended. The whole business of examination and speaking only occupied one day, their was then one weeks vacation given.

Please present my most respectable respects to Governor Swain and assure him that I sincerely regret that I cannot say more on this subject, that it would give me great pleasure at all times to add to his convenience in any way that I possibly could.

I am dear Sir with sentiments of respects and regards

Your Obt Servt
H. James

Mr. Owen
Chapel Hill
Orange County

Their was no particular dress for the students directed by the Trustees or faculty during my stay at the I[nsti]tution. They dressed as fancy or convenience dictated.

HJ[6]

ooooo

Letter from John and Ebenezer Pettigrew to Charles Pettigrew

Skipperton Feb. 23, '95

Hond. Father,—

After a long and tedious journey we have at last arrived here safe. We found things very different from what we left them. There was hardly one boy but what had chang'd his room; and among the rest we lost ours. I confess that I was much displeas'd at it at first, and spoke to Mr. Kerr concerning it; and he told us that he suppos'd we must have it again; but, upon

Hark the Sound of Tar Heel Voices

a second consideration, we concluded that we would move into another room, where ther[e] were but four boys; two of them are sober young men, that We like very well and the other two are small boys.

Mr. Hardy's son is also in a room just above us that had but four boys in it. There was but one more room in the university but what had its number of beds in it, and I preferred this far before the other.

There are now 73 or 4 students at the University. They come very fast, and there is not room for more than nine or ten more; so that those who propose comeing up from Windsor had better set of[f] as quick as possible.

We met with a series of misfortunes upon the road, as many as would fill a small volumn. I will acquaint you of one of the worst, and you can make Glasgow [a slave or body servant] inform you of the rest. The worst was, when we got to the guts of Roanoak the mare gave out entirely, and would pull none attall, but I believe that it was nothing but stubborness, so that we were obliged to get one of Mr. Lyscum, and leave the young horse to plough in his room, for he was not able to go in the fills [fields], but we have made their mair pull before all the way. I will leave Glasgow to tell you all the rest, as I have not time.

We have not yet settled with the steward, but we expect to do it tomorrow. I am much afraid that we shall be much pushed for provisions this year; for I am told that Mr. Taylor buys corn by bag-fulls; so that in case of necessity, we shall have to get in hollow trees, and do as the bears do; for it would never do, to set off home, we should perish upon the roads. Mr. McCorkle is not to be here this year, and I shall send his letter back enclosed in mine.

All our class study *french* one half of the day, and *latin* the other half; but we shall be in a class in *latin,* and study *greek,* when they study *French.* We shall be under Mr. Delavo [Delavaux] reading *latin,* but Mr. Kerr or Hombs [Holmes] in the *Greek.*

Please to give our duty to our mother and compliments to those who ask after us.

John and E. Pettigrew[7]

ooooo

> Damn you, you will hear from me again.
>
> Future senator
> Thomas Hart Benton,
> upon being expelled from UNC
> at the age of sixteen in 1799

Excerpt of Letter from John Pettigrew to Charles Pettigrew
APRIL 12, 1796

Cursing & swearing is carried on here to the greatest perfection; even from the smallest to the largest they vent out the oath's with greatest ease immaginable. They have lately got a supply of bo[o]ks, & those are chiefly Payn[e]'s *Age of reason*, they prefer it to all the books that were ever wrote since the creation of the World, they also say that he was sent into the World to set menkind to liberty; but I would not have you think that they are all of this opinion but there are . . . a greaty majority of this cast.[8]

ooooo

Excerpt of Letter from John Pettigrew to Charles Pettigrew
JUNE 27, 1797

You desired me to give you a full and just statement of the management of affairs, & also with regard to the conduct of the Students in general. . . . In compliance with your request I shall give you as true an account a[s] possible. The Students in general have nothing very criminal in their conduct except a vile & detestable practice of cursing & swearing, which has become very fashionable here, there can be hardly a sentence spoken without some of these highflown words which sailors commonly use to pirvert each other. As to study, I believe those who are in the senior classes, & far enough advanced in years to study their own interest ap[p]ly themselves perty closely, but on the contrary there are here a great many small boys the half of whom do little or nothing with regard to improvement; those are the ones that make the greatest proficiency in the art of swearing.[9]

Hark the Sound of Tar Heel Voices

1800
—
1809

The New University Enters a New Century

Campus misbehavior, as manifested in the cursing and swearing of the earliest students, grew in practice, scope, and range as the university emerged from the eighteenth century. Disciplinary hearings before the faculty became commonplace for offenses that included drunkenness, drawing guns and other weapons, dueling, assaults, theft, overturning outhouses, removing gates, barring doors to classrooms, insulting citizens and faculty members, stoning residences, and gambling. Anxious to quell the rampant misconduct, the trustees enacted an ordinance in 1805 whereby student monitors were authorized to enforce discipline by restricting speech and imposing a military regimen at mealtimes. Any student who offered opposition to a monitor engaged in his duty was subject to suspension.

Reaction by the student body to the campus monitors (who were required to take oaths) was swift and demonstrative. Kemp Plummer Battle eloquently described it: "If our students had been a colony of wax-dolls they might have submitted to this law without a murmur. If cruel tyranny had crushed out all their instinctive sense of right or wrong and had made them a colony of liars and sneaks, they would have cringed, promised obedience and straightway systematically fawned upon and deceived the professors; but, being American boys with independence of thought and abundance of pluck, they received the ordinance with angry disgust and determination not to submit."[1]

A series of disturbances in protest of the monitor ordinance followed. In its aftermath, forty-five young men—a majority of the student body—departed the university for good. The unrest caused by the ordinance (repealed in December 1805) compelled William R. Davie to correspond with John Haywood, a fellow trustee who served as treasurer of the state of North Carolina for forty years. In his letter, Davie expressed his opposition to the ordinance, his opinions about the causes of student disturbances, and his ideas concerning ways to improve campus conduct.

One of the students who survived the turmoil was William Hooper, who graduated in 1809. Hooper, the grandson of the man of the same name who signed the Declaration of Independence for North Carolina, began teaching at his alma mater in 1818 and served as a professor of ancient languages and rhetoric and logic until 1838. Years later, he provided a rich account of his days as a student at the university and a detailed description of the faculty and campus in 1804, on the eve of the disturbances.

Joseph Caldwell assumed the role as the first president of the university in 1804, at the very time when student unrest and misbehavior were mounting. Stern but compassionate, Caldwell carefully guided the campus through difficult times. Although the subsequent graduating classes were extremely small (three in 1805 and four in 1806), the university overcame its early woes, and the first president spent the remainder of the decade in pursuit of academic excellence. A letter from Caldwell to a friend on June 3, 1807, gave his intimate assessment of trials and tribulations at the university.

Just two days later, six students appreciative of Caldwell's efforts offered their gratitude and praise in a letter to the university president. Their letter not only serves as a barometer of campus thought and opinion but also gives some indication of the writing abilities of university students in the first decade of the nineteenth century.

> If God is not a Tar Heel, then why is the sky Carolina blue?
>
> Anonymous

Hark the Sound of Tar Heel Voices

Excerpt from Letter of William R. Davie Addressing Student Unrest and Misbehavior

Halifax, Sept. 22nd 1805

My Dear Sir,

The late unfortunate occurrence at the University is much to be lamented on many accounts, and most of all for the ill advised measure of the ordinance which gave birth to the conduct adopted by the students. . . .

I have reflected much and seriously since the event on the causes of this spirit of insubordination and the means of preventing it. It has always existed in a considerable degree, the ordinance may be considered as only an accidental cause; I think the real causes may be found in the defects of Domestic education in the So. States, the weakness of parental authority, the spirit of the Times, the arrangement as to vacation, and some errors of the Board which I will notice hereafter.

Every man of discernment, who has lived 40 or 50 years, must have observed and lamented the general decay of parental authority, and the consequent presumption and loose manners of our young men. Boys of 16 or 17 years, without judgment, without experience or almost any knowledge of any kind arrogantly affect to judge for themselves, their teachers, and even their parents in matters of morality, of Government, of Education, in fact in every thing. The effect of the other general cause is visible throughout the whole of their remonstrance. Nothing can be more ridiculous than *Boys at school* ta[l]king of "a sacred regard to their right," "the high and imposing duty of resistance," and of "denouncing laws," &c., &c., the genuine Slang of the Times culled from the columns of Newspapers; yet these very sounds were attended with the most mischievous consequences. Over all these causes the Board of Trustees have no power or influence, but they must be considered to be counteracted as far as possible.

I have understood and observed ever since the establishment of the University, that the disturbances have generally manifested themselves about this period of the second session, and that when a general resistance to authority did not take place, a spirit of insubordination always shewed itself more or less at this season: This I attribute to the great length of time the students have been confined at Colledge; they become tired and disgusted with study, their minds gradually acquire a sour, gloomy, and restive *temperament producing* a general predisposition to any measure that may break up the session, or interrupt business and distress the Faculty. Two or three fellows more daring and unprincipled than the rest seize on this Disposition and artfully turn it into the channel of a general revolt against all authority: To remedy this Evil I would earnestly recommend tha[t] an ordinance be passed at the next annual meeting establishing the vacations on the same footing as they are at Princeton whatever that may be. . . .

The Difficulty we have continually experienced in the management of youth at this Institution has often obliged me to reflect on the means we have used, and the nature of the Government of such Institutions. I am now perfectly convinced that the best governed Colleges are those which have the most respectable Faculties, and the fewest *written* Laws, and that we have committed a serious error in making an ordinance for *every thing*, or in other words legislating too much. It is now my opinion, that after describing the kind of punishment to be used on the Establishment, and reserving in all case the punishment of *Expulsion* to be confirmed by the Board, all the rest should be left to *discretion* of the Faculty.

Your Wm R. Davie[2]

○○○○○

William Hooper's Description of the University

When I first knew Chapel Hill in January, 1804, the infant university was but about six years old. Its only finished buildings were what are now called the East Wing [Old East] and the Old Chapel. The former was then only two stories high, capable of accommodating one tutor and sixty students by crowding four into a room. The faculty consisted of three: President Caldwell, Prof. Bingham, and tutor Henderson. Their college titles were "Old Joe," "Old Slick" and "Little Dick." "Old Joe," however was only thirty years of age and possessed . . . a formidable share of youthful activity. "Old Slick" derived his cognomen, not from age but from premature baldness, and the extreme glossiness of his naked scalp. And "Little Dick," a cousin of the late distinguished Judge Henderson, though he was a brave spirit, was not very well fitted by the size of his person, to overawe the three score rude chaps over whom he was placed as solitary sentinel. As a nursery of the college there was a preparatory school, taught by Matthew Troy and Chesley Daniel. All things were fashioned after the model of Princeton College, and that probably was fashioned after the model of the Scottish universities, by old Dr. With- erspoon. If this were the case, it would seem to account for the small quantum of instruc- tion provided for us, if Dr. Johnson spoke the truth when he said of Scottish educa- tion, that "there every body got a mouthful,

> You must desire it, believe in it, and put in the resources to achieve it. That's what it takes to build a Chapel Hill.
>
> William C. Friday

but nobody got a belly-ful." Into this preparatory school, it was my fortune to be inducted, a trembling urchin of twelve years, in the winter of 1804. It was then a barbarous custom brought from the North, to rise at that severe season of the year before day-light and go to prayers by candle-light; and many a cold wintry morning do I recollect, trudging along in the dark at the heels of Mr., afterwards Dr. Caldwell, with whom I boarded, on our way to the tutor's room, to wait for the second bell. In that year I read Sallust's *War of Jugurtha* and *Conspiracy of Cataline*, under the tuition of Mr. Troy, of whom my recollections are affectionate, for he was partial to me, and taught me well for those times. But I can recollect some of my classmates, grown young men, upon whose backs he tried a blister-plaster, made of chinquepin bark, to quicken the torpor of the brain. Nor was he singular in his discipline. Whether boys were duller or more idle than now, I know not; but at that time whipping was the order of the day....

The South building . . . was then in an unfinished state, carried up a story and a half, and there left for many years to battle the weather unshel- tered; but it was inhabited. "Inhabited!" you will say, "by what? By toads and snails and bats, I suppose." No sir, by students . . .

As the only dormitory that had a roof was too crowded for study, and as those who tried to study there spent half the evening in passing laws to regulate the other half, many students left their rooms as a place of study entirely, and built cabins in the corners of the unfinished brick walls, and quite comfortable cabins they were; but whence the plank came, out of which those cabins were built, your deponent saith not. Suffice it to hint that in such matters college boys are apt to adopt the code of Lycurgus: that there is no harm in privately transferring property, provided you are not caught at it. In such cabin your speaker and dozens like him hibernated and burned the midnight oil. As soon as spring brought back the swallows and the leaves, we emerged from our dens and chose some shady retirement where we made a path and a promenade.[3]

ooooo

Excerpt from Letter of Joseph Caldwell

Chapel Hill June 3rd 1807

My dear Friend,

In 1796 I received an invitation while I was studying at Princeton and acting as tutor there, from an old friend to come to N. Carolina and fill his place as Professor of Mathematics in the University. After further correspondence I determined to accept and answered him on the last day of October. There I have continued ever since, and am likely to spend here the remainder of my days. The difficulties, trials, and anxieties I have encountered through this lapse of time, are too numerous to be recounted within a short compass. About three and a half [years] ago, I married, and at the end of two years had a daughter who with my wife has a few months since been surrendered into the hands of Him who gave them.

When I first came here I found the University just commencing business, and it took two years afterwards to render the highest class fit for its degrees. There was no president, and I suffered myself to be persuaded, young and inexperienced as I was to take the superintendency of the institution. After a year's experience, I determined to resign, and stated to the Trustees that thus was the only condition upon which I could consent to act any longer. . . . At that time there was but one officer in the University beside myself. On this resignation, I continued as professor of mathematics, and another professor was appointed to whom the superintendence was assigned. In little more than eighteen months he left us, and the consequence was that I was obliged to assume his business anew. For four successive sessions I continued to solicit of the Board the appointment of some other person to the chief professorship, but a person was not to be easily had, and the trustees still insisted that I should continue. At last finding it no longer to any purpose I went on in the business, and had the good fortune to give general satisfaction to the Trustees, the students, & the public. In July 1803 I married, and a year afterwards was regularly elected President with a salary of $1,000.00. This is a small sum for such an office, and the heavy duties annexed to it; but the buildings of the University are not all finished, and the Trustees are forced to apply their funds to that object as far as possible. I was made happy by a daughter, who died six months ago when she was 14 months old, and my wife soon followed her to the grave. Such is the fallacy of human expectations, and the transition of present happiness!

About 8 or ten months ago the trustees of Columbia college in South Carolina elected me to the professorship of mathematics in that college with a salary of $2000 but finding my attachments grown to this place, and disliking change I declined my appointment, though they held up as an inducement the prospect of a speedy succession to the Presidency which is endowed with a salary of $3000.[4]

ooooo

Letter from Six Students to Joseph Caldwell

Chapel Hill 5th June 1807

Mr. Caldwell,

Having so long witnessed your exertions in behalf of this institution of your Country and religion; having so sensibly experienced the advantages of your fostering care & attention, we cannot consistently with our feelings omit paying you this tribute of respect. Your situation involves a variety of interesting and important duties. When we behold the relations in which you stand, when we witness your capacity and fidelity in training to habits of piety, of temperance and industry the youth committed to your care, it is

> No institution in this state or in the country for that matter, has done more to seek out the truth and make it available for all, than the University of North Carolina.
>
> *Shelby Daily Star*

a spectacle we think which superior natures may contemplate with delight. You have been the *director* of the youthful pursuits, our *guide*, our *teacher*, and our *friend*. Under your guardianship and inspection we have acquired the rudiments of that knowledge which is to fit us for the active and important scenes of life. You have often inculcated upon our minds with the zeal & solicitude of a parent the great and instructive lessons of moral rectitude. "You have taught our young ideas to shoot, our wayward passions how to move."

When viewing such essential services, how cold and lifeless, how insensible to every generous motive must be that heart which does not swell with the strongest emotions of gratitude and love. Be assured, Sir, that we duly appreciate your *worth*. We fain would hope that the sentiments inspired by your lessons, "may never be erased." Your admonitions shall be remembered when we are far removed from your presence, they shall rise in our minds like the light of the evening to guide and refresh us.

That you may live in health and peace and see these plants of your care, blossom and produce much fruit; and that you may long continue a blessing to religion and to the world is the sincere [and] the hearty wish of your *friends* & pupils.

Green H. Campbell
John L. Taylor
John R. Donnell
John G. Montgomery
Gavin Hogg
Stephen Davis[5]

1810
—
1819

Challenges for the Young University

*A*s the Chapel Hill campus began the slow transition from infancy to youth, the attendant growing pains presented a variety of challenges. Efforts to curb misconduct and to discipline rowdy students met with a measure of success, although punishment in some cases resulted in suspension or expulsion. Trustees soon found themselves faced with the dilemma of filling campus vacancies with new enrollees or with disciplined students who sought readmission.

One such contrite student was John Ambrose Ramsey of Moore County, North Carolina. He had studied in Chapel Hill from 1803 until the last term of his senior year in 1810, when he was suspended as the result of an incident involving a gun. Ramsey's successful plea to the trustees for reinstatement, dated June 28, 1810, included an admission of wrongdoing, an explanation for his behavior, and a description of his recent academic work. Following his graduation, Ramsey served in the state legislature.

In 1816, the university found itself embroiled in a controversy involving the rights of students with regard to academics and speech. Dr. Robert H.

Chapman, the Princeton-educated Presbyterian minister who assumed the presidency in 1812 during Joseph Caldwell's four-year respite, was an unabashed "Peace Federalist" throughout the War of 1812. His views on the war were in direct contrast with those held by most of the students, who favored the American military policy against Great Britain. The ongoing dispute between the Chapman administration and the student body came to a head on September 16, 1816, when William Biddle Shephard delivered his senior speech, entitled "On the Massacre at Dartmoor Prison."

In the manuscript for his speech, Shephard, an outstanding student from an influential family in eastern North Carolina, condemned Great Britain for its savage attack on Hampton, Virginia, and for its treatment of prisoners at Dartmoor in Devonshire, England. Prior to Shephard's speech, President Chapman examined the manuscript, excised several sentences containing favorable references to the Republican Party, and ordered Shephard to refrain from uttering any of the censored sentences.

When the student delivered his address before the faculty and his peers, he proceeded to present the uncensored, unedited version. Dismayed by what he heard, Dr. Chapman immediately demanded that Shephard halt his oratory and leave the rostrum. But the speaker persisted, goaded by scores of students who offered encouragement by screaming, "Go on! Go on!" Shephard defiantly completed his speech. The following day, a large group of students met in Person Hall, where they adopted resolutions in support of Shephard and his cheering section.

Shephard, who became a noted attorney, state legislator, and congressman, was subsequently suspended from the university for six months as a result of his disobedience. Some of his supporters received varying degrees of punishment, including expulsion.

Iveson Brookes, a freshman in 1816, offered his thoughts about the Shephard affair in a letter to his father just days after the speech.

Anxious to dispel public dissatisfaction over the university's handling

> And so, in concentric circles, as if from a pebble tossed into a pool, the influence of the University of North Carolina at Chapel Hill moves outward to the farthest corners of our state, and far beyond its boundaries.
>
> Charles Kuralt

Hark the Sound of Tar Heel Voices

of the controversy, an unidentified professor offered a defense of the administration and faculty in a communication published in the *Raleigh Minerva* on October 18, 1816.

Unable to survive the lingering strife wrought by the dispute, Chapman resigned as president on November 23, 1816. Joseph Caldwell resumed the top administrative position. Despite some initial misgivings, Caldwell was energized by a burning desire to earn for the university a national reputation as a distinguished place of scientific as well as classical learning. He thus embarked upon a campaign to develop and fund a chemistry department. Caldwell's letter to William Polk, a trustee, on April 1, 1818, signaled the beginning of the university's superb chemistry program, which in time would boast the likes of Venable, Kenan, and Morehead.

ooooo

Plea from John A. Ramsey for Reinstatement to the University
JUNE 28, 1810

To the Trustees of the University of N.C[.]

Gentlemen—

Having been debarred for some time past from the privileges resulting from your institution, I take this method of informing you my sentiments and lay open the cause that leads to this address. Probably some of the members of your honorable board have not heard my situation, or the relative circumstances of my unfortunate punishment. It was during the agitations and commotions which happened at College in the month of March last that I was seduced to take a part in those disturbances; a part which I long have sorely repented that I ever bore, as it gave reason to the faculty to imagine that I wished greatly to add to the confusion which universally spread itself.

The reason upon which was founded my suspension appeared to have been the act of firing one pistol and if it is any palliation of the crime, it did not take place within the hours prescribed by law for study, nor at night when the cracking of a pistol might have caused greater tumult.

This I mention with the hope of convincing the Board that I had no settled plan of annoying and disturbing the business of the University, and that it was an act of wantoness which I have been sorry for ever since the commission; and had I been called upon to make confession for that fault, I should have been ready even before the infliction of my punishment.

I shall now go on to Solicit of the Trustees a reinstatement at this time, also that I may be allowed a diploma. I have read of the books studied by the Senior class of College the following: Blair's *Rhetoric*, Helsham's Lectures upon Natural philosophy as far as the Lecture upon sound; Paley's *Moral [P]hilosophy* through the third Book, and Ferguson's *Astronomy* to Equation of time, upon which I suppose the Trustees would choose I should be examined. I have also to mention that should this request be agree'd to, I have not pretended to commit to memory any part of my studies as is done at College, only to attend to general subjects, and that being deprived of the aid before afforded by the distinguished abilities of President Caldwell and destitute of much necessary explication.

Having been ever since the beginning of the year 1803 under the protection of your guardianship, and having received the first rudiments of my classical education at this institution, having long been inspired with an affectionate fondness for its prosperity; and never before during that time being censured by the Faculty for the least offence, whilst scores of my fellow-students have been suspended and admonished (some even expelled) and again readmitted[,] these things being considered, I fervently hope that the Trustees will confer upon me that honor for which I have been laboring these seven years, and if not which my situation will absolutely preclude the possibility of prosecuting farther. It is unnecessary for me in my humble Capacity to extend and dwell upon situations formerly presented so like my own. Should my presence at any time be thought requisite, I shall wait with pleasure to answer any interrogations which may be deemed necessary.

With Sentiments of the Most profound respect, I Remain yr obt st

Jn A. Ramsey[1]

> More than any other institution or agency—even the public schools—the University of North Carolina depicts the brain and the heart of the state.
>
> *High Point Enterprise*

ooooo

Letter from Iveson L. Brookes
to Jonathan Brookes

Chapel Hill Septr 1816

Dear Father

As a favorable opportunity of writing by Mr. Morehead, (who will pass
by the neighborhood) offers unexpectedly, I cannot let it pass without giving you a few lines (though I have but a few minutes to write in)[.] We have
lately had a considerable commotion in college which has terminated in
the suspension of 27 of the students. It origin[at]ed from a speech delivered by one of the Senior Class which had been corrected by the president
and the Student neglected the alterations made & persisted to speak as he
had composed it, after he was several times ordered to stop upon the publick stage. The students generally supposed the corrections on the speach
were wrong & many of them at the close of it showed their approbation of
the young man's conduct by clapping & making open plaudits in the publick Hall in the presence of the assembly in which were several strangers[.]
On the next morning they met in the Chapel for the purpose of consulting
on some measure to shew their further contempt of the President for the
corrections of the speech & his conduct towards the Speaker[.] In short
many of them manifested a spirit of open rebellion if the Speaker should
be punished for his disobeying the President[.] The Faculty proceeded
to ascertain those who were more particularly engaged in the tumult &
suspended them for six months as they obstinately refused to make any
concession; They then suspended the speaker W. B. Sheppard & all who
were concerned in the offence except those who made necessary conces-
sions. . . .

I have been long anxious to hear from you. I wrote you a letter some
time ago but know not whether you received it as no answer has come
to hand. We have had dreadful accounts of the drought in the upper
Country. I should be extremely glad to hear how crops are with you
and neighbors[.]

The Session will end about the first of December at which time I shall want to go home. I am at present thro' mercy enjoying very good health and my studies are becoming some more easy tho' yet difficult. I hope however to maintain a respectable standing with the class tho' I may not obtain any particular [dis]tinction. I feel more anxious daily to prosecute my studies, could I be fortunately favored the necessary funds. [T]his place is very expensive; but with regard to dress the Students are plain.

Iveson L. Brookes[2]

ooooo

The Published Response of the University to the William B. Shephard Controversy

University of North Carolina.
Communication.

Correct information is very important and desirable, especially in those cases where the interests of society are so materially concerned. You will therefore insert in your useful paper [the *Raleigh Minerva*] the following observations. Feeling fully justified in the proceedings in the case by the laws of the University and a firm determination in the strength of God, to discharge duty amidst every opposition; the attention of the public is invited to a plain candid statement of facts. . . .

On these grounds [the speech of William Shepard was ex]amined, and corrections were made by the President. Some of these were considered by him and known by the Speaker to be important and some unimportant. It has been the invariable practice of the President in his corrections to signify the first by erasure and insertion, and unimportant verbal alterations by placing the corrections above, without erasing the words of the speaker, leaving it at his option to use his own language or adopt the suggested amendment. . . .

It is proper, then, to state to the public that at the conclusion of Wm. Shepard's speech, in defiance of authority, there was a general plaudit in the Hall in token of approbation. That at the end of the speakin[g], as the students went to the College, there were noisy shoutings for Wm. Shepard, and the great noise and riot in the buildings during a great part of the night[,] that the next morning the Faculty were grossly insulted by the students, individually and as a body[,] that as business was at an end, and authority despised and insulted, that a public notification was placed on the Chapel door inviting the attendance of the students at a precise hour that only 27 attended, & that these when discovered by the Faculty, avowed it as the object of their meeting, in the express language of one of their leaders "to form measures to express their indignation against the proceedings of the Faculty." This avowal they seemed afterwards to palliate and conceal. They all had opportunity given them by the Faculty to state their object, to disavow such a design, and withdraw from the combination; but they chose to maintain their connection. Finding them engaged in such business, the following law of the University was the ground of procedure; "if any clubs or any combinations of the students shall at any time take place, either for resisting authority of College, interfering in its government, shewing disrespect to the Faculty, or to any of its members, or for concealing or executing any evil design, the Faculty are empowered and directed to break up all combinations as soon as discovered, and to inflict a severer punishment on each individual than if offence intended had been committed in his individual capacity, whatever be the number concerned or whatever be the consequence of the College.["]

Chapel Hill Oct. 15, 1816.[3]

ooooo

Letter from Joseph Caldwell to Colonel William Polk

Chapel Hill April 1, 1818

Dear Sir,

In a letter which I wrote some time ago to Mr. Treasurer Haywood, I took occasion to suggest to the Committee the probability that you would be called on this year for the expense necessary for erecting a laboratory, to accommodate the professor of chemistry by the beginning of the ensuing year. It has occurred to me however that this may be rendered unnecessary. The dining room here, as you may recollect, was enlarged by an addition of I think, 16 feet to the length of it, just a[t] the time when the measure was adopted of permitting the students to board in the Steward's hall, or in the village. The whole length of that room at present is probably more than 60 feet. Were a partition run across through the middle of it, 30 feet would undoubtedly be amply sufficient for the purposes of Mr. Burton, or any other person who may occupy the premises, and 30 feet would be enough for the lectures & experiments of the professor, in the presence of his class. The room is more than wide enough for two ranges of tables, and I believe Mr. Burton never has need of one table of the length of 25 feet. It is for the Committee then to consider, whether they may not in the present circumstances, look to the retention, in their next contract for the dining room[,] of so much for their own use, as may answer the purpose of a laboratory for some time.

Mr. [Denison] Olmsted in a letter to Mr. [Elisha] Mitchell has mentioned the specifick sum of 700 dollars as competent to the purchase of such apparatus as will be sufficient for his experiments, for the illustration of a course of lectures. He has had an opportunity of sending to Europe by a gentleman on whose skill as a chemist, and on whose fidelity he can rely, for procuring such parts of apparatus as cannot so well be obtained in this country. As such an occasion might not hereafter occur, he concluded to furnish the necessary funds from his own purse, calculating upon the approbation of the Committee. He did not state, as I understood from Mr. Mitchell, the sum he should send: probably it might be 400 dollars. . . .

I am Dear Sir, yours very sincerely

Joseph Caldwell[4]

> There is no adequate means of determining or measuring the influence of this University upon the progress and development of our Commonwealth and our Republic. Suffice it to say that in all matters affecting the sound progress of our people, its alumni are always to be found in the forefront, striving always for a higher level of intellectual, economic, and spiritual attainment.
>
> William B. Umstead (class of 1916),
> United States representative,
> United States senator, and
> governor of North Carolina

1820
—
1829

The University as a
Home Away from Home

*U*nlike the Chapel Hill campus of the early twenty-first century, to which thousands of students commute by automobile or public transit every day, the university of the 1820s was a place where students, once they arrived, remained until school broke at the end of the term months later. As a consequence, the university of that era not only educated its students but also played a significant role in their social and moral training.

Because of the limited modes of transportation at the time, the young men enrolled at the university either lived and ate their meals on campus or boarded in private homes in the village that had grown up in the shadow of the school. Leander Hughes, a Virginian who enrolled for the fall term of 1823, wrote home soon after his arrival in Chapel Hill and explained his living arrangements. His letter to his father, typical of many written by new students throughout the history of the university, begged for mail.

Long months of separation from homes, families, friends, and the only world they had ever known often led to homesickness, loneliness, disenchantment, and daydreaming. Franklin Lafayette Smith of Charlotte expressed the sentiments of many homesick students in a letter to his cousin in 1828. This piece of correspondence, written while Smith was in his second full year at Chapel Hill, furnishes an understanding of the mind-set of disillusioned students far from home. Despite the misgivings set forth in his letter, Smith endured and graduated at the top of his class in 1829. He offered the Latin salutatory at the commencement exercises.

To qualify for admission to the university in the 1820s, students were required to pass examinations in Greek and Latin. Upon admission, their academic regimen included physics, mathematics, geography, English (grammar, composition, and literature), declamation, logic, rhetoric, philosophy, chemistry, geology, mineralogy, and astronomy, as well as further study in the classical languages. Most classroom instruction involved a teaching method known as recitation. Students were expected to memorize their textbook lessons and then recite them when called upon by their professors. One student, apparently tired of the rigors of academic life, poetically expressed his delight at the completion of the term in 1821. Lucius J. Polk's poem, entitled "College Rules," was left unfinished by its author, but it survives as an excellent example of contemporary student creativity and thought.

In his address at commencement in 1827, Archibald D. Murphey, a member of the class of 1799 and a champion of the young university, advocated that the institution play a vital role in molding the moral character of the young men in its charge: "The next great object, after the improvement of the intellectual faculties, is the forming of a moral character. . . . We must look to our constitutional temperament, to our passions and feelings as influenced by external circumstances; and for rules of conduct, we must look to the sermons and parables of Christ; they are worth more than all the books which have been written on morals; they explain, and at the same time apply that pure morality which is founded upon virtuous feeling."[1]

Considering Murphey's remarks, it is little wonder that the students of the time were required to attend daily prayers and chapel exercises conducted by the administration and faculty, composed primarily of Presbyterians. In many ways, the university served *in loco parentis* for the students. A regular report of academic progress and personal conduct was forwarded by the institution to parents and guardians. One such report, prepared by presiding professor Elisha Mitchell at the close of the term in December 1828, provided the parents of Paul Cameron with a comparison of their son's diligence and deportment to those of his fellow students.

ooooo

Hark the Sound of Tar Heel Voices

Letter from Leander Hughes to John Hughes

Chapelhill,
August 23rd 1823

Kind and affectionate parent

[B]eing now at leisure I sit down to write you a few lines descriptive of my situation at this place, as it appears that you have not received my letters. I have written twice, and this is the third time since my arrival here; but had almost determined not to write anymore until I should receive some intelegence from you, yet I should have been impelled to it again by filial affection, it is a singular pleasure to me to receive a letter from you at any time and I hope it will not be long before you write to me again[.]

I board at Mrs Mitchels and shall continue there during this session. I room with a Mr Prince a classmate of mine whom I esteem and respect. [I]n one of my letters I [s]tated that I Roomed with M. Moore but prefering Prince and he appearing equally anxious that I should room with him I done so[,] while with Prince I pay nothing for lodging whereas with any person I should pay five Dollars per session[.] I have obtained a trunk by sending to Raleigh about two weeks after coming here. I am quite well and have enjoyed a very good health since my arrival here[.] I will now give you a detail of some of the occurencies that have taken place since I came here; there have been two of the students dismissed from college one for having a pistol for the purpose of exploding gunpowder the other for allowing him the privlge [to] load in his room. There has also been a very severe engagement here between a r[e]sident of this place and one of its vicinity[. T]he latter unfortunately had his entrails cut out while engaged in the contest and walked from the spring to college or nearly so before it was discovered[,] a distance of nearly two hundred yards. [H]e has mended much, and it is thought will entirely recover.

The session expires on the fifth of December as you may have probaly learned while here; at the end of this term I hope to have pleasure to return home.

Leander Hughes[2]

ooooo

Letter from F. L. Smith to Gustavus A. Miller

Chapel Hill Febry 1st 1828

Dear Friend

Your letter was received last mail. I thank you for your good wishes. But Adolphus I have little hope or even a strong wish to reach that height of fame which your kindness would assign to me[.] In youth we are too often apt to look forward to our passage through life as one decked with flowers and calculated to render us happy in every condition. Yet we find as we advance that these expectations are nothing but the illusions of a youthful imagination and that our present situation [is] far different from that which we had anticipated. This is indeed a world of disappointments. The little boy as he cons over his grammar looks forward with buoyant hopes to the time when he shall enter college[. H]is imagination paints to him scenes far different from those which then surround him. When the time arrives, how much he is mistaken! He finds college instead of the Elysium which he had expected, the same dull routine of studies, that his brains are bothered with something worse than ... the lessons of a dictionary. He now looks back with feelings of regret upon the many happy moments spen[t]

> What a joy it has been to live and learn in Chapel Hill—the hospitable home of the creative spirit.
>
> J. Carlyle Sitterson

among his young academical friends and longs to be restored to the home of his childhood. Here however fresh hopes arise in his bosom, he may look forward with pleasing anticipations to the time when he shall depart from these somber walls and enter the world a candidate for distinction in some profession. His lofty and visionary dreams make him completely successful. He thinks of the approving smiles of his doating parents or perhaps of an object even dearer than these. Fortune too smiles on his endeavours and crowns them with all the blessings of wealth. He becomes popular [and] is elected to the legislature[. T]his is but a stepping stone to congress! How much farther might I follow the young devotee in his vain hopes!—But how seldom are these hopes realized? I might say never in their full extent. He finds the world far different from what his imagination had painted[.] Instead of being disposed to encourage and honor his talents (should he have any) he finds [people] ready to criticize and disparage[. T]hey prove to be cold, callous and in many cases villanous. Such are the disappointments attendant on him who kneels at the shrine of hopeful ambitions and he is fortunate if his perseverance overcomes them, and he is not driven by them to seek releif in the haunts of dissipation.

Yours &c

F. L. Smith[3]

ooooo

Excerpt of "College Rules," a poem written by Lucius J. Polk in 1821

1 Now we are freed from College Rules,
From common place book reason,
From trifling syllogistic schools,
And systems out of season:
Never more we'll have defined
If matter think or think not,
All the matter we've to mind,
Is see who drinks or drinks not[.]

2 Metaphysically to trace,
The mind or soul abstracted,

Or prove infinity of space,
By case or cause affected;
Better souls we cant become,
By immeterial thinking—
And as for space we want no room
But just enough to drink in.

3 Plenum, vacuum, minus, plus
Are learned words and rare too,
Those terms our tutors may discuss,
And those who may please hear too,
A plenum in our wine we show,
With plus and plus behind, Sir.
And when our cash is minus low,
A vacuum soon we find, Sir.[4]

ooooo

Letter from Presiding Professor Elisha Mitchell to the Father of Paul C. Cameron at the Close of Session

Chapel Hill, Decr 9th 1824

Sir,

In conducting the education of the youth committed to our care, we, as the Faculty of the University, and as individuals, are accustomed to look around with solicitude, for the most efficacious means of attaining our object. The students of a college, are most of them at a distance from home. With many, the period of entering within its walls, is the first at which they have been left to choose, or at least to continue their own associations and friendships. Amidst the dangers to which they become exposed, the only means of preventing evil consequences, or of recovery to such as have incurred them, must be found in previous habits, and if these should fail, in such motives only as may be addressed immediately to the understanding and the heart. No means, then, should be neglected, by which such motives may be fortified, that the utmost assurance may be given to the prospects and anxious wishes of parents, in the education of their children. . . .

We propose therefore to address a letter to you, at the close of every session, while your son, or the son of a friend, now under your guardianship and parental direction, shall continue in the college, containing statements from which you may form a judgment of his standing and progress during the past session. This to many will be valuable, by preventing or putting an end to needless anxieties, if not by imparting the richest enjoyment which a parent can feel. . . . From much experience in colleges the Faculty have found it to be a general rule, that the fidelity of a student in the prosecution of knowledge, and in most cases too, the correctness of his morals, are to be estimated by the regularity of his attendance on all the exercises and duties of the college. When a youth is frequently absent from prayers and recitation, there is reason to apprehend that he is falling into evil company, irregular habits, and a disregard, if not a spirit of opposition to the laws and authority of the college. On the other hand, punctuality in these duties is most commonly accompanied with a proper deportment in general, and is a presage of ultimate success in the accomplishment of a good education.

> And when we left Carolina, Carolina stayed with us. Like a beacon, it pointed the way to excellence elsewhere. It still reminds us of our obligation to do our best.
>
> Alexander Julian, II, class of 1969

Paul C Cameron
No. Of times.
Your son has been absent from prayers—12
Your son has been absent from recitation—39

There are 143 students. Of these 25 have not been once absent from prayers, and 26 not once absent from recitation.

33 persons have been absent more than your son from prayers.
5 persons have been absent more than your son from recitation.

E. Mitchell, Presiding Prof^s

1830

—

1839

Ups and Downs and in Between

*F*or the university community as a whole, the 1830s were marked by a series of high and low points. By the onset of the decade, more than 450 men had graduated from the Chapel Hill institution, yet the total enrollment in 1831 barely exceeded 100. And while admissions would steadily increase the study body by almost a third at decade's end, the university grieved over the loss of beloved personnel and a challenge to its continued existence in Chapel Hill.

In a letter dated October 23, 1837, Alpheus Jones, a student from Wake County, North Carolina, offered his observations about the state of affairs at the university to a recent graduate who was studying law in Virginia. Jones intuitively noted, "As soon as our University rises in one respect, it appears to decline in another."

One of the lowest points in the early history of the university came on January 27, 1835, when President Joseph Caldwell died in the parlor of his home on Franklin Street. In the wake of Caldwell's death, his stepson, Professor William Hooper, was presumed by many to be the likely successor to the presidency. However, Governor David Swain, the choice of the trustees, assumed the post in January 1836. A year later, Hooper departed

Hark the Sound of Tar Heel Voices

Chapel Hill to serve as president of the Furman Theological Institute (now Furman University) in South Carolina.

As his departure neared, Professor Hooper received homage in a poem by George Moses Horton, a black man who earned nominal sums from university students by writing personalized verses for them. Born into slavery in eastern North Carolina in 1797, Horton, at the age of twenty, began making his way on Sundays from nearby Chatham County to Chapel Hill, where he sold produce and his creative work to earn money to purchase his freedom. Entitled "Farewell Address to Prof. Hooper," his stanzas of tribute were published in the *Raleigh Register* and the *North-Carolina Gazette* on October 9, 1837.

Prior to the death of Caldwell and the departure of Hooper, the university had survived a scathing indictment by one of its own. In November 1834, Walker Anderson, a professor of natural philosophy and astronomy, transmitted a letter to the president of the university's trustees in which he enumerated the many defects of the school as he perceived them—poor scholarship, a lack of student discipline, and the need for a relocation of the campus. His proposed remedy—moving the university to Raleigh or another town larger than Chapel Hill—fell upon deaf ears.

Amid the rumblings caused by the changes in administration and faculty and the concerns expressed in Anderson's letter, students experienced the ebb and flow of college life. On the positive side, Charles L. Pettigrew corresponded with his father, Ebenezer, at the beginning of the term in 1833 to inform him that he had a pleasant roommate, that he was studying hard, and that he ranked high in his class.

At the other end of the spectrum, Joshua Perry was forced to provide his father an explanation of his behavior in connection with an incident on the campus in 1839. Even in those days, bad news had a way of making its way home. Perry's letter, dated May 18, offered a classic defense by a student who was in trouble both at school and at home.

But for most students, day-to-day life was one of long, hard hours of routine. Kenelm "Kelly" H. Lewis, who graduated just months after he penned a letter to his sister on February 28, 1838, provided his

> The University has made enduring contributions in developing the pioneers indispensable to the decisive forward movements in the common life of the State— men and women willing boldly to step in the lonely front for a cause later to be the triumph of the people.
>
> Frank Porter Graham

sibling with an excellent overview of the daily tedium experienced by students of his time.

ooooo

Excerpt from Letter of Alpheus Jones to Peter W. Hairston

Chapel Hill 23rd. Octr. 1837.

Dear Peter:

It would appear, (for I very seldom hear from you), that you have fallen in with so many of the noble sons of Old Virginia, that you have almost entirely forgotten your old acquaintances at this University. But probably some of the circumstances herein mentioned may serve to arouse your memory, and, by bringing to your recollection many past scenes, render more perfect those pleasures which I hope you now enjoy.

It may be somewhat cheering to you to learn, by the Catalogue, of the flourishing and still more promising condition of the University at present. The number of Students is 142; and, if every "Fresh" Class continue to have as many members as the present one, by the time my Class graduates, the whole number of Students will amount to 200 or more. And I know that it is still more pleasing to you to learn that the number of members of the Dialectic Society has increased so much; but all our rooms are completely filled up. . . .

But so soon as our University rises in one respect, it appears to decline in another; for while the number of Students has been increasing, it seems that other Colleges have been attempting, by offering larger salaries (I suppose) to deprive us of our Professors. Professor W. Hooper has resigned, to become President of a College in South Carolina, (which you may have seen published in the *Raleigh Register* together with a farewell address to him by our Poet, George Horton.) Also the Professorship of Mathematics has been offered to Pro. [James] Phillips by a College in Mississippi. But I believe that he takes interest enough in our University not to accept it. . . .

The present "Fresh" Class, is the most pugnacious and wild set that I have seen in some time. They have [had] no less than three [fights] in it this Session; and a few mornings there was a half-grown steer in the bull-pen in the old chapel, at prayers, which I suppose was placed there by the "Fresh."

It happened, that he was placed there in the absence of our President, Gov. Swain, or I suppose we would have had a speech from him on the subject.

Your friend &c.

Alpheus Jones[1]

ooooo

Poem of George M. Horton
SEPTEMBER 1837

Farewell Address to Prof. Hooper

Farewell, if thou hence wil't depart,
And leave us, dull brooding behind,
The thought of thy flight, is a veil to each heart,
And clogs all the wheels of the mind.

If thy race in this College is o'er
And duty forbids thy delay,
Farewell! but thy conduct we still shall adore,
When fortune shall waft thee away.

We still shall thy powers proclaim,
And thy deeds we will ever admire;
Here, no mortal tongue shall extinguish thy fame
But kindle its taper, still higher.

The Sun of our language must set,
Gladly to rise on some distant shore;
He leaves us in gloom, with tears of regret,
And will illumine this College no more.

The honor'd Professor, farewell!
May the joys of life be thy lot;
And though grief may our sad bosoms swell,
Thy virtues shall ne'er be forgot.[2]

From the coming of the first student to its open doors . . .
the University of North Carolina at Chapel Hill has been
a magic gulf stream flowing in an ever-widening current
through the lives of people in the cities, the counties and
the state of North Carolina and beyond—tempering the
customs, traditions and habits of the people it serves and
lifting them to higher levels of living wherever it has
gone.

Albert Coates,
founder and first director
of the Institute of Government at UNC

ooooo

Excerpt from Letter of Professor Walker Anderson to the President of the Board of Trustees

Univ. of N.C. Nov. 1834

The defects of the present organization of our University, seem to the subscriber to be so fundamental, that in preparing to lay before the Trustees, his views of the condition, he is tempted to enter more at large into the subject & to suggest more extensive alterations. . . . Though I speak of defects, it will be seen when I enter into detail, that they are not of a character to bring the smallest censure upon the gentlemen who have had charge of the institution. . . .

1. The first defect to which I shall allude is radical & unfortunately too obvious to need any proof—it is the low standard of scholarship in the University, not perhaps as compared with other colleges, but with that estimate of the good scholarship which is formed in every plain practical understanding. Our graduates in a large majority of classes carry with them from college the most slender & superficial knowledge of what has

occupied them for years & in all our examinations it is difficult to find a problem in mathematics, a principle in physics or morals, or a passage in the classics simple or easy enough not to present an impossible obstacle to the candidate. . . .

2. The second defect to which I shall allude grows in part out of the efforts made to correct the first. The subjection of young men & boys to the same kind of discipline, is almost certain to be attended with mortification to the disciplinarian & irritation and alienation on the part of the young men. . . . The young men are alienated by a discipline, of which they cannot understand the motives—while the boys soon detect its inefficiency & set at nought its requisition. . . .

3. The third defect I shall mention arises out of the location of the University. . . . I am persuaded that a village may abound with all the temptations which are supposed to be peculiarly dangerous to young men in a larger town, while it is destitute of all those countervailing influences which are furnished by the latter in restraints imposed by the countenance of an enlightened & Christian community. . . .

I propose then that the institution under the care of the Trustees be divided into two departments, the one to be called the "Collegiate Institute of N.C.," & the other "the University of N.C.," the former to be located at Chapel Hill under the charge of a Rector & three tutors & organized after the model of the High Schools of Europe & our Northern States. . . .

The University proper I would have located in some town, perhaps the capital of the State would be preferable to any other. . . .

Respectfully,

Walker Anderson[3]

> From the very first moment, my memories of Chapel Hill carry with them a quality of magic which is present to this day. As soon as I step on campus, I am filled with that feeling of respect, of awe, of magic.
>
> Michael Hooker

Excerpt of Letter from Charles L. Pettigrew to his father
AUGUST 19, 1833

I have a room-mate who is quite a pleasant young man generally; the reason I took a room-mate was because I expected the college would be ful[l] and I would therefore be obliged to take one so I thought it better to have one of my own choosing but I now find that I might have had a room by myself if [I should] choose, but I shall now continue with him all the session and it costs less, however it costs more than I expected; I suppose it is because there is but one good store here and they knowing that students are obliged to have certain things ask their own price. I study tolerable hard and am among the best in the class though there [are] some who sit up very late at night and have their books in their hands untill night. I am in very good health. I would write more but it is so late, being past ten and I am so sleepy that I must quit.[4]

ooooo

Excerpt of Letter from Joshua Perry to Jeremiah Perry

Chapel Hill, May 18th 1839

Dear Father

The astonishment with which I met, in the perusal of your letter, induces me to write to you immdiatly. I find your letter, that I am accused of neglecting my studies, and also of disorder, both of which charges, I deny, and can prove at any time to be false, by those to whom I recite and also by my whole class. I have consulted with Governor Swain concerning the affair, and he says, that he knows nothing against me. As to being disorderly, I am verry certain, how that originated; some three or four weeks ago

Swain was absent from the hill, and one evening at pray[er]s, something took place, which created a great laughter, and Old [Elisha] Mitchell, (to be smart) got up, and spoke verry harshly, and in return, nearly every fellow in college commenced stamping; and those whom he did not see, he reported on suspicion. . . . [D]aily observation proves to me, that the Faculty are a set of rascals. I hope when you receive this, that you will have no further doubts as to the dissolute course which, some of the Faculty would have you believe, I have been pursueing.

I still remain your faithful Son

J Perry[5]

ooooo

Excerpt of Letter from Kenelm H. Lewis to Emma Lewis

University of NC. Feb 28th 1838

Dear Sister

I received your letter dated 23 Inst. Yesterday, and should have answered it immediately but was prevented by the report that a balloon was to make its' ascension that evening. I attended but it was a failure. . . .

My health at present is very good[. I am] very well situated & have every opportunity both of reading, and learning the course of Studies prescribed in College. [W]e have in our library about three thousand five hundred volumes. History, Novels Biographys &c. &c. I am very desirous to remain here next vacation for the purpose of reading.—

I must now say a word or two in regard to the ordinary routine of daily life at College. Very early in the morning the observer may see lights at a few of the windows of the buildings inhabited by students. They mark the rooms occupied by the more industrious or more resolute, who rise and devote an hour or two to their books by candle light on the winter mornings. About day the bell awakens the multitude of sleepers in all the rooms, and in a short time they are to be seen issuing from the various doors with sleepy looks and a few with books under their arms to attempt to make up as well as the faint but increasing light will enable them, for the time wasted in idleness or dissipation on the evening before. [T]he first who come down go slowly, others with quicker and quicker step as the tolling of the bell proceeds; and the last few stragglers run with all speed to answer to their respective names. One of the Professors reads a portion of Scripture by the mingled light of the reddening beams which comes in from the eastern sky. He then offers the morning prayer. The hundreds of young men before him exhibit the appearance of respectful attention[. W]hen prayers are over, the several classes repair immediately to the rooms assigned to them, and recite the first lesson of the day. During the short period which elapses between the recitation and the breakfast bell College is a busy scene. [P]arties are running up and down the stairs two steps at a time with the ardour and activity of youth. And now and then a fresh crowd is seen issuing from the door of some one of the buildings where a class has finished its recitation and comes forth to disperse to their rooms[.] The breakfast bell brings out the whole throng again and gathers them around the long tables in the Steward Hall, or else scatters them among the private families of the Village[.] An hour after the breakfast bell rings to mark the commencement of study hours . . . the students are required by College laws to repair to their respective rooms, which answer the 3fold purpose of parlour bedroom and stud[y, to] prepare for their recitation at 11. o'clock[. T]hey who choose to evade this law can do it without any detection. The great majority comply, but some go into their neighbour[s'] rooms to receive assistance in their studies, some lay by the dull book and read a tale; and others farther gone in the road of idleness and dissipation steal secretly away from College and ramble in the woods or skate upon the ice, evading their task like truant boys, they of course are marked absent but pretended sickness will answer for an excuse. [T]hey go on blind to the certainty of disgrace which must soon come.—

Your. Brother.

K H Lewis[6]

Hark the Sound of Tar Heel Voices

Students, Students, Students

*I*n relative terms, the student population exploded in the university's sixth decade of operation. More than fifteen hundred students enrolled during the decade, and commencement exercises counted nearly forty graduates each year. Much of the growth reflected the increasing sectionalism in the United States. Affluent North Carolina families who in earlier times had sent their sons to established schools north of the Mason-Dixon line began to choose instead to enroll them in their state university. In addition to sectional pride and patriotism, university enrollment benefited from the advent of the public school system in North Carolina in 1839.

Among the students who graduated in the 1840s was a man considered by many historians to have been one of the most brilliant men ever born in North Carolina. James Johnston Pettigrew descended from a family that had been associated with the university from its inception. During his magnificent four-year academic career in Chapel Hill, Johnston, as he was known on campus, received a grade of "excellent" in every course, establishing a standard that has rarely been equaled at the university.

On his visit to participate in the commencement exercises at his alma mater in 1847, American president James K. Polk was highly impressed with Pettigrew, who graduated as valedictorian of his class. Polk convinced the young scholar to return with him to Washington, D.C., where Pettigrew was promptly appointed as professor at the National Observatory. Sixteen years later, Pettigrew, then a Confederate general, died in the Southern retreat from Gettysburg (where, just days earlier, he had played a prominent role in leading a division in what is popularly known as Pickett's Charge).

Two letters written by Pettigrew in 1844—one to his father, Ebenezer, and one to his older brother Charles, an 1836 graduate of the university—provide a look at the academic and social life in Chapel Hill during the final term of the scholar's freshman year.

Not long after James Johnston Pettigrew penned the letter to his brother, the campus readied itself for a great influx of visitors to the commencement exercises of 1844. In an attempt to attract a sizable number of females to the campus for the graduation festivities, an anonymous writer for the newly established *North Carolina Magazine* crafted a romantic, albeit tongue-in-cheek, description of the campus and its students.

One year later, a party atmosphere filled the autumn air as students enjoyed a "spree," a multi-week time of fun, merriment, entertainment, and sometimes mischief. William E. Blake, a senior, described the spree of September 1845 in a letter to a friend who was then a student at Randolph-Macon College in Virginia.

Accompanying the growth of the student body were problems associated with boyish high jinks and outright misbehavior. When students got out of hand at a campus dance and a freshman party in August 1840, their unruly behavior threatened bodily injury to Dr. Elisha Mitchell and Manuel Fetter, the professor of Greek. Dismayed by the events, Mitchell turned to Charles Manly (the secretary-treasurer of the university's board of trustees, who would become governor of North Carolina before the end of the

> Measured in terms of her greatest dimensions, interpreted in terms of the profound realities for which she stands, judged on a national basis, and by national standards, I believe that the University of North Carolina is the best product of her civilization that North Carolina has to show to the world!
>
> Edward Kidder Graham

decade) for guidance and support. Mitchell's letter, dated September 11, 1840, paints a vivid picture of student activities gone awry.

ooooo

Letter from James Johnston Pettigrew to His Father

Chapel Hill Jan 13th 1843 [1844]

Dear Pa,

I arrived here the evening of the day I started and received my trunk that night by stage; I came very near losing it, and if I had not been down there at the time it came in, it would have gone onto Hillsboro for the bar-keeper did not get up to examine the way-bill, but slept on till the stage went out. I delayed writing thus long, that I might know whether I should room by myself or not, so as to write you, and so many new students have arrived, that it is impossible to do so and I have concluded to continue in the same room. A great many persons have joined College this session, which I believe is unusual, the number of students, generally, being less the spring session than the fall one. One class consists of forty-five, being eight or ten more than last session and it is now the largest class in College and most of our old recitation rooms cannot hold us. Some of the students went down to the Governor's last week and he told them the same thing he told you, that my marks were better than any one else in our class.

We have had very bad weather ever since I have been here; it has rained almost every day and sleeted, and came very near snowing twice. It has cleared off however and I hope we shall have some good weather.

The place is a great deal more dissipated in the vacation than in the session and the night I came they were all of them intoxicated in some degree, which, together with cardplaying constituted the principal amusement. Governor Swain had some of them up before the faculty for their conduct in the vacation, but I believe did nothing to them.

Your aff. Son

J. Johnston Pettigrew[1]

ooooo

Letter from James Johnston Pettigrew to His Brother Charles

University of N.C.
May 5th 1844

My Dear Brother,

I received your letter in due time and intended to have answered it sometime ago, but have neglected it as yet. For this negligence I have no excuse, except that when one has studied all the week and . . . attended society meetings of Friday night and Saturday morning, he feels very little like writing a letter, in the evening.

The studies of the Freshmen class are considerably lightened by carrying up the mathematics, and instead of five Algebra recitations a week we have only three. The Faculty have decided that the present course is to[o] difficult for minds so young and untrained and on that account have transferred the study of Astronomy and Natural Philosophy to the Senior year. . . .

> In its dedication to excellence and its commitment to justice, the University may well be North Carolina's best hope for a brighter future.
>
> J. Carlyle Sitterson

Our [Philanthropic] society has been progressing and the Dialectic retrograding ever since 1837[. L]ast commencement, every Phi member of the Senior class obtained a distinction and of the . . . ten, who spoke on stage, seven were Phi's. At this commencement, we are divided about equally, but one-half of our members have a distinction, while only one-third of the other society have, and of the five who take distinction, three are Phi's.

They have a large superiority in the Junior, which is the worst class, that has been here for some years. In the sophomore they have one first-distinction man to our three. In the Freshman they have none.

The graduating class is the most talented that has been here for some years and is quite large. . . . Both societies, with the assistance of the trustees are making great efforts to build new halls, and I hope they will suc[cee]d, for, our present one is much smaller than the Di's; and being next to the campus is exposed to every man who will attempt to listen.

The Bell is ringing for church now. Give my love to Pa and brother William and believe me to be

Your aff brother

J. Johnston Pettigrew[2]

ooooo

Description of the Campus in June 1844 and an Invitation to Graduation

For the benefit of those who have never graced this classic spot with their noble presence, we will give a small description of the Campus.—It is an area of ground containing about four acres; it is enclosed on the North and South sides by a rock wall of singular strength and beauty, whose solid materials promise to defy the ravages of both time and weather; the Eastern side is bounded by a rail fence, and flanked by a group of neat white buildings, denominated the "Steward's Hall," which from contrast, renders still more lovely this enchanting spot; on the Western side is another faint attempt at a stone wall, which seems to have been ashamed of its impudent obtrusiveness, and shrunk back in despair of rivaling the peculiar elegance which characterizes those on the North and South sides. The Campus is ornamented with a variety of trees of the noblest order; giant old oaks, the pride of American forests, decorate this seat of Learning; here and there may be described a venerable hickory, which claims the right of being ranked side by side with the oak; and one spot more highly honored than the rest, boasts a lordly old poplar, whose lofty head towering high above all others proudly proclaims its pre-eminence. We were preparing a few cantos; and in truth had already written the first, to commemorate this monarch of the grove, when a reckless editor rendered our poem a work of supererogation, by inserting in the first number of this Magazine a miserable doggerel dedicated to the very "Auld Patriarch" himself; thus anticipating our purpose, and robbing the readers of this periodical of a most delicious treat.

We despise the spirit of innovation which is stalking abroad through the land. We despise the new-fangled notions of taste. When we were matriculated, the College grove presented one of the most delightful prospects we ever saw; trees were as thick as they were in the forests of the West before daring pioneer has laid his axe to the root; during the summer when the leaves are in full maturity, the dense foliage cast a shade as dark, gloomy, and romantic, as that of the valley of the Mississippi. But alas! "how changed the scene," in four short years this beautiful place has been purloined of many of its most magnificent decorations. In vain did we cry out against such wilful destruction of life; we supplicated, we remonstrated, we threatened; our prayers were unheard, our opposition over ruled, and our menaces scorned. With a mind determined upon murder, a dignified Tutor strutted about, dooming this and that tree to death, and soon the country, for miles around, responded with the thrilling cry of the wounded and dying. An idea got into the heads of the Faculty—by the way its a wonder it did'nt run them all crazy—that the appearance of the place might be greatly improved by removing half the trees; alledging as a reason, that they obstructed a view of the College buildings, from the gaze of stage-coach passengers. And this—the ruination of the Campus— is the "grand improvement which has been effected" and "the grander ones which are in contemplation," with which they have so successfully humbugged the Legislature—the guardians of the institution—and the good people of North Carolina, for ten years.

Annually this place is graced with the wealth, the beauty, and the talent of the State. And will you not, gentle reader, make one of the attractions at our next Commencement? If you are a lady, we can offer irresistible arguments why you should be present; if a gentlemen you will need no incentives. If a lady, we promise you a beau who will answer your loftiest expectations. The reflective and dignified senior is at your service; the gay and gallant junior would esteem it the highest of honors to be favored with your company in a stroll through the Campus, through the Literary Halls, and to the Chapel; the erudite Sophomore will discourse learnedly to you, on the beauty of the classics, and talk loudly of the sublimities of Calculus and Astronomy; and the susceptible Freshman, with a pair of exceedingly high heeled boots pressing his corns just sufficiently to remind him that he has on a pair of boots, will make love, quote Byron and Shakespeare, and talk of stars in the middle of the day. From a crowd of such fascinating youths, you will doubtless be at a loss to make a choice, but if you'll allow an interference on our part, we would modestly prefer the claims of

Seniors. Not because we are a Senior ourself, but because, oh! Because, ah!—. But should none of these tickle your fancy we have at your command a few straggling Irregulars, who can do a little at almost any thing. If you prefer a white ribbon [the color of the Philanthropic Society] to a blue [the color of the Dialectic Society]—fifty are instantly soliciting the honor of your hand; if a blue—a hundred would go into ecstasies at an approving smile. Should you condescend so far as to make yourself agreeable, gold badges will be showered upon you with the most extravagant profusion:

> Lives there a woman with soul so dead
> Who to herself hath not yet said
> I'll come, I'll come, I'll come.

As to the gentlemen—the young ones we mean—it matters very little whether they come or not; we have a plenty already, to entertain five hundred ladies, better than they have ever been before; so we will not be pressing upon them "to favor us with the honor of their company, the 6th of June."[3]

ooooo

Excerpt from Letter of William E. Blake to Richard Irby
OCTOBER 3, 1845

My time has been occupied in preparing a senior speech for my debut on stage. My subject is "The Shade of the Past." It opens up a wide field for the imagination as well as for historical illustration. There are thirty seniors and among them are some very good declaimers and writers. We expect a very large audience. . . .

The ladies both of Hillsborough and Pittsborough (the one town 12, the other 18 miles distant), have engaged rooms in the village for the occasion. We have, besides, 13 young ladies in Chapel Hill. I suppose there will be about 30 or 40 young ladies and as many matrons. We have engaged a band of musicians. We have also succeeded in getting the faculty counsel to allow us to speak at candle-light; so that it will occur three evenings in the week; and such gallavanting as there will be.

I will venture to say that for the last two weeks, Chapel Hill has been the gayest place this side of the Potomac. We have had a delegation of the

Pittsborough girls here on a visit, and, taking them altogether, they are ahead of any thing I ever saw. The prettiest, loveliest, liveliest, and most heart-breaking, bone-cracking and study killing images of female sweetness, that ever bustled in a crowd . . .

There were three parties as a token of welcome on the part of the villagers, and the visit was interspersed with walks, rides, et cetera, morning, afternoon, and evening. The visitors left here yesterday and seven of the students accompanyed them up to Pittsborough. As such sprees occur rarely, it is not surprising that the fellows make the most of them. . . .

Our regular Sessional Spree came off last Friday week. About 20 or 30 fellows disguised with calico coats and pants, and paper hats, plumed with chicken fellows [feathers], sallied out in the campus about 11 o'clock at night. They commenced ringing the bell, blowing horns, shooting pistols, and then, forming a line, would charge against the trees and piles of rocks with a savage vengeance.

The faculty came on the ground, and one attempted to enter one of the passages. The fellows ducked him with two buckets of water, pelted him with apples and finally threw a wash basin at him. This made him leave.

They had up about 20, but only 5 were dismissed; the others were too silver-tongued to be caught. While there are occasional sprees here, generally very good order prevails.[4]

ooooo

Letter from Elisha Mitchell to Charles Manly

University of N. Ca. Sept. 11th 1840

To Charles Manly, Esq.
Dear Sir,

Three weeks ago, there was an affair in which Professor Fetter and myself were concerned of which some account appears to have reached you— true perhaps [but in] the main untrue in some of the details. A Bull dance was got up on the second story passage of . . . the West building. A pail and wash-bowl[,] I believe it was out of water[,] were placed in the landing place of the stairs to wet such member of the Faculty as might attempt to interfere. It was Prof. Fetter's evening to be there for the preservation of order. The noise of the dance was so great that after it had continued for some time I went down and was upon the ground a little before Mr. Fetter escaped the proposed ducking, but the lights were immediately extinguished. I obtained a light in the third story and . . . it appeared that the persons who had been engaged in the disturbance ran down and escaped from the building. After I left, the annoyances were kept up and directed particularly against Professor Fetter. Water, books, tables, or parts of tables were thrown down from above and a charge of pusillanimity is attempted to be got up against him for not having put these disturbances down and for having run[,] as it is (untruly) said[,] from the building when he left it over to Dr. Graves. The running Mr. Fetter positively denies any farther than he passed rapidly out of the building and to the distance of a few feet from it with the view of avoiding anything that might be thrown from above. My own recollections are that the night was too dark to admit of any person being seen either running or standing still at the distance of an hundred yards in the grove. Before he went out of the building Mr. Fetter's position was one of difficulty. The upper stories—the second and third were quite dark—if he ascended without a candle he could see no one—if with a candle he became a mark for a pitcher of water or other missile by which the candle would have been extinguished. . . .

The affair having gone off so well gave additional spirit to those of the next Saturday night. A freshman treat was had after dark in the woods . . . from which the company came up hallooing and shouting. The Faculty went round to the rooms to see who was absent, and it not appearing to be much use to stay longer went home. Some stones and brick bats were thrown before they retired. Afterwards the belfry having been broken open, the bell was rung indefinitely. They also began to batter in pieces the doors of the sophomore and junior recitation rooms and of the laboratory. The door of the library[,] yielding by bursting off of the box of the lock to the first application of force[,] was not broken. Fearing that great injury to the apparatus might be done in the laboratory I went down with a view if possible of having an interview with the rioters and *persuading* them to desist. I had plenty of brick bats thrown at me, masses weighing from one to two pounds thrown with a hearty good will and flying on all sides of me. The Faculty afterwards went through the buildings between the hours of two and three in the morning with the view of detecting some of the authors of these disorders who had taken our horses out of the stables and were riding them about the campus, but in consequence of some delay in our movements nothing important was accomplished. I have spoken of what I myself saw because I do not know exactly what befell the other members of the faculty.

What is to be done? . . .

. . . [T]he Faculty are I suppose entitled to that protection when engaged in the discharge of their appropriate duties which the laws of the land are held to afford the meanest citizens. The ordinances of the Trustees do not encourage or even warrant a criminal prosecution on our part. . . . But it seems desirable that the students should be told in very plain terms that they are amenable to the laws of the land and that the Trustees will of their own notion proceed against them if these things are repeated or others like them are engaged in.

Yours Respectfully,

E. Mitchell[5]

The Calm before the Storm

*I*n the decade before the War Between the States, all outward signs from Chapel Hill seemed to indicate that the university was about to enter a golden age. Burgeoning enrollment brought students from many other states, particularly Tennessee, Louisiana, Alabama, South Carolina, Mississippi, Georgia, and Texas. Growth in the student body enabled the administration and the trustees to enlarge and maintain an able faculty and to expand the size of the campus.

Not only were more students enrolling, but larger numbers of them were completing the requirements for graduation. In 1858, the graduating class neared one hundred for the first time in school history. A year later, President James Buchanan accepted the invitation to speak at the commencement ceremonies in Chapel Hill. His remarks, intended as a charge to graduates, hinted of the brewing storm that would temporarily delay the university from attaining its high aspirations: "I would advise these young men to devote themselves to the preservation of the principles of the Constitution, for without these blessings our liberties are gone. Let this Constitution be torn to atoms; let the members of this Union separate; let thirty Republics rise up against each other, and it would be the most fatal day for the liberties of the human race that ever dawned upon this land. Let this experiment fail, and every friend of liberty will deplore the sad event."[1]

During the decade, the university developed the leadership skills of many of the young men who would assume prominent roles in the war that would engulf America in 1861. Three of these students left interesting accounts of their days in Chapel Hill.

In 1850, James Lee, Jr., came to the university from his home in Tennessee with an intense desire to succeed at a school he deemed one of the best in the nation. Through the assistance and compassion of President David Swain, Lee gained admission and subsequently became a prominent attorney and statesman in his native state. Though he was defeated in the 1853 gubernatorial contest by one Andrew Johnson, Lee went on to be elected to the Congress of the Confederate States of America. His letter to a friend and mentor in Tennessee in October 1850 chronicled Lee's dogged determination and boasted of the high academic standing of the university.

David Swain was the glue that held the school together in the years before the maelstrom, as well as the impetus behind the quest to achieve national fame and recognition. Aside from his responsibilities as president, Swain taught a number of classes and befriended many a student. In 1851, a prospective student from Swain's beloved North Carolina mountains requested a loan from the university president in order to come to Chapel Hill for an education. Swain complied with the request, and soon thereafter, Zebulon Baird Vance, one of the most remarkable men ever produced by North Carolina, arrived in Chapel Hill. James W. Wilson recalled his classmate's debut: "I remember well Vance's first appearance at the Hill— homemade shoes and clothes, about three inches between pants and shoes, showing his sturdy ankles; quick and rough at repartee; and mostly remarkable for his jokes."[2]

Indeed, Zeb Vance acquired a well-deserved reputation as a campus prankster. His antics in David Swain's classes were legendary. Dr. Richard H. Lewis, Vance's seatmate in international law, penned a delightful account of the mountaineer's wit and cunning in class.

After leaving Chapel Hill, Vance emerged as a dominant figure in the

I speak for all of us who could not afford to go to Duke, and would not have even if we could have afforded it.

Charles Kuralt

history of his native state. From the outbreak of the War Between the States until he was elected governor of North Carolina in 1862, Vance served on the battlefield as the colonel of the Twenty-sixth North Carolina. His political career, which included several terms as governor and service in both chambers of the United States Congress, was both long and distinguished. Through it all, Vance never forgot the valuable lessons he learned from his friend David Swain. In one of his speeches, he paid special tribute to Swain and offered warm reflections on his classroom experiences in Chapel Hill.

Vance's junior officer in the Twenty-sixth North Carolina succeeded him as the commander of the regiment. Likewise, he had followed in the footsteps of Vance at Chapel Hill. Henry "Harry" King Burgwyn, Jr., the son of an aristocratic planter in northeastern North Carolina, graduated from the university in 1859 at the age of sixteen with an impeccable academic record. As he listened to the words of President Buchanan at the graduation exercises, Burgwyn was yet desirous of a military education, preferably at West Point. Two of his letters, written to his mother while a student at the university, evince that desire.

Burgwyn's brief but heroic military career came to a tragic end on July 1, 1863, when "the boy colonel of the Confederacy" died while leading the Twenty-sixth North Carolina in one of the most famous charges in the Battle of Gettysburg. His dying words—"Tell the General my men never failed me at a single point"—were directed to James Johnston Pettigrew, a fellow alumnus who ironically would die less than two weeks later.[3]

ooooo

Excerpts from Letter of James Lee, Jr., to Major G. A. Henry
OCTOBER 20 AND 21, 1850

University of North Carolina Oct. 20th/50

Maj: G. A. Henry

When I joined the college I was deficient on every thing and in consequence of which I was at first rejected, being informed of my rejection I did not know what step to pursue, I disliked to return home and I thought it would be a bad chance to get in any other institution so you may judge how I felt far from home, in the midst of strangers and not being able to get in college. A thousand thoughts in a moment presented themselves to my consideration, and finily I arose from my meditation and straight way I went to our president Gov Swain and told him I had come from Tennessee to join this institution and I was going to do so if they would only give me half a chance and all I asked was to let me enter on probation until I could make up my deficiencies, he consented, and immediately I . . . rolled into hard study to keep up with my class and also to make up my deficiencies. The first two weeks I studied until two o'clock at night and never laid down before one no how and was compelled to rise at half after four to prayers, at [the] end of two week I was perfectly exhausted and my health began to decline. . . . I saw my critical situation and conducted [concluded] it was perfect folly for me to wear myself out in pursuit of an education and after having obtained it to go home with a shattered constitution to lay down and die[. W]ith this view of the matter I ceased studying and from that time I commenced improving and now *my coat wont meet on me*, having resumed [m]y studies I am now marching up the fair hill of science like some proud ste[a]mer up the mighty bosom of the father of waters, and will never rest satisfied until I have climbed the last round of the ladder of fame and can stand upon the topmost pinnicle of human glory. As the ten o'clock is ringing I shall take your advice and retire.

Sunday morning October 21st/50

I suppose you would like to learn some of the particulars of the University of North Carolina as you are a literary character some what. In the first place it is situated upon the top of the highest situation in the whole country in the midst of a delightful grove. . . . The vicinity is so poor that when a man dies they are compelled to *maneuvre* his grave to enable him to arise in the judgment day. The institution is of long standing and extensive character[. I]t was founded in the year 1787 and received the name of University in 1816 and can without transcending the bounds of reason or varacity boast of having sent out a greater number of prominent men than any institution in the United States. Our faculty is the best that can be had any where and to show you a test of our old institution[, a] young man came here from Cambridge to join college (he left there on account of his ill health)[,] he left the Junior class there and was compelled to make up some studies before he could enter here. The faculty here is as tyranicle as they are smart for in the beginning of the session we had about two hundred and fifty students [and] we have only two hundred now[. T]he rest have been sent off or quit on their own accord. The rules are very rigid indeed for if a student misses recitation even once when he is sick he must make it up before he can get a diploma and many other things too tedious to mention.

Your &c

James Lee Jr.[4]

ooooo

An Account of the Classroom Antics of Zeb Vance by Richard H. Lewis

One day, in the recitation on international law, in Gov. Swain's room, we were called upon to give a list of the cases bearing upon the question of "contraband of war." There were some thirty or forty cases cited in the textbook, all of which were required to be accurately memorized. Having no memory worth speaking of, I had written all these cases, in pencil, upon my left boot, foot and leg. Vance, who always sat by me, saw me reading the cases. "Lewis," said he, "lend me your leg." Without waiting for my consent, he jerked my leg up into his lap, and rapidly read the names, and returned my limb. In a few minutes I was called upon to recite the list. I think I gave three or four, not more, and sat down covered with confusion. "Mr. Vance, advance to the front and cite the cases bearing upon this point," said Gov. Swain, with an appreciative smile at his own pun. Vance rose promptly and

Chapel Hill fostered and nurtured me. I took solace and strength from those numerous campus evenings when thick fog hugged the lampposts. . . . My first night on campus was one of those nights, and I knew from the first evening that I'd come to the right place. I thought, "God, this is a dream."

Novelist Leon Rooke,
winner of Canada's highest literary award

gave every one of the cases with the weary air of one who had been know-ing the thing for ten years. When he sat down he gave me a dig in the ribs with his elbow, saying: "Lewis, why don't you study your lesson, you lazy fellow."[5]

ooooo

Tribute to President David L. Swain by Zeb Vance

How well do I remember the many occasions during my sojourn at the University when he, as my preceptor, esteeming such influences of greater importance to the class than the tests of the lessons, would for the time give his whole soul to the stirring up of these generous and emulous senti-ments in the hearts of his pupils. The very first recitation in which I ever appeared before him was one such. I shall never, never forget it! In 1851 I entered the University and joined the Senior class as an irregular. This first class was in constitutional law. A single question was asked and answered as to the subject in hand, and then he began to discourse of Chancellor Kent, whose treatise we were studying; from Kent he went to Story; from Story to Marshall, repeating anecdotes of great Americans who had framed and interpreted our organic law, and touching upon the debate between Hayne and Webster. From these he went back and back to the men and the times when great principles of Anglo-Saxon liberty were placed one by one as stones polished by the genius of the wise and cemented by the blood of the brave in the walls of the temple of human freedom. . . . Warming as he went with glowing theme, walking up and down the recitation room, which was the library of the "old South," with long and awkward strides, heaving those heavy passionate sighs which were always with the witnesses of deep emotion, he would now and then stop, reach down from its shelf a volume of some old poet, and read with trembling voice some grand and glowing words addressed to man's truest ambition that thrilled our souls like a song of the chief musician. A profound silence was evidence of the deep attention of the class, and the hour passed almost before we knew it had begun.[6]

ooooo

Excerpt from Letter of Henry "Harry" King Burgwyn, Jr., to His Mother

AUGUST 25, 1857

Chapel Hill Aug 25/57

My Dear Mother

I also with the single exception of my sleeping apparatus . . . am probably as well fixed as any other person. I have good luck in being with such clever & steady young men as Walker Anderson & George Johnston. They are both extremely kind & Attentive to me. George Bryan also is very kind but with all that I don't like the place half so much as West Point but I don't mean to say that I am dissatisfied with it[. O]n the contrary I like it much better than I thought I would. I room about a half mile from the college & do not hear much of the noise which a person rooming there has to put up with. I think that this place is fast improving & in point of dissipation the faculty are trying to put it down as much as possible & I hear they caught twenty students last night either drunk or with liquor in their possession. I should think that, if the trustees would make it incumbent on the faculty to expel every student who was caught in that state & have it carried out, they would soon have this college equal if not superior to the university of Virginia which stands second only to West Point. Two or three days ago we had a heavy storm & ever since the weather has been cool & delightful[,] so cool indeed that it reminds of the near approach of autumn. . . . I study mathematics in the Soph & senior class in order to get along faster. I also study french in those with my latin & chemistry occupy[ing] almost my entire time. What little there is left[,] & there is none but on Saturday & Sunday[,] I employ either in reading or writing. . . . I suppose I can leave here by the 25th of November[,] a little over three months from now. . . . Give my love to all. Write me also *s'il vous plaît* about plantation news & so forth.

Ever yr most affect. Son

Henry King Burgwyn, Jr.[7]

ⲟⲟⲟⲟⲟ

Excerpt from Letter of Henry "Harry" King Burgwyn, Jr. to His Mother

MARCH 6, 1859

Chapel Hill March 6th/59

My Dear Mother

Another week has passed & . . . I am again at my post as every one should be who adopts *"Semper Fidelis"* for their motto. The great event of the week has been the summoning of thirty four men before the Faculty for irregular attendance at morning prayers. I however though I had snapped [skipped] more than my regularly allowed number fortunately escaped. Of the whole number however only one man was sent off & he probably will get back in a week or two.

I gave my measure a week or ten days ago to a tailor from Baltimore who came here for the purpose of getting orders for clothing from the students & who has given a good deal of satisfaction here & I wrote him yesterday to send me some samples of his spring goods. Shall I order a suit from him or not? The price will probably be about thirty dollars[,] from twenty five to thirty. I think I had better. It is getting quite warm & I will need a spring suit. What color had I better select[?] . . . I received last Tuesday a catalogue of the Virginia Military Institute. It does not say anything about how old or how young a person must be to enter. I am very much in hopes that I may get the appointment to West Point. . . .

I am quite ashamed my Dear Mother of my letters to you when I contrast them with yours to me. They really appear very diminutive but the entire absence of any thin[g] which could in the remotest degree interest you as well as my very limited time[,] which prevents me from taking a sentance & then writing a composition on it as it were & thus lengthening out my epistles[,] must be my excuse. Next Sunday however I will endeavor to be more communicative.

Ever Your Most Affect Son

H. K. Burgwyn Jr.[8]

Promise Turns to Despair

*I*n 1860, the sky appeared to be the limit for the first state university, now one of the largest institutions of higher learning in the United States. All seemed well that year when a student writer for the *University Magazine* offered this idyllic description: "The College Campus is now arrayed in all the charms of Nature assisted by the fostering hand of Art, and the soft, balmy air is perfumed by the almost eternal flowers that bloom in vernal beauty along the walks that lead from the Buildings to the Village. If it be true that the noblest traits of character and intellectual progress and development are the effects of such natural scenery—if it be true that it is owing to such scenes as these that a Wallace and Tell were reared, and if 'the untrammelled element of liberty, the safeguard of religion and virtue' be there nourished to bloom and bless the world—then, surely, it is fortunate for students here that such gay, smiling landscapes are spread out before them, with forests, hills and valleys extending in majestic grandeur and the freshness of perpetual morning far away to the distant limits of the horizon."[1]

The promise and hope of one spring gave way to a sense of urgency and unease the next as North Carolina reluctantly joined its fellow Southern states in seceding from the Union. Before the spring term ended in 1861, dozens of students left school to volunteer for service in the Confederate armed forces. Others remained on the campus, torn between their desire to attend to patriotic duty and their parents' wish for them to remain in school. In a letter to his father on April 20, 1861, Edward H. Armstrong, a twenty-year-old junior, expressed his strong conviction to cease his studies so that he might shoulder a musket for his native state. Not long after writing the letter, Armstrong followed the dictates of his conscience. He ultimately lost his life fighting as a Confederate captain in Virginia at the Battle of Spotsylvania Courthouse.

In the wake of the departure of students who would be soldiers, President Swain issued a circular in May 1861 wherein he attempted to assure the university community, parents, and the public that the Chapel Hill campus would remain open: "Whilst the Faculty of this Institution have no disposition to quench patriotic ardor, or to withhold from public service, at the proper time, any one capable of performing the duties of a soldier, they beg leave to intimate to parents and guardians the propriety of restraining the anxiety so natural to the young and inexperienced to rush prematurely into military service. . . . The Faculty are at their posts, endeavoring to discharge their duty faithfully to the young men committed to their charge. There will be no suspension of duties, and no reasonable pains will be spared to render the approaching Commencement attractive."[2]

By the beginning of the fall term in 1862, the detrimental effects of the war on the student body were in evidence. Preston H. Sessoms, who was starting his sophomore year, provided a description of the forlorn state of affairs in a letter to his sister in late August. Sessoms joined the Confederate army a year later and served for the duration of the war.

In the meantime, David Swain, as determined as ever to preserve the university and spare its remaining young scholars—"the seed corn of the Confederacy," as he called them—from bloodshed, sent an appeal to Confederate president Jefferson Davis in October 1863 to exempt students from conscription. Though the Confederacy was then in desperate need of able-bodied soldiers, Davis acceded. In a letter to his sister several months later, Henry A. London, a junior, alluded to the exemption. Eventually, though, London decided to

> This institution has been eminently useful to the State. It has contributed, perhaps more than any other cause, to diffuse a taste for reading among the people, and excite a spirit of liberal improvement. It has contributed to change our manners and elevate our character.
>
> Archibald Debow Murphey, the "father of North Carolina's public schools"

interrupt his education at the university to serve as a Confederate courier.

That the war had ended in defeat for the South was clearly evident upon the appearance of hordes of blue-jacketed troops in Chapel Hill in the spring of 1865. Charles P. Mallett, the owner of a store selling stationery and books near the campus, wrote a letter apprising his son of the day-to-day events as they unfolded during the Union occupation of Chapel Hill.

His campus spared from wartime destruction, David Swain busied himself in an effort to keep the university afloat in the grim aftermath of the four-year conflict. J. B. Mitchell, a young Confederate veteran, returned to the campus in 1866. During the Christmas season that year, he offered a dreary picture of the university and the South in a letter to a friend.

By the end of the decade, the days were even darker for the struggling school. Cornelia Phillips Spencer used her pen to assail the new president, Solomon Pool, and his administration, thus launching the campaign that would in time bring new life to the campus. Her letter to *The Sentinel*, a Raleigh newspaper, dated April 6, 1869, survives as a classic example of her relentless crusade on behalf of the university in its bleakest days.

ooooo

Letter from Edward H. Armstrong to Thomas G. Armstrong

Chapel Hill
Saturday Apr 20th 1861

Dear Pa

To day I went to the office, but no letter was there to cheer my spirits, by telling me to come home and hasten to the war. I was anxiously expecting one, and the disappointment went quite hard. . . . There was a flag raising here to day. The ladies of the place made and put up the Flag. The citizens raised the pole in which I had the pleasure of assisting. Two young ladies made speaches and were followe[d] by the following noted gentlemen, S. F. Phillipps, Capt. Ashe, Gov Swain, and Sidney Smith, together with quite a number of students. Gov Swain in alluding to the war said that the south was invincible by any force that our enemies can send against us. He thought that further blood shed could be avoided, by every man in the South shouldering his musket. Lincoln would then see our strength and would know that it would be useless to attempt to coerce us. Such being the case I beg you to let me be one to proceed to Federal Point, and frighten Lincoln out of his witts, if possible[,] and if the Gov's prediction should prove untrue and war should actually be necessary, I should be happy to bear my part, humble though it be, in defense of my country. The flag raised to day contained nine stars, the last two in honor of Virginia and N.C. This is probably the first flag raised, on which N Carolina has been numbered with the seceeding states. God grant that she may soon take her place among her southern states in reality. . . .

Can I stay here and pretend to study, when I am continually hearing news from the war and when my country needs [me?] . . . There is a company formin[g] here to go to Washington City, composed of students. As my state needs my services I shall not volunteer. Please write to Capt Cowan immediately and see if he will except me. I am co[m]pelled to go somewhere.

Another of my classmates Lyon of Edgecombe leaves tomorrow morning. Several will leave during the week.[3]

ooooo

Letter from Preston H. Sessoms to Penelope E. White

Chapel Hill N. Carolina
August 28th 1862

Sister Bett.

I have again reached this place in safety, and found all things as they were when I left last January, except there has been a great deal [of] change among College affairs. For such a place as this, which is called a university,— there had ought to be no less than three or four hundred students, but there are only fifty now, a very small number. Very soon after I left last January nearly all the students left and went to war; some were called out by the draft[,] some were taken by the Conscription law and some went voluntarily[.] So nearly all left; if there had not new students come this session, there would be hardly twenty students here now. I call it [a] very dull and lonesome place; if it was not for one thing I would not stay h[e]re[.] There is but two or three boarding houses now, all have gone down, and board is very high, and but very little to eat[.] The college expenses are the same as the[y] have always been. I have heard something about the second call for conscripts; if there does come another call, this college will certainly break, it will take all, sweep it clean. . . . There is no pleasure in staying up here unless everything was more free, and cheaper[.] I would like it great better to stay at home, I suppose that the Yankees are thicker up there than when I was there. There is no chance of their getting up here, but they may cut off the rail road[. T]hen I should be locked up in a place, hard to break out. If the Yankees were to cut me off up here, when I got ready to come home, I should surely come, Yankees or no Yankees[.] If there was no chance of getting around them, I would got through them. . . . Believe me to be your brother

P. H. Sessoms
Chapel Hill N. Carolina.[4]

ooooo

Letter from Henry A. London to Lilla London

University of NC Feb 16th 1864

My Dear Lil

Although you have never answered the letter, which I wrote you nearly four months ago, yet I will write this, hoping it may be answered, as you will not be so busy as you were in So Carolina. I wrote Pa last Saturday a week ago, which letter I hope he received, and will answer, in the course of time. I arrived here, without breaking down, though I expected to do so every moment, as the old buggy was very ricketty, but driving slow we got along tolerably well, and I hope John [Rutherford London] got back home without breaking down. I have been kept pretty busy since my arrival, "making up" the time I was absent, but I am through now, and breathe free. . . . We had quite an excitement here last week, and which we enjoyed very much, it was this: The Sheriff of the County summoned a "Posse" of about thirty of us to break up a camp of run away Negroes, which we most effectually did, capturing the camp with all its contents, taking 7 prisoners and wounding one, without a man of us scratched. We had another one, but of a totally different character, namely the carrying away to Raleigh of about [a] half dozen Students who were eighteen. You know it is only the Juniors & Seniors who are exempt and so last Tuesday the Enrolling Officer took to the Conscript Camp the Sophs and Fresh who were liable to conscription, and who had been skulking here for sometime with the hope of being let alone till they were Juniors, when they would be exempted by the President [Jefferson Davis]. Tell Pa not to be afraid of their taking me, as Gov Swain says there is no danger of it, but I would not care much if they did, as I hate the idea of skulking, as it were, out of the army, when my Country needs my services so much, but yet when an exemption is proferred a man, he can scarcely be blamed for taking it. Ask Pa not to forget to send the candles, I wrote him for, the first opportunity.

Henry A. London, Jr.[5]

ooooo

Excerpts from Letter of Charles P. Mallet to Charles B. Mallet Describing the University at War's End

Chapel Hill 18th April 65

My Dear Son

I was at Church in the afternoon [on Easter Sunday, April 16]. Mr [Andrew] Mickle called out, and when I met him in the street, found that another parolled prisoner from Lees Army had come in, and reported Yankees approaching in force on the town road, which of course produced great excitement. The citizens met and appointed a committee to meet them and ask a safeguard; between sun down and dark some forty or fifty under a Lieut—came dashing into the village and enquired for [Confederate general Joseph] Wheelers men—some few s[ep]arated from the others and behaved badly, took away some watches &c; but when the Lt was informed he called them off, and returned to Headquarters, appointing 8 oclock the next morning to meet the Army, and make our terms. I was on the committee, and if Gov Swain did nothing more on his mission, he procured favorable terms for Raleigh and Chapel Hill.

Monday 17. [T]he committee met the column on the Hill [and] were very courteously received by Genl. [Smith D.] Atkins who upon being assured that all of Wheelers men had gone, and that no resistance would be made, called a halt, and informed us, that his orders were positive to respect all private property; (provisions and forage excepted)....

Friday morning 21st—fifth day occupation—I feel provoked to hear the college bell sounding as though the college was in full blast—a miserable set—not one true man among them and they desire to hand it down in History that the dear Yankees, did not interfere with the regular exercise of the college,—when in truth there were not five students here when Wheeler left us. Gov. Swain has over 500 bus[hels] of corn, and I learn he has lost nothing....

Sunday, 23rd—Seventh day of occupation[.] The College bell rang for prayers as usual. I know there is but one Senior and one in the junior classes, and I am incredibly informed there is but one other student in college. We will see, (maybe) what the Faculty will publish on the subject[. E]very thing [is] quiet and I hear nothing wrong in the village. Young ladies are getting over their fright—and becoming quite sociable[.] I learn that Misses Fetters are walking the streets with them, and Miss Ella Swain sent [for a] side saddle to ride out with some officer....

Tuesday morning, 25th April, 9th day of occupation[.] What can be more ridiculous that the continued ding dong of the College bell for prayers and all the usual recitation hours, when there are now but one Senior and one junior in College—and besides in my usual walks to visit Anna and Mary I pass through the campus and between the college buildings, and I can always hear the Yankees at nine pins or some other such game on the several floors and passages....

My guard has just come in—says the camp rumours confirm the death of Lincoln on the 14th and that the man escaped, that Andy Johnson has refused to accept the terms of capitulation &c; &c.[6]

ooooo

Excerpt from Letter of J. B. Mitchell to Ruffin H. Thomson

Chapel Hill N.C.
Dec 20h/66

Dear Ruff

I am pained to see you so much disposed to melancholy because I am in the same condition myself & consequently unable to offer consolation. I cannot say that I percieve any light ahead. Those old wiseacres who during the war were always crying out, "Never mind Boys, keep a good heart. You know the darkest hour is just before the day" have disgusted me with hope. I believe the only way to be happy now is to content ourselves with the old aphorism that "whatever is right" and endeavor to make the best of it. To day I know I am comfortably seated in a pleasant room before a cheerful fire, and outside all is cold & disagreeable[,] the ground being covered with snow & sleet. I can remember the time when it was different, when I had nought but the ground for a bed and rocks for a pillow, and in this I percieve a blessing. But the blessing ends here and my limited vision is incompetent to pierce the thick darkness further. The future of the South

> I love the University. I love the University because she is my Alma Mater. I love the University because she taught me much beauty and truth in the days of my youth. Over and above all these things, however, I love the University because she has diffused light and proclaimed liberty to her students and her state throughout the generations.
>
> Sam J. Ervin (class of 1917),
> United States senator

is to me a mysterious horror and I decline to contemplate it. My imagination has not even shaped my own future but awaits the development of events. In College I am pursuing an irregular course which comprises all the studies of the Senior & Junior classes with the exception of Latin & Greek. Having but one year to employ here I thought I would during that time approximate finishing the whole course as nearly as I could. . . .

. . . The number of students in College is very small[,] not more than seventy five. Many of them have been soldiers and consequently are not very remarkable for orderly behavior. Of the old students there are only two besides myself. . . . The old corps of professors are still retained and all look as well as ever. They are always glad to hear of their old scholars & take great pleasure in tracing their whereabouts. Old Gov. Swain during one [of] his lectures to us last session in speaking of Judge Ruffin mentioned your father & yourself & gave us the reason why you were called Ruffin.[7]

ooooo

Letter of Cornelia Phillips Spencer to The Sentinel Criticizing the New University Administration

Raleigh
April 2, 1869

Mr. Turner:

I have read your correspondent "&c., &c.," on the University and take leave to differ with him decidedly. I have just returned from a few weeks visit to the Hill. No North Carolinian with any manhood in him can go there now, and see what it has come to with[out] mingled rage and mortification. The President is a little formal arrogant prig, without two clear ideas in his brains beyond his own selfish aggrandizement, and his own two penny schemes. Mr. [Solomon] Pool is not even a grateful man, as Gov. [William] Holden will one day find out. He is without respectable capacity either as a scholar or as a man of business, nor even as a disciplinarian of old field school. The adventurers who make up the Professional corps are quite worthy of their head. There is not a man among them of any reputation or any ability to make a reputation as a man of learning or as a

Hark the Sound of Tar Heel Voices

teacher. They are however busy settling themselves for life—cutting down shade trees in their new abodes right and left, as if oaks grew every year like pea-vines. Between whiles they exercise themselves in teaching Long Division and the Rule of Three and the Latin and Greek Grammar's to six or eight village boys. Mr. Pool has two little nephews "in College" also, who are not quite as large as he. These are the "students"; this is the University. . . . Is the General Assembly to appropriate one sixpence to the support of these needy adventurers? I trust not for the honor of the State. . . . Let them be made to understand unequivocally that North Carolina scorns them and their pretensions to be a University. The whole troop ought to be led to the extreme verge of the State and dismissed into the Atlantic with a harmless but ceremonious kick.[8]

1870
—
1879

From the Ruins

When the fall term of 1870 commenced in Chapel Hill, the university was yet alive, but barely. Although fifteen students enrolled that September, most were long gone by the time President Solomon Pool submitted his ill-considered "Plan for Continuing the University" to the new trustees on December 1. His proposal, as recorded in the minutes of the trustees, advocated, among other things, the creation of a "State University" comprised of every existing college in North Carolina. Under Pool's scheme, the Chapel Hill campus would be put up for lease.

Several months later, the university officially closed its doors. From all corners of North Carolina came lamentations from citizens who had nurtured the school and recognized its supreme importance to the state and its people. Zeb Vance warned from his law office in Charlotte, "This noble property of the State is fast sinking into ruin. Many of the grand old trees have been laid low for firewood. Doors are off their hinges and broken down, windows without blinds or glass, carpets torn up and carried off, the halls (Society halls) are measurably stripped of their furniture and adornings; and almost everything portable is either injured, destroyed or stolen. . . . An air of melancholy, or *ruin*, pervades everything where once there was so much active and intelligent life, where so much of North Carolina's moral and intellectual greatness were found and fitted for her advancement, where were centered so much of her hope and her pride."[1]

In the eyes of its most stalwart supporters, there remained a glimmer of hope for the university. Cornelia Phillips Spencer, the sagacious lady with the boundless affection for the Chapel Hill campus, ended a missive to her friend Zeb Vance in late September 1871 with the suggestion that the university might be reorganized and live anew.

Over the next several years, Spencer, Vance, Kemp Battle, and a host of other university loyalists waged an aggressive campaign to resurrect the school. In the midst of their quest, lightning struck and damaged the Davie Poplar, one of the most beloved campus landmarks. When in August 1873 Cornelia Spencer notified friends of the university of the damage to the old tree, two symbolic questions could be answered only by the passage of time. Would the strike doom the landmark and spell a foreboding omen for the campus? Or would the bolt serve as a spark to rekindle the flames of a living, breathing university?

Almost two years later, the dark clouds of doubt yielded to a Carolina blue sky when the campus came to life once again. Two accounts of the joyous reopening for the fall term of 1875 provided unique observations of the historic time. Cornelia Spencer, one of the true champions of the grand event, ended her narrative with a challenge to the citizens of the state to rally to the aid of the university and give to it their support and resources. William Joseph Peele, class of 1879, experienced the rebirth as a member of the inaugural freshman class of the restored university. His subsequent recollection of the reopening provided a glimpse at the campus, the faculty, and the activities in those September days of 1875.

Just months before Peele graduated with honors in 1879, another student, Henry William Faison, offered positive reassurances that the university was alive and well in a letter to his father.

ooooo

President Solomon Pool's Plan for Continuing the University

University Plan, Dec. 1, 1870

I. That a committee of the Trustees confer with the authorities of other colleges with the view of bringing them under the head of the State University.

1. The corporations of the several colleges to still retain their present chartered rights.

2. To receive such aid, as colleges of the University, as may be agreed upon.

II. To effect the lease of the property at Chapel Hill upon such fair and equitable terms as the following.

1. Lessee to give bond for the Security of the property and its safe return at the expiration of the time of the lien, natural decay, and accident by fire &c excepted.

2. Free tuition to be offered constantly to fifty youth of the State.

3. The leading religious sects of the State to be offered a representation in the college, and the discussion of party politics to be constantly forbidden.

4. To be one of the University Colleges, submitting reports of the operations of the college &c, to the Trustees of the University at such times as the said Trustees may require.[2]

ooooo

The university is like a lighthouse which throws a beam out to the far horizons of the South, yet dark at its own base.

Paul Green

Letter from Cornelia Phillips Spencer to Governor Vance about a Plan to Reopen the University

Chapel Hill, September 30, 1871

To Governor Vance,
My Dear Governor:

Last Monday I was favored with a call from Mr. Lassiter, Secretary of the Board of Trustees of the defunct University, introduced by Professor [Alexander] McIver. His object, he stated, was to request me to suggest some plan for the restoration of the University, and to prepare a manuscript for him to submit to the Board at their next meeting. I think I may be excused for smiling at this turn of affairs.

I endeavored to feel not unduly elated by the honor thus thrust upon me. "A Plan."

I told Mr. Lassiter that the only plan occurring to my mind was that the present Administration resign unconditionally, and call on the Alumni to take charge of the Institution.

Mr. Lassiter has few ideas, and a limited horizon bounded chiefly by "Our Party." It was, to say the least, nauseating to hear him talk about "party" in connection with this matter.

He objected to my plan on the ground that the Alumni were "all Conservatives" and it would be giving the University over into the hands of this "Party." I suppose he is an honest man, and means well according to his lights, which lights are few.

His favorite word next to "party" was "co-operation." He wants everybody to co-operate with the present board in a generous effort to re-animate and restore the University. I said I did not think that would be done. They must abandon the whole concern, before anyone else would move. And Mr. McIver rather surprised me by seconding this declaration very vehemently and declaring, if he had a million dollars, he would not give one, while the present trustees held on, or the present administration retained.

Professor Patrick is gone, *abiit, evasit, erumpit [erupit]* . . . his creditors being numerous and desperate. Chapel Hill people have had to come to the rescue and send in food to the family.

An entire breakdown. Mr. Brewer remains. Says he means to be on the ground when reorganization takes place. He has openly expressed his hope of being able to secure this place for a negro college. Says the money for this would be forthcoming from the North at once.

Mr. McIver is fighting him. I do not know what Mr. McIver will do. He is thoroughly sick of Mr. Pool and the rest. I think he is honestly anxious to undo any mischief he may have done in coming here. Some think he is playing a game to secure himself with the Alumni in case they come into power.

Some time when you have a spare half-hour—and Mrs. Vance does not need you; for I do believe she cooks "all by herself" as the children say, though of course she is willing to take the credit—some spare half-hour then, between setting the table and bringing in the dinner, you would do me a great favor if you would say what you think about the chances for the reorganization of the University. . . .

I am Dear Governor with much regard,

C. P. S.[3]

ooooo

Cornelia Phillips Spencer
Describes Lightning Strike of Davie Poplar

Chapel Hill
August 4, 1873.

The old students of Chapel Hill and friends of the University generally, will be grieved to learn that in one of a late series of severe thunder storms, the great poplar in the campus identified with the very foundation of the college was struck by lightning; and though not shattered, yet as the path of the bolt is visible from top to bottom of the immense bole of the tree on the northwest side, and a shorter track on the south side, evidently from a return stroke, it may well be feared that the noble old tree is doomed.

The poplar measures 14 feet 6 inches in girth, two feet from the ground, and carries up a magnificent trunk some twenty-five or thirty feet without a branch, spreading at the top its crown of leaves, and golden cups. I have often heard from Miss Nancy Hilliard the late George Mendenhall's account of the lunch taken at the foot of that tree by the committee appointed to

> Her place firmly fixed in the Constitution and laws of our State and in the hearts of its people, her orbit determined by the counsels of those who guide its destinies, under God, it is my prayer and the prayer of all our children that our Alma Mater shall see the night of eclipse no more.
>
> William Joseph Peele,
> class of 1879

select a site for the University eighty years ago. They were on horseback, riding leisurely through the country, and stopped in that grove for their nooning. Water was brought from a spring that rose freely among the roots of some fine oaks about a hundred yards distant, (at the corner of what was once Miss Nancy's property,) but which the unaccountable taste of one of the college gardeners long ago filled up.

Here the newly appointed executive committee reposed for an hour or two in the shade of a vast unbroken forest, and decided that nowhere in all their wanderings had they seen a more fit or beautiful spot than this for the location of the new institution. . . .

The poplar has been celebrated in song and praise, and was the northe[r]n limits of the grand procession which in the old days was formed on commencement day and marched to its foot and thence west by Dr. Caldwell's old monument, where the members were directed to remove their hats in homage to the memory of the staunch old President whose remains lay beneath it, and thence southwest to the Chapel where the ladies were assembled crowding the windows and standing on the benches to see the march. I have before me one of those commencement day Programmes, to read which brings back a gush of warm sweet spring air, crowds the silent campus with glowing ardent youth, lights the halls with the fresh Beauty and Grace that once adorned them, sends the music of drum and trumpet floating through the tree tops, and crowns our riven old poplar again with bud and bloom.[4]

ooooo

Cornelia Phillips Spencer
Describes the Reopening Ceremonies

The friends of the University of North Carolina have every reason to thank God and take courage. The ceremonies of the *reopening of the Institution* have just closed, and as I write, the two Literary Societies are in session, having been reorganized by the committee appointed for that purpose. The day has been bright and beautiful, September was never more charming. The old college has donned her new dress, a delicate fawn relieved with brown. The repairs and improvements of the buildings and the grounds reflect the highest encomiums on the diligence, thoroughness, and perfect good taste with which they have been carried on. Those who saw the college last spring are amazed at the transformation. The noble gravel walks have been reopened, the grounds smoothed and cleared, the trees and shrubberies trimmed, while the buildings have been nearly all entirely renovated, repaired, white-washed and painted and the works are still going forward. The College Chapel is as neat and fresh as paint can make it, and two days ago a party of Chapel Hill ladies took possession of it, and decorated it for the Reopening with such taste and appropriateness as the ladies alone can show on these occasions. They obtained permission to bring down the portraits of the worthies who in former times adorned and illustrated the annals of the College. These were hung round the face of the gallery with evergreen wreathes festooning the space between. The pillars also were wreathed. Over the rostrum were placed Gen. Davie and Dr. Caldwell, the founder of the institution and its first President. Within the recess was Gov. Swain, opposite him at the other end of the Hall was Gov. Graham and around were Drs. Mitchell, Phillips, Hawks, Judge Ruffin, Manly, and Badger.—Their familiar faces looked down on the familiar

> I would suggest that the University is outstanding because it is a leader. It has exercised leadership in the unceasing fight for higher standards of education throughout North Carolina, and its influence has been felt in every corner of the state.
>
> Governor Luther Hodges, 1960

Hark the Sound of Tar Heel Voices

scene benignantly, and their presence seemed not only a tender reminder of the past, but a significant pledge for the future of an Institution to which they had given their best thoughts and the best work of their lives. A single motto in letters of evergreen on a white ground over the rostrum, "*Laus Deo*" expressed the feeling uppermost in every honest man's heart there present: "Thank God."

... The people must now endow and sustain this Institution. It is their own, devoted to their best interests, fostered by their best men, appealing to their best feelings, no sordid or vindictive motives have been shown by those who have revived it, they call on all classes, all parties to unite in the effort to sustain them.

We devoutly trust it will be done.[5]

ooooo

William Joseph Peele Describes the Reopening of the University

On my arrival in Chapel Hill, I noticed that there was a subdued silence throughout the grounds. A few lonely looking students could be seen going in and out of the old buildings, selecting their rooms, which were now musty from long disuse. Occasionally might still be seen relics and reminders of old student life. I saw written in chalk in one of the old recitation rooms a memorandum of the brief and disastrous attempt to continue the University after the death of Governor Swain by those unfamiliar with its traditions. It read: "This old University has busted and gone to hell today," and then the writer fixed the day and date of the catastrophe. ...

At the formal opening Col. W. L. Saunders was present, and he it was who reorganized the Phi Society. He gave into our keeping with becoming solemnity its books and archives, which he had preserved from the destruction which attended Sherman's army. His strong, full face, his round head, his serious, anxious eyes, and his pathetic voice mellowed by suffering were all fitted to inspire the young men with the reflection that they were helping to make history. ...

Of the Faculty of the University, it is not my special province to speak. The Chairman, Dr. Charles Phillips, or "Old Fatty," as we called him, was the most impressive looking man among them: head massive, face leonine, and his heart big as a water bucket. His expression was good natured, his gait gouty, his coat short. The boys sported with his nickname and infirmities, but respected his character and learning.

Professor [Adolphus W.] Mangum was essentially a preacher, and, though he had a good natural literary instinct, he was never fully at home unless in his pulpit, or the lesson in Moral Science allowed him to make a pulpit of his chair and his class a congregation. We all knew that in his heart of hearts he would rather see us on the "King's highway of holiness" than in the way of getting our diplomas, and some of us took the occasion to appear pretty regularly in his congregation to advertise the fact that our hearts were right anyhow.

Professor [J. DeBerniere] Hooper was a model of decorum, gentility, scholarship, and culture. His dignity and urbanity, did not, however, suffice to protect him from his nickname, "Old Frog." Nothing ever ruffled his temper or rattled his understanding. He was never sick; or if so, he never complained. He was never in a hurry, but never behind in his appointments. He had cultivated away his enthusiasm, but not his charity. He spoke evil of none and had no outspoken enemies; he never flattered and had no friends. Envy was too busy with easier game to waste much time on his reputation.[6]

ooooo

Excerpt of Letter from Henry Faison to His Father
JANUARY 20, 1879

For the past week the College has been terribly stirred up on account of elections. One week ago the campaign commenced and day by day additional warmth was added to the contest and finally last Saturday it resulted in the election of good commencement officers. There was scarcely any studying done last week. I myself missed four recitations. The excitement was interesting and I like it very much. . . . I was elected to introduce the Speaker at commencement. I will have to go down to Durham, hire a fine "turn out" and "blood" the Speaker up the Hill. The day after we arrive I attend him in the procession, and finally I appear on the rost[er], and introduce him to the audience. Now this is a position which many desire, because it gives a man a chance to wear fine clothes and to put on kid gloves. Three fourths (¾) of the voters of the society have chosen me for the place, and they expect me to wear "low quarter pumps," "red socks," "white cravats," and a "stove piped hat." They have selected me to "fill this bill"—toes pinched by "box toed gaiter," lungs compressed by a "buttoned frock," neck sawed by a "starched stander," and hands sweating terribly under my kids. I had rather meet the man in a neat homespun suit. How in the world did they ever select me for the place! Am I guilty of making false impressions? . . . The Society pays my travelling expenses. You, Pa, will have to foot my dressing bills. If you can afford to dress me up nicely for the occasion I would like to serve my fellows; if you think not, I am happy to reconcile my self to the best wishes of my father. . . .

Well the excitement is about over and we will begin to work Monday morning. Most of the Old boys have returned, and about 20 new students have come in. There will be nearly 200 on the Catalogue.[7]

1880
—
1889

The "Frosh" Life

$\mathcal{U}$nder the skillful leadership of President Kemp P. Battle, the university made rapid strides in its second life as the state and the South emerged from the throes of Reconstruction. Once parents regained confidence in the stability of the institution, they began to send scores of their children to Chapel Hill, swelling the ranks of the freshman class year by year.

One of the most important innovations of the Battle administration was the creation of the normal school, designed to educate badly needed teachers for the state's growing public school system. Through this avenue, the Chapel Hill campus formally enrolled women for the first time in its history. In a letter written in June 1881 to the young lady he would subsequently marry, Leonard Anderson Southern of Rockingham County, North Carolina, made mention of several of the female students in the normal school as he offered his first impressions of the university.

The initial appearance of women students was short, as the normal school was temporarily suspended in 1884. In a speech entitled, "The Seventy-fifth Anniversary of the Coming of Women to the University of North Carolina," Gladys Hall Coates, the renowned historian of the female experience at the university, offered a poignant look at the attitudes toward female students in the 1880s.

For most of the young men who came to Chapel Hill during the decade, hazing was a rite of passage of the freshman class. In a letter to his mother in 1883, Richard Hackett informed her of his survival of hazing activities: "I arrived here safely last Thursday and have been well since. I think I will like Chapel Hill very much indeed. I am rooming with Mr. Alexander and think he is a very nice man. The boys have not hazed me any eccept in the fresh treat in which I got hit with a few rines [rinds]. I have entered the Freshman class on every thing but Greek and will stand my examination on that this evening. I have not been home sick any yet."[1]

In 1882, another freshman provided his mother with a more in-depth description of the ritualistic pranks and "tests" to which first-year students were regularly subjected in the early 1880s. In the first of his two letters on the subject, Neil A. Sinclair recounted how President Battle had personally intervened on his behalf to prevent a showdown over hazing.

Kemp Battle took a dim view of hazing during his fifteen-year tenure as president. In his mammoth treatise on the history of the university, Battle clearly noted his opposition to the harassment of freshmen. His concern about and disdain for the "special" treatment of first-year students by upperclassmen were ultimately borne out during the presidency of Francis Venable, when a death during freshman hazing brought a measure of shame and disgrace to the campus.

Contrary to Battle, the *University Magazine* offered an editorial that endorsed hazing and urged a continuation of the campus tradition.

Freshmen and upperclassmen alike experienced intercollegiate sports for the first time near the middle of the decade. Prior to that time, there had been little time or resources for organized recreational activities on

Our Alumni have been, are now, and if we do our duty to the University, [will remain] among the foremost leaders of public opinion and thought in the State and the pioneers of every good work.

John Manning (class of 1850),
attorney and United States congressman, 1884

the campus. A member of the class of 1882 explained why: "It is no reflection on the University that no recreational facilities were provided. It was no time to think about recreation. Existence was the important thing at that time. The University had not been re-opened long, the student body was a mere handful, less than two hundred, and legislative appropriations were meagre, and existence was too precarious to think about recreation. There was no demand on the part of the students for recreation, for the reason they had come to the University at a time of severe economic stress and reconstruction. They were there for the serious purpose of getting an education. They were there to work, rather than to play."[2]

The university first played baseball on the intercollegiate level when its team challenged Bingham Military School in the spring of 1884. Four years later, a gridiron contest against Wake Forest College in Raleigh initiated the Carolina football program. Ironically, the school that has boasted a winning record in virtually every one of its varsity sports lost both of its initial games, 12–11 to Bingham Military and 6–4 to Wake Forest.

Francis Venable, who had a great interest in campus sports, opined that the first cheer for a Carolina athletic team took place at the close of the loss to Bingham Military, when the Chapel Hill faithful yelled, "Three cheers for the University nine." His excellent overview of the birth of intercollegiate athletics at the school was first published in the *University Magazine*.

ooooo

First Impressions of L. A. Southern upon His Arrival in Chapel Hill

University Normal School
Chapel Hill, N.C.
June 28, 1881

Miss Bettie Caruthers
Dear Friend

I will drop you a few lines to let you know that I have not forgotten you all, but have nothing that I suppose will interest you much to write of—except it be something concerning my trip, what I have seen, etc.

Hospitality prevailed in the University village of Chapel Hill, and it would be hard to find a place in the world of such elevated social life.

Josephus Daniels (class of 1887),
secretary of the navy, United States
ambassador to Mexico

I enjoyed my ride finely on the cars coming down here. I left Kernersville at 8 o'clock A.M. and arrived here half past 3 in the evening. This is a beautiful place and the school buildings beat anything I ever saw. There are eight in all. To recite we have to go from one building to another. Here are the largest Librarys in the state. They are opened on Saturdays & Tuesdays. I never saw as many books before. I have also been in the Museum—it is full of wonderful curiosities, many things from France, Spain, Italy, Egypt. Various species [of] reptiles, fresh and salt water fish, shells, minerals, metals, woods, etc. besides large numbers of ancient relics, etc. I am enjoying myself fine, am boarding and rooming at [a] widow lady's—two young ladies are boarding there—one from Pitt County, the other from McDowell. There are in all about 200 students here from all parts of the state and I have formed many acquaintances from among them. I am the only one from Rockingham [County].

I was disappointed in not meeting Prof. Bradfield down here. I guess he is busy thinking about book publishing. I think I will learn a good deal down here. I am studying vocal music, Drawing, Philosophy, Physiology, Nat. History, Geography, Arithmetic, Grammar, Elocution, etc. I don't really studie. All we are required is to read over our lessons several times then those great teachers lecture on it and ask questions and they never fail to make every thing to[o] plain. They also . . . tell us how it must be taught to be successful in public schools.

Our boss is from Baltimore, one teacher from New York and there is one to arrive on the 23rd from England so you can see my opportunitys to learn are very good and I want to make use of my time while here.

We are having very warm weather down here but we have an abundance of good water, plenty of good things to eat, and I eat so much, so as to get my moneys worth that I think I will weigh about ten pounds more when I get back. So I must close—there is so much noise that it bothers me—some playing croquet, some singing, talking, etc. so I hope you will excuse my bad composition and all mistakes. Tell Sam to hunt up his pen and write me the news. Tell all inquiring friends the same. Would be pleased to hear from you.

Your friend,

L. A. Southern

My address is as the heading of this letter—Chapel Hill, N.C.[3]

ooooo

Observations of Gladys Hall Coates on Female Students at the University in the 1880s

In 1877, the first summer normal school conducted by the University, and said to be the first summer school in the United States connected with any university or college, was opened, and women as well as men were invited to attend. The invitation read somewhat condescendingly:

Females

Although the law requires that the money paid by the State shall be devoted to the uses of males, the females are cordially invited to attend all the exercises of the school free of charge. . . . We earnestly appeal to every teacher and every man and woman in the State who desires to teach to come forward and attend this School.

Of the total number of 235 enrolled in the first summer school, 107 were women and 128 men.

The number and eagerness of the women teachers who grasped this opportunity impressed the students, and their observations are reflected in debates, editorials, and articles throughout the period. A *University Magazine* article, in 1882, agreed that some women should have a sound education but doubted the wisdom of co-education because of the difference in the minds of men and women. An editor of the Magazine in 1883, however, came out strongly for the education [of women] as the solution to the problem of the poverty of the State.

Hark the Sound of Tar Heel Voices

> I believe in coeducation at the University of North Carolina because I believe that education in a university is not a sex right but a human right.
>
> Frank Porter Graham

"As early as 1795, North Carolina established a University for her boys," he wrote. "Ninety years, we may say, have elapsed and she has done nothing for her girls. Our people are growing tired of this discrimination. The State is expected to aid in female education. How must this be done? For those communities able to support a double-system of colleges and universities, we prefer separate education, but for North Carolina, who is too poor to support a respectable system of public schools or give her University a shilling, we advocate Co-education."

In 1882, two girls, graduates of Fayetteville Public Schools, prompted by their superintendent, Dr. Alexander Graham, had applied for admission to the University. Etta May Troy and Fannie Watson took the entrance examinations but, though making higher grades than the boys applying from the same school, were not admitted. The girls, said their superintendent, came "asking no quarter on account of age, sex, or previous condition of servitude . . . [and] were sent back to the braes [hillsides] of Cumberland [County] because they were girls."

When the summer normal school was discontinued in 1884, University students raised the question of admitting women to the University's teaching course in the regular session. The Dialectic Society passed a resolution heartily endorsing such an innovation but the Magazine editor of that year, though declaring himself for the higher education of women, wondered if co-education was the answer.

There were mixed feelings throughout the student body at [the] possibility of women in the University. Some gallant students, said one writer, thought women would help "to polish boorish ways" and were favorable to their coming; others, fearful of falling in love, were against it![4]

ooooo

Excerpts from Two Letters of Neil A. Sinclair to His Mother Concerning the Hazing of Freshmen

September 9, 1882

There has been [a] good deal of "freshing," but I've been troubled but very little. The first of the week, while going to supper one evening, a fellow thought he would be smart and stepped up in my path & drew his fist as if he were going to knock me down. He came meeting me, but I deliberately walked on till we met & ran up against each other, but instead of backing off I stood firm & looked him square in the eyes. He seemed rather disappointed & after a while asked what I was looking at him so hard for, thinking he would create a laugh, but I said, "I was just going to keel you about 10 ft. out there on the grass if you had touched me," & I would have done it too[.] He saw I was in earnest and he got *mighty small* & slunk around to one side of me & passed on[,] leaving me in possession of the field. Then I started on without even looking back & the crowd first yelled at the Sophomore about allowing a Freshman to bully him. I was not troubled any more till Wednesday night. About 25 boys came around & told me I had to make them a bow, but I told them I would do nothing of the kind. They also tried to make me get on the table & speak & to dance but I would not. They said they would black [humiliate by covering with tar or pitch] me then. Ransom & 2 others about drunk were going to do the blacking. I told them that was one thing I did not propose to allow & that I would not be blacked alive & that the first man that attempted to black me would get that. I told them there was but one thing that [they] could make me do & that was to trot, that I would not think of fighting a man for such a thing as that, & I knew they could carry me by force. So they gave out their blacking notion & we started out & just as we got to the door, Pres. Battle met us & said, "Gentlemen, this devilment has got to stop." In five minutes the whole campus was quiet, & for 3 hours before you could have heard the noise for 5 miles. So I am done of it, except the "Fresh Treat" which comes off this evening. I don't know whether I will go or not yet, but think I shall[.] I promised . . . another Freshman to go with him. They have not even said "Fresh" to me since the other night. . . .

Two wagon loads of watermelons have just arrived for the "fresh treat" & there will be a right big time by & by. When they get through they turn the wagons over & cut up generally. The grand "winding up" of hazing . . .

September 15, 1882

I have not done much as yet, on getting settled & used to things. It depends altogether on the man here & not the teacher. I have been called on only once in Math & 3 times in Latin. Our Math Class has over 50. Nearly ½ of the Freshmen have to take Prep. Math, & the majority, Prep. Greek. The "News" was mistaken. We have not 100 Freshmen, but hope to have before next June. About 85 now . . .

The "freshing" is over now ie. as to the boys already here. I rather enjoyed it, but some did not. I don't like my room-mate much. He is a sour morose kind of fellow, pretty green & imagines that his equal is not on the Hill.[5]

ooooo

President Battle Expresses His Opposition to Hazing

In this year (1886) occurred a case of hazing, notable because of the three engaged in it two had left the institution and received their letters of honorable dismission. These letters were ordered to be recalled and the sentence of dismission was passed upon the student who was still subject to the authority of the Faculty.

In addition to the laws of the societies against hazing . . . the Senior Class passed a resolution to use their influence against it, bearing especially on the injury to the University by frightening off the timid. The Sophs, not to be outdone, agreed to refrain from the custom, but in language showing that in their judgment it was wrong. They said, "We blot from our speech, and from the book of our remembrance, all preconceived ideas of blacking, trotting, bull riding, and spanking, and we submit ourselves wholly to the Faculty's fatherly guidance." . . .

The persistence of the practice of hazing is difficult to understand by those who know that it is injurious to the reputation of the University, and diminishes its patronage, besides seriously detracting from the character of the participants as gentlemen.[6]

ooooo

Excerpt from an Editorial
about Hazing in the University Magazine

We say, after a four years' experience as Freshman, Sophomore, Junior, and Senior, that judicious hazing serves to inculcate respect for college discipline. When a boy enters college he is without restraint, no longer fearing the rod, or if he be from a military school the guardroom, and reasonable hazing teaches him that his deportment must be in accord with the new world in which he has entered.

Again, if a Freshman meets with naught but courtesy, he attributes it to a lack of spirit in the older students, or to superiority in himself. The effect of the stipulation between the [Philanthropic and Dialectic] societies abolishing hazing three years before, made the subsequent Freshmen classes intolerably conceited and cheeky.

A boy entering college is like a cockerel beginning to crow. He is considered brilliant at home. What better remedy for his arrogance than to force him to trot half a mile or make a speech to jeering auditors?

Hazing, then, is what a new student expects; it limits his admiration of himself; it keeps him in his room at night at his studies; it keeps quiet in the building in study hours. . . .

What student does not recall with pleasure those "Fresh treats" of the olden time, when the air was thick with watermelon rinds, and village, campus, and surrounding hills echoed with the shouts of fleeing Fresh and pursuing Soph? What more harmless fun and more replete with incidents for happy recollection in after years[?][7]

ooooo

Dr. Francis Venable Recounts the Birth of Intercollegiate Athletics at the University

"Athletics" was confined to baseball in a desultory fashion and football of the kind described in *Tom Brown Rugby* [*Tom Brown's School Days*, an 1857 Thomas Hughes novel set at Rugby School]. Besides these, muscles were hardened by walks, mainly on the road to the railway station, and secondarily to Piney Prospect and in Battle Park. Tennis was first introduced by Dr. Venable about 1884, the court located in the Grove south of his residence. About the same time a baseball team after a short practice was beaten ignominiously by Bingham School.

There was no gymnasium but at a somewhat later period an Athletic Association was formed and one of the two annual contests were held. In 1885 our first Gymnasium was erected by the aid of the alumni . . . and a great impetus was given to athletics, which proved of signal benefit to the health of the students. Before this four cases of insanity from overstudy developed, but there were none afterwards.

At times "knucks" [bare-knuckle boxing] was the favorite pastime and those who are afraid of bodily injuries in modern games should be comforted by the fact [that when] a serious injury to the knee from much kneeling resulted to one of our students, [he] was taken to Baltimore for treatment by a specialist.

In 1888 when neither understood well the modern football the University was defeated by Wake Forest. Then the University men sent for printed rules of the mode of playing and after two weeks' practice under them without a coach, unwisely met Trinity [now Duke University], whose President, Dr. Crowell, a graduate of Yale, had seen to their training.

> The constitutional obligation to foster the University is upon us. And we can gain the approval of posterity by exerting ourselves on behalf of this institution, until the University of North Carolina shall become a synonym for all that is progressive in science or elevating in education.
>
> Governor Daniel Fowle, 1889

Of course they [the UNC men] were beaten, their Captain (Bragaw) being badly lamed in the struggle. A need of coach was seen and Mr. Hector Cowan was chosen to that position. Thus far the students [had] managed the contests of their own motions. Disputes and bad blood between the University students and those of the colleges of the State were engendered. The Faculty thought best to draw in the reins. In 1889 they ordained that games should be played only on college grounds.[8]

Hark the Sound of Tar Heel Voices

1890
–
1899

The Centennial Campus Spirit

or the hundred-year-old university, the Gay Nineties were a time when a special college spirit prevailed on the campus. That spirit provided a new excitement, zeal, and enthusiasm. Amongst the revelry surrounding the centennial celebration of the nation's oldest state university, myriad other events took place about the campus, each indicative of the infectious school spirit.

From its modest beginnings in the previous decade, the intercollegiate football program quickly gained stature and attracted widespread attention from friends of the university throughout the state. In 1892, the football team in Chapel Hill was positioned to challenge the squad from the University of Virginia as the best in the South. Captained by Michael Hoke, a diminutive halfback (and the son of Major General Robert F. Hoke, a Confederate hero from North Carolina), the 1892 team bested the Virginians in a contest held before a huge crowd in Atlanta in November. An anecdote from that game is suggestive of the fervor that football had engendered: "Following a 26–0 victory by the 1892 team over the University of Virginia, a Confederate veteran hailed the Carolina captain as he was making his way off the field. 'What's your name?' asked the veteran. 'Hoke,' replied the football star. 'Any kin to General Hoke?' was the next question. 'Yes, sir; his son,' Michael proudly replied. 'Well,' responded the veteran, 'you go back and tell your pa that I've seen the finest fighting today that I've seen since Chancellorsville.' "[1]

When the team returned to Chapel Hill in the wake of its convincing triumph, it was greeted by the student body en masse and feted by the university with a banquet. Kemp Battle provided an account of the victory celebration and noted the actual cheers used by the crowd.

In the course of their celebrations during the university's centennial decade, students were attracted to a variety of "vices" on the campus. Alcohol, tobacco, and dancing were the great temptations of college life at the time. In a now humorous confessional letter to his mother in 1893, Worth McAlister expressed his battle against giving in to campus enticements.

Energized by the hoopla over football and the centennial observance, the university was set to receive its most famous and appealing landmark in 1897. For many years, the ancient well in the heart of the campus had been viewed as little more than a wooden eyesore that provided water from the depths of the earth for thirsty students. Anxious to enhance the beauty of the campus, President Edwin Alderman personally designed and oversaw the construction of the picturesque symbol known the world over as "the Old Well." Alderman, in a letter to a Chapel Hill friend, related the story of how the famous Old Well came to be.

William E. Cox, class of 1899, witnessed the beautification of the well during his student days in Chapel Hill. His first impressions of the campus as a freshman recalled the unsightly appearance of the wooden-roofed structure prior to the improvements wrought by Alderman, but his words also testified to the deep affection that the institution was fostering in its students.

No student writing of the 1890s better reflected the abundant college spirit in Chapel Hill than William Starr Myers. Just before he graduated in 1897, Myers, a native of western North Carolina who later became an esteemed professor of history at Princeton University, penned the words to "Hark the Sound"—or, as he called it, "Hail to the Brightest Star." Days

> The University is the people's school.
>
> Edwin Anderson Alderman, 1897

later, Francis A. Gudger, Myers's roommate and the university Glee Club's first tenor, sang the song in public for the first time. For many years, "Hark the Sound" has served as the official alma mater of the university. In his diary entry of June 2, 1897, Myers noted, "At about 8:30 P.M., the Glee and Mandolin Clubs gave their regular concert. I managed to slide out on playing on the Mandolin Club this concert, but san[g] on the Glee Club as usual. The Glee Club sang a song—'Hail to the Brightest Star'—the words of which I wrote, the tune being the old college song 'Amici.' "[2]

ooooo

Kemp Battle Describes the Football Team

In the Fall of 1892, under Captain Michael Hoke, a son of the eminent Confederate General, R. F. Hoke, the football team won notable victories, losing only once, to the University of Virginia in October, at Richmond, by a score of 30 to 18. It then became the superior of any in the South, defeating Richmond College 40 to 0, Trinity 24 to 0, Alabama A. and M. 64 to 0, Vanderbilt 24 to 0, and the University of Virginia, a second game, at Atlanta on November 26, 26 to 0.

It is true that the University of Virginia had been victor in the first, or championship game, and our triumph was in an exhibition game, but that did not prevent the general exultation. A committee was appointed to arrange for a banquet, another to decorate and send to University Station a special train to meet the players. When it reached Chapel Hill the students enthusiastically converted themselves into equines and drew the carriages from the station to the Campus. President [George T.] Winston, Captain Michael Hoke, and Mr. Charles Baskerville, manager of the team, were in the leading carriage. The shouts of

> Rah! Rah! White,
> Rah! Rah! Blue,
> Hoopla! Hoopla! N.C.U.

rang out on the Campus until a late hour.

A few days afterwards the banquet was given to the victorious team. President Winston, absent at Asheville delivering an address, sent a stirring letter. Howard Rondthaler was toastmaster. The Faculty Athletic

Committee responded to toasts, viz., Dr. [Francis P.] Venable to "The Team," Dr. Baskerville to "Our Captain" (Hoke), Dr. [Eben] Alexander to "Our Manager," and Professor [Henry Horace] Williams to "Athletics." The students who responded were Captain Mike Hoke on "Our Sponsors," and Perrin Busbee on "Our Scrub Team."[3]

ooooo

Excerpt of Letter from John Worth McAlister to His Mother
MAY 1, 1893

Somehow I don't get the same joy out of my Christian life that I used to, I am not as good, and as consecrated as I used to be, even as I was when I left home last Summer, and I don't always follow the dictates of my conscience, and worst of all, God seems far away when I pray to him, not near like He used to. I know that is my fault, and not God's, and it makes me ashamed to say that God will not hear me, when he has done so much—everything—for me in the past[.] I seem to limit the power of God. . . . The devil is always on the watch out, and a boy is never safe until he has finished college. Now, don't get scared and let visions of barrooms and champagne suppers rise up before you, for I give you my word and honor that I haven't been—exactly drunk—no my dear little mother. I haven't touched a drop of anything, not even the cider sold down [the] street, and I haven't smoked any cigarettes or chewed any tobacco or done any of those heinous things—then what's the matter with me? The only thing I know is this, that

> Generation after generation, since the days of the American Revolution, Chapel Hill has been extremely productive of talent. As a state university, it is uniquely successful, and almost every phase of enlightenment and progress in the state, and to some extent in the South, can trace its birth to this small town.
>
> John Ehle (class of 1949), *The Free Men*

I have decided to dance at commencement, and have made my engagements which I can't get out of if I would, and wouldn't if I could. Mamma, I don't care whether I ought to do this or not—its an experiment—and here, Mama, I confess it to you. I believe I have blunted my conscience, and reasoned myself into the belief that it is all right and very little harm, if any.[4]

ooooo

President Alderman Describes How the Old Well Acquired Its Beauty

In the fall of 1897, if my memory does not fail me, I was possessed with a great desire to add a little beauty (which, after all, is the most practical influence in the world) to the grim, austere dignity of the old Campus at Chapel Hill. Looking out my window on the first floor of South Building, I beheld the old well squalid and ramshackled. I determined to tear it down and put something there having beauty. Of course, money with which to do ambitious things was utterly lacking. I had always admired the little round temple which one sees reproduced so often in English Gardens. These were spread over England by the Stuarts under the influence of the French tradition, derived largely from the Temple of Love in the Garden at Versailles. This temple of love literally descended—

1. From a Greek shrine

2. From the Tholos at Epidaurus

3. From the Temple of Vesta at Tivoli

4. From the "Pietro Montorio" by Bramanti.

Our little well is, therefore, a sort of sixth cousin of [a] Greek shrine, or third cousin of the Temple of Vesta, or second cousin of the Temple at Versailles.

I was more familiar with the Temple at Versailles. So I found a picture of it and some pictures of round temples in English Gardens derived from it, and took all of these to my ever helpful friend in all practical matters about the University, Professor J. W. Gore, and asked him if we could reproduce it, or something like it, fairly decently at very trifling cost in wood. He said he thought we could. He then drew, or had drawn, a pencil sketch based on the temple at Versailles, in scale for our purposes, took up its building with some nearby lumber company, and lo! The little structure went up, seemed to my eyes well proportioned and now, after the passage of thirty-seven years, has stolen into the hearts of people [as] beauty in any sort of form has a way of doing, and is also by way of becoming somewhat mythical as to its origin.

I recall a fine shindy [quarrel] I had with a very distinguished professor who intimated broadly to me that I was foolish to spend money (about $200) for such luxurious gewgaws when so many vital things—sewers, waterworks, electric fixtures—cried out for improvement. I recall intimating to my distinguished colleague that he would do well to attend to his own "damn" business. . . . It was the day of small things in money matters but of full grown ideas about great permanent sins. The whole incident, the building of the little Temple, was a pitiful, yet beautiful, illustration of the way Democracy cries out for beauty to give it backbone—spiritual backbone—that will make it so strong that it can and will defy self gratification, mobs and red terrors.

Beauty
Old yet ever New
Eternal Voice
and
Inward Word[5]

Our first duty is to enable the students to catch the spirit of the great masters of thought; our next is to the people, to aid in developing our resources. We owe a duty to our women, and should open our postgraduate courses to them.

Edwin Anderson Alderman, 1897

ooooo

William E. Cox's First Impressions of the Campus
SEPTEMBER 1895

Immediately after breakfast I set out eagerly for a glimpse of the University about which I had heard so much. I entered the campus at the West Gate and for a bird's-eye view of the place as a whole followed Cameron Avenue entirely across the campus to the East Gate, then came back to the well for a close-up view of the buildings. . . . The artistic columned cover over the well, familiar to students of more recent years, was not there then. If my memory serves me correctly there was a square box curb around it with chain and two buckets for drawing water, and an octagonal roof over it. The new round-top cover was put there by Dr. Alderman shortly after he was made President, and while I was a student there.

As I stood by the old well and looked across the tree-studded lawn toward the rustic rock wall on Franklin Avenue I thought it was the most beautiful place I had ever seen, and the thrill of that moment has never left me. The old rock wall, the first of its kind I ever saw, possessed a beauty all its own, for it seemed to me to be a real work of art. It was made of loose rocks of various shapes and sizes piled one upon another without cement or mortar of any kind to hold them together, yet top and sides of the thick sturdy wall were straight and even. Through my whole term at the University the beauty of that wall continued to fascinate me. I sincerely hope that it will be allowed to remain there as a symbol of the simple but substantial character of the earliest of State Universities.[6]

ooooo

William Starr Myers Writes the University's Official School Song in 1897

Hark the sound of loyal voices
Ringing sweet and true,

Telling Carolina's glories,
Singing NCU.

Hail to the brightest star of all!
Clear in thy radiance shine,
Carolina, priceless gem,
Receives all praise as thine.

Hark the echo of those voices,
Boys of long ago!
Singing Carolina's praises,
As through life they go.

So with the future generations
That shall know thy love
All will join the happy chorus,
Their affection prove.[7]

1900
—
1909

Vision for the Twentieth Century

idding adieu to his alma mater in 1900, President Edwin Alderman offered words of wisdom as the university embarked upon the twentieth century. He concluded an eloquent commencement address with a challenge for the community he left behind: "The University of North Carolina is an honest, faithful force. North Carolinians need it as Virginians, Texans, Louisianians need theirs. The time has come to decide what sort of University we are going to make out of this noble institution. While I do not believe that any Yale or Harvard can be built here, yet I do believe that the State of North Carolina has the opportunity to make here a far reaching and powerful institution."[1]

Alderman was succeeded by Francis P. Venable, a farsighted, pragmatic administrator who believed that the remarkable heritage of the university could serve as a springboard to future greatness. To prepare the university for the mighty work that was before it in the new century, Venable reminded the faithful of the remarkable recent half-century in his University Day speech on October 12, 1900:

The truest democracy in the State is found right here—a wise toler-ance for all shades of opinion and belief. . . . When I enter yonder Me-morial Hall and read on those tablets the roll of our Confederate dead a great wave of pride and deep emotion fills my heart. . . . Twelve in each hundred of all her sons fell, one in every eight. Of the Freshman Class of 1859, all but one, who was unable to bear arms, entered the service. Of the Freshman Class of 1860 one in every three gave up his life. . . .

The story of the University during the last quarter of a century is one of which any people might justly be proud. It required pluck and en-ergy and brains to keep up that fight against poverty and ignorance and narrow hostility. Prejudices were overcome by masterly tact and care. The University grew until from a handful of professors and a few dozen students it has come to be recognized as a leader among educational in-stitutions of the South[. I]ts walls are overflowing with students, taught by an able and enthusiastic Faculty, seven times as large as that twenty-five years ago. It is with its meager income doing the work of thrice its wealth.[2]

John Sprunt Hill, an honors graduate of the class of 1888, envisioned a new library as the centerpiece of the university of the twentieth century. In 1903, he made an impassioned plea to his fellow alumni to provide such a facility: "Will not some great hearted son or daughter of the Old North State give our people a great library, the head of the library system of the State, to illumine the homes of all the people of every creed and every sta-tion, and show them the hidden paths to the kindly fruits of the earth and to the eternal blessings of Heaven? Pearls and palaces, diamonds and din-ners will vanish with the tolling of a bell, great fortunes will be made and lost in a century in a whirlpool of luxury and extravagance, princes will follow princes in the lengthening cycles of debauchery and corruption, but the rich fruits from this, the most beautiful flower of philanthropy in the garden of fine nativity, will give ever-increasing hope and happiness to your people and prove immortal and divine."[3]

For President Venable, the most critical needs of the modern Univer-sity of North Carolina were a world-renowned library and a distinguished faculty. His relentless efforts to land quality faculty members paid hand-some rewards in succeeding decades, and the quest for a new library was attended by success in 1907.

Not satisfied with a new library building, Venable wanted to fill its shelves and vaults with documents and manuscripts about North Caro-lina. He joined forces with his outstanding librarian, Louis Round Wilson, and his noted professor of history, J. G. De Roulhac Hamilton, to assemble

> Surely no institution in American life more clearly exemplifies the truth that "Great oaks grow from little acorns." The University of North Carolina stands today as a "Giant Oak" in the field of letters and in cultural leadership and achievements.
>
> *Kinston Daily Free-Press*

what was to become the famed North Carolina Collection. Their 1909 appeal to the public for materials related to the state was instrumental in the formation of the prized collection, the largest assemblage of North Caroliniana in the world. John Sprunt Hill, in response to this appeal and his own plea, would subsequently provide a generous endowment for the North Carolina Collection.

Intercollegiate basketball has long been acclaimed as the sport that has brought the most fame to the university. But at the dawn of the twentieth century, the school had not yet fielded a basketball team. In its edition of December 5, 1901, the *Tar Heel* envisioned the advent of the sport that is now synonymous with the Chapel Hill campus: "An attempt is being made to arrange a basketball schedule, games to be played during January, February and March. It is desired that the classes take up this game and make it a part of the athletic life of the University."[4] The team finally took the court in 1910.

A proper venue for basketball was completed in 1905. Bynum Hall, a gymnasium given by Judge W. P. Bynum in honor of his grandson, was dedicated that May. At the dedication ceremony, President Venable read a short letter from Judge Bynum, and Dr. Richard H. Lewis accepted the gift on behalf of the university. In his remarks, Dr. Lewis expressed the desire that the gymnasium and the athletic program would stand "four square to all the winds that blow." Ironically, decades later, Dean Smith, the legendary head coach of the men's basketball team, would revolutionize the college game with his four corners offense.

Meanwhile, the university was educating a native son whose vision, intellect, character, and courage would endear him to the Chapel Hill family as one of its most loved, admired, honored, and distinguished leaders. Beside his photograph in the 1909 *Yackety Yack* was an almost prophetic description of the man who would render a lifetime of service to his state, his nation, and his university—the incomparable Frank Porter Graham.

ooooo

> The University of North Carolina is the lengthened shadow, not of one man, but of a whole people, the "freest of the free," united in a grand struggle for civil and religious liberty.
>
> John Sprunt Hill, 1903

President Alderman's Last Commencement Address

Four distinctive traits of institutional character mark the life of the University.

First. Its freedom from academic aloofness. It has from the first seen the relation of culture and training of social service. Of the United States Senators from this State, forty-four per cent went from this University, of the Representatives in Congress, forty per cent; of the Governors of the State, fifty-eight per cent; of the Lieutenant Governors, fifty-nine per cent; of the Speakers of the House of Representatives, fifty per cent; of the State officers, twenty-two per cent; of the Judges of the Superior Court, thirty-eight per cent; of the Judges of the Supreme Court, fifty-two per cent. . . . In the Civil War, forty per cent of the total enrollment from 1825 to 1867 were in the Confederate Army. . . .

Since the reopening of this institution in 1875, two thousand eight hundred and ninety-six students have matriculated here [and] five hundred and sixty-two have graduated. There is no arithmetic that can calculate the good these men have done, or can estimate the loss to the State if this army of trained men had not been sent out into its life. Ninety-three per cent of these matriculates have come from this State. Fifty per cent have been the sons of men who never knew the advantages of college training.

Second. The University has accomplished greater results on smaller means than any American institution. Its annual income from the State is $25,000.00, from all sources $48,000. It has thirty-five members of the Faculty, students five hundred and twelve. It maintains a continuous session and a summer school for teachers. It has opened its doors to women. No Southern institution on so small an income can exceed this result.

Third. There is the spirit of freedom, toleration, and equality in its life. Three-fourths of the students are the sons of poor men or are here as the result of money borrowed or earned. All sects, parties and conditions meet and mingle on an equal footing.

Fourth. The passionate affection of its alumni. A boy comes, hard of hand, strong of face, ungainly of dress. But he has faith shining in his eyes. Four years go by and something rich and strange comes into his face, something subtle enters into his motions and speech, and he stands erect and free, that noblest of God's creatures, an effective, cultured gentleman. Whenever a true conception of what a real university is gets into the bone and marrow of North Carolina this institution will have the finest chance in America to realize its ideal.[5]

ooooo

Letter from Three University Officials Regarding the Genesis of the North Carolina Collection

The University of North Carolina
Chapel Hill, N.C.
Sept. 25, 1909

To the Alumni and Friends of the University—

With the completion of the new Library in 1907, the University outlined a plan by which it hopes to build up here and place at their service of investigators a great collection of material relating to North Carolina. To this end, it equipped a fire-proof vault in the Library stack-room with specially designed steel cases for the more valuable manuscripts, pamphlets, and volumes, and set apart one large upstairs room for the general collection of North Caroliniana. This is considered the first essential—a suitable, fire-proof home.

All the original collections belonging to the University have been consolidated and placed in the new quarters. The North Carolina Historical Society, organized in 1844, has transferred to the Library its store of valuable documents and books. Through the gift of an alumnus, an annual income of $250.00 is available for the increase of the collection. Other alumni and friends of the University have thought favorably of the plan and have shown their approval by many much appreciated gifts.

We are confident this undertaking will be sanctioned by all North Carolinians who would like to see at their State University such a body of material relating to the State's life as would encourage scholarly research in North Carolina history. The difficulties attending its collection must be obvious to you. In every locality in the State, there are files of newspapers and collections of letters, manuscripts, pamphlets, and books which we could use to great advantage in the way indicated if we could only procure them.

If you have such material in your possession, or know of its existence in your locality, we urge you to inform us concerning it and aid us in our endeavor to secure it. Here it will be protected from injury, will be carefully indexed so as to render its contents easily accessible, and will, through its growing extensiveness, be of great service.

May we rely upon your cooperation and assistance?

Very sincerely yours,

Francis P. Venable, President
Louis R. Wilson, Librarian
J. G. De Roulhac Hamilton, Alumni Professor of History[6]

ooooo

Letter from Judge W. P. Bynum on the Erection of a Gymnasium

Charlotte, N.C., May, 1905

To the Board of Trustees of the University of North Carolina.
Dear Sirs:

With your permission, I have caused to be erected on the grounds of the University, a gymnasium, intended for the use and benefit of the students, and in memory of a grandson who died before his graduation at this school.

Naturally, the place desired and selected for this building was the University of North Carolina, an institution that has accomplished and is accomplishing so much for the educational growth and prosperity of the whole State.

With the hope that this building will be of some assistance in this great work, I respectfully and cordially present the gymnasium to the Board of Trustees of the University of North Carolina.

Most respectfully,

W. P. Bynum[7]

ooooo

Remarks of Dr. Richard H. Lewis upon the Acceptance of Bynum Gymnasium by the University

No gift could have been more opportune. A suitable gymnasium was sorely needed in our athletic life. Not infrequently one hears that boys are sent to college to study, not to play ball. Such are incapable of feeling the wild delight that follows a home run in the ninth with a short score and the bases full, or the delirious joy of the touchdown which brings victory. . . .

The aim of this University is to train men—not one-sided men, but well-rounded men—for the honor, support, and protection of the State and for its own lasting glory. And this cannot be done without the athletic feature.

It may be mere fancy, but the architectural style of the building, it seems to me, is most appropriate. While very handsome, it is very simple, as befits a people whose motto is *Esse Quam Videri*. It is a square building, and in this respect I trust symbolical. It stands firm and strong "four square to all the winds that blow." And so I hope will ever stand the Athletic Association of the University of North Carolina to the athletic world, straight and true, firm and strong, four square against all temptations to achieve success by trickery or deceit, remembering that defeat with honor is worth a thousand victories that are besmirched. The general Athletic Association, which is essentially the student body, is the chief maker of college opinion. May this beautiful building of theirs be to them a temple of honor, from which emanate such influences that no man guilty of dishonorable conduct, either on the athletic field or in the class room, can continue to live within its shadow.[8]

ooooo

Profile of Frank Porter Graham from the Yackety Yack of 1909

Frank Porter Graham, Charlotte, N.C.

A man to all the country dear.

Age 22; height 5 feet 6 inches; weight 125. Law. Di Society; Y.M.C.A.; Golden Fleece; Gimghoul; Odd Number Club; Cosmopolitan Club; Mecklenburg Club; Secretary W.H.S. Club; Class and All-Class Baseball Team (1); Scrub Baseball Team (2, 3); President of Class (2); Soph-Junior Debater (3); Class Historian (3); Assistant Editor-in-Chief of *Tar Heel* (3); Secretary of Phi Beta Kappa; President of Y.M.C.A. (4); Editor-in-Chief of *Tar Heel*, Fall Term (4); President of Class (4); Secretary of Modern Literature Club; Chief Cheerer (4); Editor of *Yackety Yack* (3).

Frank, Laddie Buck.

Everyman's friend, confidant, and playfellow. Couldn't do what he is supposed to do to-morrow if he were to live his whole life in one day. No settled tradition in college can be carried through without him, no new movement can be successful without him at its head. And, curiously enough, with the burden of college upon his shoulders, he bears it without losing himself in it all. Out of it all he comes a little worn, but still the same good fellow of his lazy, less-occupied days.[9]

1910
–
1919

Of Students and
Their Teachers

*A*ttracted to Chapel Hill because of the university's growing reputation for academic excellence, a number of exceptional professors accepted faculty positions in the second decade of the new century. Among this distinguished group were Edwin A. Greenlaw in English and Frederick Koch in drama. These two innovative scholars joined long-serving professors such as Horace Williams to mold some of the finest minds in the South while the university and the nation endured World War I.

Horace Williams, Chapel Hill's renowned philosophy professor, used his classroom gifts to encourage his students to be freethinkers. Archibald Lee Manning Wiggins, a prominent American businessman and railroad tycoon following his graduation from the university in 1913, warmly recalled his "adventures in thinking" with Professor Williams in a subsequent speech to the Horace Williams Philosophical Society.

Professors Williams, Greenlaw, and Koch teamed their masterful talents to train two of the most revered American authors of the twentieth century. One was Paul Green, who interrupted his education at the university to serve in World War I. He won the Pulitzer Prize in 1927 for *In*

Abraham's Bosom, a play written while he was a professor at his alma mater. And, too, there was Green's celebrated classmate, Thomas Clayton Wolfe. Acclaimed by William Faulkner as the best writer of the Lost Generation, Wolfe attributed much of his success to his undergraduate education and experiences at Chapel Hill. About Professor Horace Williams, the novelist opined in *You Can't Go Home Again*, "He was a great teacher, and what he did for us, and for others before us for fifty years, was not to give us his 'philosophy' . . . but to communicate to us his alertness, his originality, his power to think."

Wolfe arrived on the campus from his home in western North Carolina in the fall of 1916. Never one to shrink from the spotlight, the lanky, high-spirited lad made a memorable entry into the Dialectic Society. It was customary for the older members of the organization to initiate freshmen with embarrassing practices such as head shaving. In the midst of the humiliation, sophomore students would demand speeches from the initiates. As a freshman, Tom Wolfe was the first to be called upon. As he stood to deliver his "talk," Wolfe took notice of the portraits of distinguished men who had once belonged to the society. Hanging over the rostrum where Wolfe stood was the likeness of Zeb Vance. In a self-assured tone, the freshman told his audience that he was happy and proud to be in their distinguished company. He boldly ended his oration by proclaiming that he hoped his portrait would someday hang alongside that of Vance.[1]

In *Look Homeward Angel*, Wolfe termed his impetuous speech "an inexcusable blunder." However, his portrait now adorns the north wall of the very Dialectic Society chamber where he made his bold claim.

Albert Coates—who like his classmate Wolfe attended Harvard after graduation—was witness to the clever genius and remarkable wit of the

> Sometimes when the springtime comes,
> And the sifting moonlight falls—
> They'll think again of this night here
> And of these old brown walls,
> Of white old well, and of old South
> With bell's deep booming tone,
> They'll think again of Chapel Hill and—
> Thinking—come back home.
>
> Thomas Wolfe

budding author. His description of Wolfe the student offers colorful insight into a complex personality.

During his student days in Chapel Hill, Paul Green observed Wolfe's raw talent. He recalled, "His procrastination usually kept him in hot water. He would wait until the night before he was to read his play, then sit up until daybreak dashing off page after page of dialogue scrawl that only he could decipher. Then he would come in to class hollow-eyed, shaggy-bearded, unkempt and stuttering, and babble through the reading of his play. And always there was enough in the piece for 'Proff' and the rest of us to praise."[2]

Frederick Koch, known to Wolfe and his fellow students as "Proff," played an integral role in fine-tuning the rough talents of the young writer. Proff fondly recalled his opportunity to work with Wolfe in the fall term of 1918.

Following his Chapel Hill days, Wolfe maintained a cordial relationship with his professors at the university. One of his favorites was Edwin Greenlaw. Affectionately known as "Eddie," Greenlaw paid what Wolfe considered the highest praise to *Look Homeward, Angel* when he wrote his former student, "I didn't find a line of shoddy in it."

In *English at Chapel Hill, 1795–1969*, Dougald MacMillan observed, "As head of the Department of English and Dean of the Graduate School, Greenlaw did more than any other person has done, and as much for the University as any one person has done this century." At the dedication of the classroom building named in Greenlaw's memory, former chancellor Robert Burton House recognized the special qualities that had endeared the English teacher to so many: "As the going got tough under his strenuous discipline, some students indulged in snap judgments of Dr. Greenlaw as a bear or tyrant. But they learned that the bear had a tender heart,

> At six o'clock in the morning when I finally finished the last of the 864 pages of *Look Homeward Angel*, I knew that the only college I could attend would be Thos. Wolfe's alma mater, The University of North Carolina.
>
> Richard Adler (class of 1943),
> two-time Tony winner

Hark the Sound of Tar Heel Voices

and that the tyrant tyrannized over himself in their interests. Nothing ever overcame his infectious humor and merry laugh with them over incidents in each day's happenings."[3]

ooooo

Archibald Lee Manning Wiggins Reflects on Professor Horace Williams

In class one day, he [Professor Williams] opened the discussion by asking in his simple and disarming manner, "Mr. Wiggins, why does a dog catch a rabbit?" Well, here at last he was speaking my language. This was something I knew about and could give him an answer which would stand up. Before I realized what had happened, the trap was sprung. The entire period of that class was devoted to efforts to find an answer to the question of why a dog catches a rabbit. Most of his questions were directed to me. I dangled at the end of his hook the whole period. He made no effort to get me off and every effort I made drove the hook deeper. I was humiliated, disgusted and boiling mad. But that was the turning point. After weeks of struggle over the question, "Why does a dog catch a rabbit?", a little light broke through. Then followed that long, laborious unending effort in intellectual development and gradually some understanding in the long search for truth. . . .

The greatest shock Horace ever gave me was after our last class. We were walking across the campus to the Post Office and I asked him one more question. It was a final effort to prize out of him a direct answer to what today might be called the $64 question. I said, "Now, Professor Williams, after all you have taught us these past two years there is just one more question and I hope you will give me an answer. I am graduating next week and will get to work. I want to know what in life, after all, is really worthwhile? What are the eternal values we should seek?" I'll never forget the old man. He immediately recognized that I was lost. If that's all I had learned after two years in his classes, I was sunk. He stopped and looked down at me with those sad compassionate eyes and here is what he said, and I think maybe you will be surprised at what he said: "Mr. Wiggins, I would give anything to know." His answer rang in my ears throughout the years that followed.

He failed to wrap up and hand me a package, a finished product, by

With the close of the football season of 1913 all eyes are now turned to basketball. It is a sport that is practically new with the University, having been in vogue here for only a few years, but one that is gaining ground.

Tar Heel

replying to my question as to what in life is really worthwhile—what are the eternal values we should seek—by saying, "Mr. Wiggins, I would give anything to know." The plain implication was that he had not discovered the ultimate, but that the search would go on and on. . . . This great philosopher, this wise old man who worshipped at the shrines of the gods of truth, goodness and beauty would give anything to know the eternal values of life. Many years passed before I realized that in his reply he was still the teacher and not the philosopher, the stimulator of his students' minds in their search for truth. What he had really meant when he gave that reply is clear to me now. It was, "Mr. Wiggins, no man can answer that question for another—you must find a satisfying answer for yourself."[4]

ooooo

Albert Coates, Class of 1918, Describes His Days with Thomas Wolfe at Carolina

From the beginning of his freshman year he attracted attention on the campus by his slim figure, great height (6 feet, 3 inches), light weight (115 pounds), long strides, loping walk, a two to three inch gap between his trouser cuffs and his shoe tops, outgrowing one suit of clothes after another—he added three inches to his height during his four years in Chapel Hill.

His vaguely comical appearance in the beginning invited wisecracks from various and sundry college mates—but not for long. Tom could take care of himself in any encounter which involved a battle of wits and a use of words. Nobody could make a fool out of him, and anyone who tried it was more than likely to find himself the victim rather than the victor. I was a casual passerby and witness to one such incident which turned his adversary into the laughing stock of the group. It is told in one of his novels and is literally true. . . .

Prof. [C. Addison] Hibbard told me that Tom would pull a handful of handbills off a telephone pole post on the way to a class in English Composition, sit on the back row, write his theme there, and turn it in at the end of the class, and the quality of his writing was so far above the run of the mill themes that Prof. Hibbard said he would accept it no matter what it was written on.

He had no lack of confidence in himself to begin with, and his confidence in himself grew as he went along. In a meeting of *Tar Heel* reporters in his sophomore year, someone asked him if he had a middle name. "Yes," was the reply. "Why don't you use it?" Tom replied: "Who ever heard of William J. Shakespeare?" And he wasn't joking!

He could laugh at himself as quickly as he could laugh at anybody else. One day . . . he went to Dr. Greenlaw's class in writing and read his theme from the back of envelopes, sheets from memorandum pads, and toilet paper, which he pulled solemnly out of his pocket, one after another, to the ill-suppressed laughter of his classmates. Dr. Greenlaw responded with the observation that the quality of his creation was worthy of the paper on which it was written, and Tom led the class in appreciation of the jibe.[5]

ooooo

Professor Frederick H. Koch Describes Tom Wolfe As a Student

The only male member of the first playwriting course at Chapel Hill in the fall of 1918 was Thomas Wolfe, "Tom" to us, a lanky six-and-a-half-foot tall mountain lad with burning eyes. The other twelve members of the class

> My own conviction constantly deepens that the next great creative chapter in the history of the nation is to be written here in the South. . . . Somewhere in the South there must inevitably grow up an institution . . . which typifies and serves and guides this new civilization. . . . My dream for the University of North Carolina is that she be nothing less than this.
>
> Henry Woodburn Chase, 1919

were co-eds. After the meeting of the class that first day he said, by way of apology, "Proff, I don't . . . think that this Ladies Aid Society represents Carolina. We have a lot of he-men seriously interested in writing here, but they are all disguised in army uniforms now. I tried to get into one myself but they didn't have one long enough for me."

His first play—and his first published work—*The Return of Buck Gavin*, a tragedy of a mountain outlaw, included in the second volume of *Carolina Folk Plays*, was one of the plays in our initial production that first season. We couldn't find anyone to play the part and I said to him, "I guess you'll have to play it yourself, Tom. You may not know it, but you really wrote that part for yourself!"

"But I can't act, Proff, I've never acted."

"You're a born actor," I assured him, "and you are Buck Gavin."

I shall never forget his first performance. With free mountain stride, his dark eyes blazing, he became the hunted outlaw of the Great Smokies. There was something uncanny in his acting of the part—something of the pent-up fury of his highland forebears.

In his foreword to *The Return of Buck Gavin* Tom wrote to all beginners: "It is fallacy of the young writer to picture the dramatic as unusual and remote. . . . The dramatic is not unusual. It is happening daily in our lives."

Of his playwriting that first year he wrote: "I have written about people I have known and concerning whom I feel qualified to write. They have suggested a train of thought that intensely interests me, and is, I believe, of vital importance to me. My writing, I feel sure, has been made easier and better by their production. If they have affected my writing to this extent— if they have indirectly caused an analysis of my work, and a determination of my future course—are they not worthwhile, even though they may be but the amateurish productions of a youngster!"

It is interesting to recall now the first efforts of the young writer. Like [Sherwood] Anderson, he wrote what he knew. Though crude, those who have followed him through the years cannot fail to see in his first hastily written little plays the indications of his later achievement in *Look Homeward, Angel* and *Of Time and the River*.[6]

ooooo

Robert B. House's Tribute
to Professor Edwin Greenlaw
at the Dedication of Greenlaw Hall

The man in the profession is immeasurable. But Edwin Greenlaw can be appreciated, thanked, and loved by the student generation of his time here—1913–1925.

He put the capstone on our University years. He came to us as a master spirit of the great Elizabethan Renaissance. He gave body, bone, muscle, mental amplitude, and determined will to our aspirations and efforts toward a rebirth of freedom and culture in North Carolina. . . .

He was a superb teacher, somewhat formidable to students on first acquaintance. He was master, but no driver. He was stern and unyielding in his standards of learning, discipline, and hard work.

But he had a discerning eye for the individual aptitudes of students. He was delighted by those apt in scholarship, but he was not shocked by the crassly ignorant ones. Those gifted with a passion for pure scholarship he sought to recruit for the Graduate School as teachers and researchers. These he regarded as the saviors of civilization at its roots.

Those brilliant but unlikely for pure scholarship, he guided into the upper ranks of the professional schools.

Those without particular motivations he counseled with compassionate good humor into academically less arduous pursuits.

All the three echelons are equally grateful to Dr. Greenlaw. . . .

His students observed him, pipe in mouth, raking autumn leaves in his yard, with his baby close by in a carriage. They admired him walking

To you who read this: whether ye be Carolina students or prospects, let it have this significance: it may not be our lot in our lives here at Carolina to take part in the more spectacular activities of our college life, in athletics. But if we are not naturally endowed with athletic requirements, if we may not go out on the football field and cover ourselves with mud and glory— remember: They also serve who only sit and write.

Thomas Wolfe

up Hooper Lane, entranced by spring bloom and the perfume of honeysuckle. They sang Christmas carols at his door and responded to his fellow spirit as he came out to join them. They gave him the affectionate nickname, Eddie.

We are a gladder and better University that Eddie joined. His spirit was universal. His mind was cosmopolitan, his heart, his home, his grave all in Chapel Hill.[7]

1920
–
1929

Tar Heels at Work and at Play

For much of the Roaring Twenties, the university enjoyed a respite between the close of World War I and the financial distress of the global economic depression on the horizon. Campus life returned to normal, and students found time for both the serious and amusing sides of the college experience.

Despite its growing reputation as an institution of national significance, the university lacked a non-textbook bookshop at the onset of the decade. Nor was there one in the village of Chapel Hill, which today boasts innumerable shops. To fill the void, Howard Mumford Jones, an instructor at the university, established the famous Bull's Head Book Shop on the campus. He recalled the dire need for the store:

> When I was a member of the English faculty at the University of North Carolina in the twenties, liberal forces in the South were stirring themselves in an effort, among other matters, to throw off Mencken's reproach that we were living in the Sahara of the Bozarts.
> Chapel Hill had its folk-play theater; it had Addison Hibbard's weekly syndicated column "The Literary Lantern;" it had Paul Green; it had Howard Odum making his modern sociological analyses of Southern life; it had a distinguished faculty in history, including Robert Connor and Roulhac Hamilton; it had Louis R. Wilson, one of the

leading librarians of the United States; and it had developed a capacity for attracting to itself all kinds of conferences on Southern economics, Southern culture, Southern history, and so on.

The only difficulty was that you couldn't buy a book in either the village or the university unless it were a textbook stocked by the competent student cooperative or unless you ordered it especially.[1]

On the lighter side, the university acquired its unique mascot in 1924, thanks to the ingenuity of Vic Huggins, its head cheerleader. Rameses the First made his debut in Chapel Hill at a football victory over the Virginia Military Institute in the fall of 1924. Soon thereafter, the ram made his first and only appearance at a Carolina basketball game. Huggins, who wrote one of the university's most cherished fight songs, "Here Comes Carolina," provided a humorous anecdote about Rameses.

Huggins's successor as head cheerleader was Kay Kyser, the enormously successful Big Band leader who retired to Chapel Hill once his brilliant career in radio, motion pictures, and the recording industry came to a close. Kyser, a member of the class of 1927, was one of the key players in the birth of public television at the university. His enduring love of the athletic program prompted him to write another of the school's familiar fight songs, "Tar Heels on Hand." In an interview with William C. Friday in 1981, Kyser recalled his humorous audition to become head cheerleader.

By the middle of the decade, new construction was in evidence over much of the campus. Torrential rains in the fall and early winter left the landscape awash in red mud. Students groused about the soupy morass so much that the campus newspaper felt compelled to weigh in on the situation. In an editorial entitled "Red Mud and Cultural Mud" and in an open letter under the name of one Percival Sylvester DePeyster, *Tar Heel* staff members used their pens to urge the university "to lift itself from the mud." In an effort to add levity to the controversy, President Henry W. Chase offered a delightful response to the DePeyster letter in the *Tar Heel* in early 1925.

Matters were far more serious in January 1927, when the state legis-

> This institution remains a man's university and has no ear-marks of a co-educational college.
>
> Editorial in the
> *Tar Heel,* 1923

Hark the Sound of Tar Heel Voices

lature began consideration of a bill designed to make it "unlawful for any professor, teacher, or instructor, to teach in any school, college, or educational institution within the State of North Carolina, receiving aid from the State, any doctrine or theory of evolution, which contradicts or denies the divine origin of man or of the universe as taught in the Holy Bible." Alarm over the threat to academic freedom spread throughout the university community. Near the close of a tense, heated three-hour legislative hearing on the bill on February 10, Paul J. Ranson, a young law student at the university, was recognized to speak. He made his way to the front of the House of Representatives and delivered a dramatic appeal against the bill. His speech generated thunderous applause and spelled doom for the proposed legislation, which officially went down in defeat two days later. About the same time, the *Tar Heel* printed Ranson's memorable words.

ooooo

Howard Mumford Jones Describes the Birth of the Bull's Head Book Shop

I went to Harry Woodburn Chase, then president, and dwelt sorrow upon this lack [of a general campus bookstore]. Fortunately, a university that operated its own laundry, its own hospital, and its own bakery was not afraid of economic experiment.

"What," said Mr. Chase, "do you propose to do about it?" "I will, if you permit me," I replied, "open a book store in my office." Which, with the aid of the student cooperative, I did.

The office was about the size of an ordinary classroom, but it had shelves around the walls. My first consignment of books was from the University of North Carolina Press, and dealt mainly with Southern themes. I wrote to everybody I knew in the New York publishing world and to a great many persons I did not know, explaining that I was opening a bookstore in a college community and that the student cooperative textbook store would serve as my fiduciary agent until I made enough money to pay the bills. Books somehow came in.

The Carolina undergraduate of the twenties was characteristically book shy. A book was something you studied for a teacher, and its proper dwelling place was a mysterious building called the library where you went when you had to. . . .

... Down the middle of the room there were two or three undistinguished tables, which I managed to fringe with some ordinary classroom chairs. I put the books on the shelves and a sign on the wall ..., "Please feel free to read any of these books as long as you want to. If you want to buy one of them, it is for sale." ...

As I needed a name as remote from Ye Olde Village Booke Store as I could get, after consultation with my colleagues I determined on The Bull's Head Bookshop. It seemed appropriate to a tobacco-raising state. ...

As we had no way of wrapping a book in fancy packages, customers went away content with the naked volume. And we had, if my memory is right, no charge accounts—that is, no official charge accounts, though if we caught an undergraduate longing to possess a particular book, yet lacking the immediate cash, I think we made arrangements. ...

When I left North Carolina for the University of Michigan in 1930 the Bull's Head was a relatively flourishing concern. There were no empty shelves, and the weekly receipts were healthy. I was assured that it would not be allowed to die.[2]

ooooo

Vic Huggins Describes
How Rameses Came to Be

The secret to being a good cheerleader is hard work. We tried to be enthusiastic. That student body wasn't big then and we had good rapport with the crowd. And we tried to have something different cooked up for every game. ...

You had to use a little ingenuity and get the whole student body to help you. ...

All of our rivals seemed to have a mascot. I thought it might help school spirit if we did too. One of the best players on our great '22 team which went 9–1 was Jack Merritt. Merritt was known as The Battering Ram. It seemed only natural to link our mascot to him.

Charlie Woollen, the athletic manager at the time, agreed with the idea and gave us $25 to purchase a fitting mascot. Rameses the First was shipped from Texas just in time for the VMI game. He and his descendants have been here ever since. ...

Guess what I'm best remembered for was the time I decided to intro-

duce Rameses to the basketball court. At the half, the lights were dimmed
and a huge, glittering, twirling star was lowered from the ceiling of the gym
and Rameses, with all the pomp and ceremony at my disposal, was escort-
ed in by a quartet in full evening dress. The quartet was singing "Hark the
Sound"—and everybody stood up. Believe you me, it made quite a rack-
et in the old Tin Can Gym. It scared poor Rameses silly! He forgot his
manners and embarrassed us all right there in front of everybody! Some
thoughtful soul meaning to be kind, no doubt, turned out the lights just
as the janitor slipped over with his broom and dustpan. Now—man there
was a floor show! Rameses! A dustpan! And the janitor—a one-man clean-
up squad—and a *lighted match*![3]

ooooo

Kay Kyser Describes
How He Became a Cheerleader

It was spring and they were having tryouts down at Emerson Field for
the next fall football season, and the student body that was in the stands
would vote on which of the aspirants had done the best job.

At that time, the school spirit was at a very low ebb. It was beneath the
dignity of the student body to give a vociferous expression. It was something you thought about, but just didn't give voice to. I heard each aspirant
out there trying out. They were pleading with the students, "Oh Please . . .
Now c'mon, guys, we've got to give 15 hurrahs for the team."

And they'd yell, and you'd hear "Rah . . . rah . . . rah . . ." I could just feel
that I was going to be a real big flop out there. So I said, I've gotta do something that will shock 'em, make 'em *want* to yell. So I went out, not knowing
what I was going to do. Believe it or not—with no disrespect, I didn't even
premeditate it—I heard it coming out of me: "Gang, let's give 15 rahs for
the Baptist church."

And it so shocked the guys in the stands that before they knew it, they were yelling their heads off for the Baptist church. It shocked me, too. The ones it shocked the worst were the football players. They froze from the noise coming at 'em. When they heard Baptist church, they *really* were confused.[4]

ooooo

President Chase's Response to the Campus Quagmire, As Published in the Tar Heel on January 28, 1925

Mr. Percival Sylvester DePeyster
Chapel Hill, North Carolina

Dear Percy:

You write me about mud. You write freeingly and well, with passion and yet with due restraint. Your vigor and clarity of expression, your vocabulary, are a credit to your own wide writing and to the instruction which is offered by our department of English.

However, Percival, I must confess that your insistence on the importance of pavement under your feet whenever you sally forth from your comfortable room evidences a softening of fibre which I fear is all too common in these decadent days. Not so, Percival Sylvester, did our forefathers conduct themselves. To their minds, an important, indeed an essential element in the training of youth, was that a certain discomfort, a certain hardship, should attend the process—that it toughened and strengthened both the physical and moral fibre of young men. Consult, if you like, with the older alumni of the University, and learn how definitely such a theory was once put into practice, and then you will, I know, be grateful that some few elements of Spartan simplicity and discipline still remain to us.

As for myself, I have reached a certain age. Discomfort has not the value for maturity that it possesses for youth. When, indeed, has an older generation felt called upon to itself endure the hardships it has deemed necessary for its juniors?

But, Mr. DePeyster, you not only would do away with salutary discomfort, you would destroy one of the University's traditions. It is recorded that when Hinton James, first of [the] University's students, walked from Wilmington through the mud of winter to take up his residence at Chapel Hill, his feet trod the soil of Cameron Avenue, then a road cut through virgin forest. The mud of Cameron Avenue helped to make him what he became. Since his day, as the generations have passed, picture to yourself what feet, feet that later were to bear their possessors into the high places of the State and Nation, have trodden this sacred mud. Every foot of this mud has held in its tenacious embrace some noble form. And now you, sir, would cover with a six-inch slab of concrete the soil of this *via sacra*; you would conceal it and its memories forever from mor[t]al eyes!

Indeed, Percival Sylvester DePeyster, it is time to take thought of the old traditions of this place. It is time to ask ourselves whether the urge for material progress is not supplanting the old simple virtues in our midst. Shall we, in the name of progress, abolish one of the most typical of our inheritances—that fine, rich mixture of red earth and H_2O, the memory, and often the visible traces of which, University men carry [to] the ends of the earth? I repeat, shall we?

Sincerely yours,

H. W. Chase[5]

ooooo

Speech of Paul Ranson at the Legislative Hearing on the Teaching of Evolution
FEBRUARY 10, 1927

"I think it is time for the young people of this state to speak out," he yelled, in a voice that carried into every corner of the room. "I want to say first that I was raised in a Christian home and I think it is time that the rising generation should tell the people something about all of this foolishness they are carrying on.

["]God knows it is not evolution that's driving the young people out of the churches. I haven't been driven out and I have attended the University for six years." The house rocked with laughter and applause, the first real display of enthusiasm [during] the three-hour session. "You laugh like you think I am dumb because I went there for six years. I went there four years and graduated and then I studied law there for two years.

["]I've had five brothers who went to the University," he proceeded, after clearing up his academic record, "and not one of them has turned out to be an atheist. We do not know anything about it, we want to know where we are going from here; not where we came from—we care nothing about that.

["] I'm amazed at my temerity. I don't know what made me get up here. I had an inspiration that wouldn't let me sit back there and listen to all this foolishness. People will think me crazy. . . .

["]I just couldn't help speaking out in the meeting and now I've spoken out. I've been studying law and I had connected up to work with a law firm—but I reckon now when that firm hears about what I've done it won't take me."[6]

A Benevolent
University Family

*I*n 1930, President Henry W. Chase offered a glowing assessment of the university at a time when the nation was engulfed by economic chaos:

> The University of North Carolina has attained a position among the significant institutions for higher education in America. I make this statement without qualification and without apology, for this position is the result of the activities of many devoted and competent men at work for more than one generation of University history. . . . At precisely the time . . . when the State and the South are being brought into competition in such definite ways with the remainder of the country, the University has come into a position in which it can offer to Southern youth a training that does not shrink from measurement by national standards. . . . With its great resources, this is destined to be a region of strategic importance in America. The question to what extent Southern youth are trained in ways competent to fit them to be masters of their own heritage is probably the most significant question with which the South is now face to face. That an institution achieves national recognition is at least some testimony to the fact that it is helping toward a proper answer to this question.[1]

While the Great Depression cast its dark shadow, the university enjoyed support from people of every walk of life. Over the course of a long history, the campus and the student body were the beneficiaries of the efforts of janitors and laborers who worked long hours to keep the university operating. One such janitor was Uncle Bill McDade, who summarized his fifty-three-year career in an interview in the 1930s.

Despite the financial setbacks of the times, the campus added several significant landmarks because of the generosity of alumni.

John Motley Morehead, class of 1891, and Ruffin Patterson, class of 1893, provided the funding for the erection of the majestic 167-foot-tall Morehead-Patterson Bell Tower. Immediately before the Carolina-Virginia football game in November 1931, the handsome structure was dedicated in a ceremony broadcast live by radio station WBT in Charlotte. George Gordon Battle, a prominent New York attorney, returned to his alma mater to deliver the principal address, in which he lauded the spirit of hope symbolic of the university.

Four years later, John Sprunt Hill, class of 1889, donated the most famous hostelry in Chapel Hill. The Durham businessman had built the Carolina Inn at the edge of the campus in the mid-1920s. Through his gift of it to the university, he sought to provide support for the growing North Carolina Collection. Excerpts from Hill's letter to the university controller in 1935 and from his remarks to the General Alumni Association a year later explain the nature of his gift.

Perhaps no son of Carolina gave more of himself to the students and the world than Frank Porter Graham. Through example, he ingrained liberality into the hearts of those who represented the university. Graham's philosophy of life was infectious. One student greatly influenced by "Dr. Frank" was Vermont Royster, class of 1935. After he left Chapel Hill, Royster earned two Pulitzer Prizes and served for thirteen years as editor in chief of the *Wall Street Journal*. But it was in Chapel Hill where young Royster learned one of the most important lessons of his life, from the benevolent spirit of the university's master teacher, Frank Porter Graham.

> Everyone is proud of the University of North Carolina, and its faculty, but it is well known that within this faculty is a small group of radicals who are in an insidious manner, eternally fighting that which they frantically call "capitalism."
>
> David Clark, editor of
> the *Southern Textile Bulletin*, 1930

Royster, who joined the faculty as Kenan Professor of Journalism after his retirement from the *Journal*, recounted his magic moment with President Graham in an article in the *Alumni Review*.

A little-known incident from Graham's career in Chapel Hill came to light just prior to his death in 1972. It occurred in 1936 in Graham's office in South Building during a visit by Dr. Miguel Elias, a prominent New York surgeon who had attended the university from 1913 to 1915. During their chat, President Graham was compelled to take a telephone call from another president. Dr. Elias, after receiving permission many years later, divulged the details of the amazing conversation between the two Franks— President Frank Porter Graham and President Franklin D. Roosevelt.

ooooo

Uncle Bill McDade Recalls More Than a Half-Century of Service to the University

I didn't start to work here until the Democrats were running the state again and Dr. Battle was president of the University. A janitor's job was hard work in those days; only three janitors here then. We came to work at four o'clock in the morning and didn't get off until late in the evening. Early in the morning we had to carry water from the old well to the dormitories so the boys could wash before breakfast and when there was snow on the ground and ice on the well chain our hands and feet would about freeze. Besides carrying water, ringing the bell and cleaning, we had to cut and carry fire wood for the stoves in the rooms....

Boys haven't changed much in the 53 years I've been about here. They come to the University a little younger than they did a long time ago and they don't treat the first year men so rough. They have automobiles now and can get home or over to Durham, Raleigh or Greensboro any time they want. I remember when most of them couldn't go home for Christmas. They would come here in the fall, and because of the bad roads and slow travel, they just stayed here until school was out in the spring....

I have known men who left this place and then get to be governors, senators and judges, and when they get back to Chapel Hill, they look me up.

They didn't have but one big dance a year a long time ago, but that

> I knew that the grip of orthodoxy in the
> South must be broken. The University could not
> do its work until liberalized. With it liberalized,
> then the State could follow.
>
> Horace Williams, 1936

dance was some affair. Lots of girls came to Chapel Hill in carriages that cost more than most of these automobiles you see about here now. It was shore a fine sight to see a pair of thoroughbred horses, their harness decorated with silver and brass, stepping up and down the street. Some of the ladies even brought their servants with them. They danced the Virginia reel and waltzes that have any of these new dances beat.[2]

ooooo

Address of George Gordon Battle at the Dedication of the Morehead-Patterson Bell Tower
NOVEMBER 26, 1931

The musical notes that will come to future generations from the chimes of this beautiful tower will at once bring back the past and inspire for the future. The sound of these bells will recall the beginnings of the University, the enactment of the first constitution of the State of North Carolina in 1776, which provided "that all useful learning shall be duly encouraged and promoted in one or more universities." . . .

From those distant days down to the present the University bells have summoned the living, have proclaimed the great events of the times and have mourned the dead. They have awakened the student with their unwelcome note from the deep sleep of youth and have sent him creeping with shining face unwilling to early chapel and lecture. Through the long years in which Caldwell and Swain, Battle and Winston, Alderman and Venable, Chase and the Grahams, with other good and true men, have presided over the destinies of the old institution, these bells have sounded forth their notes of appeal, proclamations and mourning. . . .

Upon termination of . . . world-wide warfare, the sons of Chapel Hill—who had accomplished their tasks and won their laurels—resumed to the music of these same bells, the ways of peace and began that vast industrial development which has sown the State with factories and mills and power houses, which has girded our fields and hills with a system of roads unsurpassed in our country, and has added so greatly to our material resources and to our intellectual and spiritual energy. Now that this great access of prosperity has receded, and the inevitable depression has followed, the beloved old State has gone and is still going through a difficult and trying period; but the University bells still spread throughout the State the message of courage and good cheer. These bells still assure the people of North Carolina that the same stern and indomitable spirit which has carried them through the dangers and hardships of the past will still save their destinies in the future.

From this tower, these carillon chimes will announce from Currituck to Cherokee the universal and eternal truth—that true progress and security must be founded upon enlightenment and education, that the people of the State must and will support their chief and ancient institution of learning and that the future of the University will be as honorable and useful as has been its past. . . .

As were the forefathers, so the sons shall be; and the students who shall hear the music from this carillon tower will be animated by the same spirit which filled the breasts of those who heard the bell from the tower of the old South Building. They shall continue to bear high the torch of progress and to do their part for the betterment of humanity. And so the old bells and new will ring the same note on the same key.[3]

> I hope you folks keep the village atmosphere of Chapel Hill. Don't ever pave the sidewalks and keep the ivy on the buildings—there are plenty of modernized colleges all over the country, and nobody cares much about them. I'm sorta like Chancellor Bob House who says that Chapel Hill sand gets in your shoes and her soul gets in your heels.
>
> Kay Kyser (class of 1928),
> who wrote the fight song
> "Tar Heels on Hand" in 1937

ooooo

Excerpt from Letter of John Sprunt Hill to University Controller Charles T. Woollen Concerning the Gift of the Carolina Inn in 1935

Referring to the gift of the Carolina Inn property to the University of North Carolina by Mrs. Hill and myself and our three children, I herewith enclose the deed properly executed by Mrs. Hill and myself, transferring all of this property, including furniture and fixtures and equipment located on said property and vacant lot adjoining.

You will please note that the deed specifies that the transfer is made for the use and benefit of that unit of the University of North Carolina located at Chapel Hill in trust, however, upon the following uses and trusts:

The net income arising from the operation of said property shall be forever used, first, for the maintenance and upkeep of the property; the balance of said net income, if any, arising from the operation of said property shall be used for the maintenance and support of the library of the University of North Carolina, and especially for the support of that collection of books and papers known as "North Caroliniana."[4]

ooooo

This little city has become indeed the capital of the Southern mind. When the historian comes, 50 years from now, to deal with the Southern Renaissance, he will have to say, as we can say in all truth, that its primary impulse came from, and its greatest influence was, the University of North Carolina.

Mark Ethridge, general manager
of the *Louisville Courier-Journal*
and instructor of journalism at UNC, 1938

Excerpt of Remarks by John Sprunt Hill to the General Alumni Association at the Carolina Inn
FEBRUARY 13, 1936

The Carolina Inn was built to serve the University, and it has been fairly successful in rendering this service for the past 10 years. I am particularly pleased that this Association is now making it possible for the Carolina Inn to render a much greater service to the University and to the people of the State. . . .

Twelve years ago, while spending a miserably hot night in Chapel Hill, I was lying awake on the top of my bed, suffering from the heat and nervous excitement, when apparently 12 or more big rats suddenly fell upon a number of mice and chased them, squeaking with all their power, under and over my bed. I dressed, came downstairs, sat on the porch and then took a long walk to this property on the corner of Cameron Avenue and Columbia Street. Seated there on the rock on the great oak tree came the vision of the Carolina Inn. The building of it was exceedingly difficult, but, through the long days of construction, the whole work was a joy, and the vision grew out of the greater and greater service that some day it would render to my Alma Mater.[5]

ooooo

Vermont Royster Recalls Meeting Frank Porter Graham

I must confess that my beginnings here, in that autumn of '31, were not too auspicious. I had been here only a few weeks when I had my first encounter with Frank Graham, then the president.

I was then living in Old West and, as was the custom of the time, sent my clothes to the University Laundry. To my irritation it kept returning my socks with holes in them. Being irritated, I turned into a consumer advocate.

One morning I marched myself past the Old Well to South Building and asked to see "Dr. Frank." In a few minutes I was ushered into his office. Since "Dr. Frank" knew me through my father, he welcomed me into a chair beside his desk and asked, "Vermont, what can I do for you?" By way of answer I reached down, took off my right shoe, waggling my big toe through the hole in my sock. I explained that this was what his laundry was doing to me.

I do not know what "Dr. Frank" thought, but he looked at me quietly for a few moments. Then he reached into his wallet, pulled out a dollar bill and handed it to me. "Use this," he said, "to buy yourself some new socks."

I was completely outdone. All I could think of was to mutter some kind of apology, return the dollar and sheepishly depart.

That incident, I'm afraid, shows what manner of young man I was. But I was to be reminded of it 40 years later when, upon a spring day, one of my students came to class with neither socks *nor* shoes! The brashness of youth in the presence of their elders is perennial!

But that encounter of the first kind with "Dr. Frank" also showed what manner of man he was. He did not react with irritation at this bumptious freshman. He let me know that he understood my complaint and he turned away my wrath with a soft answer.

I did not realize it at the time but that was to foreshadow "Dr. Frank's" reaction to encounters of a more serious kind—some of which I was involved in and from all of which I was to learn much about this University and the ambivalent place it occupies among the people of the state.[6]

ooooo

Dr. Miguel "Mike" Elias Recounts His Visit with Frank Porter Graham

The secretary came in and said to him quietly "Dr. Graham, the White House is on the phone and wants to speak to you." With that both Mrs. Elias and I got up and started out and he [Graham] motioned for me to come back and sit down and listen in on the extension phone, which I did. And I heard the most amazing conversation that I have ever heard in my life. As I recall it there were the usual form of greetings from the White House, and the voice said, "This is Franklin D. Roosevelt, Dr. Graham. I have a very important question to ask," and Dr. Frank said, "I would be most happy—."

President Roosevelt said, "Dr. Graham, I have been following your career for many years and have been much impressed by it. I want you to do me a favor. I have given great thought to your fame and your position and I would like to ask you to be my running mate—to run as vice president on my ticket."

Dr. Graham was, naturally, stunned for a moment. He said, "Mr. President, this is magnanimous on your part, and I am overwhelmed and appreciate your thinking of me." Then he said, "Unfortunately, I have to tell you that I am not a politician—I am basically a teacher, and I do not believe that I would be able to fill the job properly." The conversation went on a minute or two, and President Roosevelt said: "Dr. Graham, please think this over. I will give you time. I know it comes as a shock to you at this particular time, but I want you to think it over and let me hear from you in a week's time." He said he would be happy to send one of his associates down to talk with him and give him full explanation. I understood that Harry Hopkins (a presidential assistant) did come down to visit President Graham about then, and perhaps this was the purpose.

I felt somewhat embarrassed when the conversation was over and I didn't know what to say. I could see that Dr. Graham was really, for once in his life, somewhat baffled.

[The two men went out and sat by the Old Well.] "Mike," said President Graham, "I'm going to ask you never to repeat this—what you have heard here today—without my consent."[7]

1940
—
1949

Fame in War and in Peace

*U*nlike the War Between the States, which decimated the student body, World War II brought students to Chapel Hill. Although the actual civilian enrollment decreased from over thirty-six hundred students to fewer than fourteen hundred during the war, more than twenty thousand enlisted military men were educated at the university from 1942 to 1945 in various training programs. Chief among these was the United States Navy Pre-flight Training School, designed for naval aviators. Chapel Hill was one of just four sites selected for the highly advanced instructional school, due in large part to the close association between President Roosevelt and Frank Porter Graham. Details of the changes to the campus necessitated by the nation's military needs were released to students and their parents in a letter from Graham in March 1942.

Among the thousands of participants in the Navy Pre-flight Training School at the university were a number of young men who would later achieve fame: Gerald R. Ford, the thirty-eighth president of the United States; Warren Anderson, the chairman of the board of Union Carbide Corporation; Ted Williams, the legendary slugger for the Boston Red Sox; and Otto Graham, one of the greatest of all professional football quarter-backs. The football team fielded by the preflight program was coached by a navy recruit trainer who in time would become one of the greatest of all college football coaches—Paul William "Bear" Bryant.

As the war neared its end in 1945, the university enrolled two civilian freshmen from very different backgrounds who would make significant marks in American society after their graduation four years later. One was a native son, the other a New Yorker.

Andy Samuel Griffith, born in Mount Airy, North Carolina, arrived on the Chapel Hill campus intent upon becoming a Moravian minister. His interest in music led him to change his major, and before he left the campus, he served as president of the Men's Glee Club. A few years after graduation, Griffith recorded the enormously successful "What It Was, Was Football," a hilarious parody about a first-time witness to college football. From the recording industry, he moved to motion pictures and television, where the weekly show bearing his name achieved such popularity that it continues to rank as one of the best-loved series in industry history. In 1995, the star donated his massive personal collection of materials related to his career to the Southern Historical Collection at the university.

Griffith's later fame notwithstanding, his life at the university was beset by trials and tribulations, as he explained in an interview.

Allard Kenneth Lowenstein came to Chapel Hill the same year as Griffith. At the university, Lowenstein busied himself in politics and was elected president of the National Student Association. An outspoken liberal, he was a great admirer of Frank Porter Graham, serving briefly as special assistant to Graham in 1949. Following his graduation from Yale Law School in 1954, Lowenstein emerged as one of the most inspirational activists of his time, championing causes ranging from civil rights to the antiwar movement. During Lowenstein's first term in the United States House of Representatives, a deranged gunman assassinated the fifty-one-year-old

> The University is liberal and that is what makes us proud of it. If the University ever ceases to be open and free it ought to close its doors.
>
> Josephus Daniels, 1940

congressman in his Manhattan office. In Arlington National Cemetery, the tombstone of the fallen son of Carolina bears a fitting epitaph: "If a single man plant himself on his convictions and there abide, the huge world will come around to him."

Al Lowenstein's letters while a student in Chapel Hill covered a wide range of subjects, from coeds to campus freedom to desegregation.

After the war, Andy Griffith and Al Lowenstein were joined on the campus by hordes of veterans anxious to begin or continue their college education. Many would also join Griffith and Lowenstein on the American walk of fame.

One such veteran was William Clyde Friday, destined to leave his mark on higher education in the United States. Friday recalled his less than graceful introduction to the study of law at the university: "Like many other veterans of World War II, Ida [Mrs. Friday] came to Chapel Hill in February 1946, with all our worldly possessions in the trunk of a small two-seated car. I was enrolling in the School of Law. Ice was on the ground and a fierce, cold wind blew. Our living quarters consisted of an attic we had managed to rent. I opened the text for my first class in Property Law and found the first five cases written in Latin. Not having attended Chapel Hill as an undergraduate I couldn't read a word of either case! I was off to a brilliant start!"[1]

Perhaps the most famous of all the veterans who enrolled at Chapel Hill after the war was Charlie "Choo Choo" Justice, whose name is legend at the university and whose exploits on the gridiron continue to fill the record books. Years after his playing days with the university and the Washington Redskins were over, Choo Choo recounted his career in Chapel Hill.

ooooo

Hark the Sound of Tar Heel Voices

Frank Porter Graham's Letter to Parents and Students about Campus Changes Wrought by World War II

March 19, 1942

My Dear Parents and Students:

The United States at war brings new responsibilities and new opportunities to the American university....

The War has brought many new things to the peaceful, freedom-loving village of Chapel Hill—the Naval R.O.T.C., the student flight-training program, the Carolina Volunteer Training Corps, courses in military science, the "speed-up" of college years from four to three, admission by examination, military and naval research projects, and civilian morale organizations.

Within the past two weeks there has come an even greater opportunity. The University is happy to be chosen, by the United States Navy, as one of the four "Annapolises of the Air." All of us here are all-out to meet the double responsibility of carrying on the regular functions and freedom of a historic and progressive state University, and of cooperating to the limit of our capacity with our country in a total war against axis powers to save the freedom and all the things for which America and our University stands. The University has, we trust, much to give to the training and life of the naval aviators, chosen as the very cream of the youth of America....

Ten of our twenty-four dormitories will be used by the naval aviation cadets. Our own students will gladly live three in a room in other dormitories, in

> In February 1949 I took the train south, heading for the University of North Carolina in Chapel Hill. I was impressed on arrival there by the red clay, the sandy walks, and the graciousness of the people.
>
> Rudolph A. Marcus,
> recipient of the Nobel Prize
> in Chemistry in 1992

fraternity houses, in "student co-op" houses, and in private homes in Chapel Hill where many University students now live. The University promises to find every student a comfortable room and to provide them with wholesome, dietitian-approved food.

The three new women's dormitories will adequately accommodate three girls in each room, permitting the one hundred and forty-six girls now living in Spencer, Smith, and Archer House to move into Alderman, Kenan, and McIver, releasing Spencer, Smith, and Archer House for use as men's dormitories. . . . Before the recent dormitory expansion in the University, many of our students lived three in a room. Their experience proved that it can be done without hardship or sacrifice in the quality of their scholastic work. . . .

I also wish to assure you that the regular work will go on unimpaired. Students now registered will have all the facilities for the continuance of their studies either at the normal pace or at an accelerated rate, as they may choose. New students will be given hearty welcome for the summer quarter or in September.

We urge you to write Dean Robert B. House for any desired information, and assure you of our complete cooperation.

Sincerely yours,

Frank P. Graham,
President.[2]

○○○○○

Andy Griffith Recalls His Days at the University

I had a wonderful time—and a horrible time—in Chapel Hill. I went through every day hoping, just hoping, they wouldn't find out how little I knew, but sometimes they did. I failed Political Science 41 twice. My counselor, a lady, called me in and said: "Andy, very few people fail political science once, but nobody fails it twice." I guess that was the only record I ever broke at Chapel Hill. But I got in a lot of singing. Sometimes I'd sing by myself, sometimes with small groups and I suppose while I was there I sang with every choir and chorus in town. And I learned some wonderful music—Verdi, Brahms, Mozart, Handel, Beethoven, Bach. Even today I get a great deal of pleasure out of it, singing or just listening.

Chapel Hill offered me another new experience when I got a part in a play. On a stage. Acting. And you know something. I thought I was just having a good time, without even knowing that I was falling in love. . . .

All along the way at Chapel Hill I was getting help from a man named Paul Young, who was head of the choral department. One day he told me if I was going to be a singer I ought to be studying singing. When I told him I couldn't pay for it he said that that wasn't a problem. If I would take care of the Glee Club music—just patch it up and keep it together—he'd teach me for nothing. I studied music with that man for five wonderful years. . . .

Then there was a graduate student there, a fellow named Bob Armstrong '46, who had written a three-act play that was going to be done by the Carolina Playmakers. I wasn't even a drama student, but Bob insisted that they let me play the male lead. . . . Ten or twelve years later, Bob Armstrong was in a stage play in New York called, *Cat On A Hot Tin Roof*, directed by Elia Kazan. One night Kazan told Bob Armstrong about a picture he was going to do. It was about this bum from Arkansas who went on the radio and began to get a big following, and then went on television and got bigger and bigger and more and more powerful . . . and the only thing was, he was crazy. Kazan asked Bob if he knew anybody who could play that part, or was like that, and Bob said, "Yeah, Andy Griffith's like that." As the result of my friend from Chapel Hill saying that, I got my first leading role in a major motion picture, a fine film called, *A Face in the Crowd*.

The first man I ever met in Chapel Hill was Edwin S. Lanier '25, who was the self-help officer there in school. He got me a job right away as a busboy in the cafeteria. Breakfast and eight dollars a week: five dollars for tuition and three dollars to live on, more or less. I was a lot thinner in those days than I am now. That went on for a long time, but then I came down with some bad back trouble and went over to Duke and got my back x-rayed. They told me it was all out of line and I'd have to wear a brace, a big old leather thing with steel running up and down. It cost thirty dollars, so I

I had never been east of Winston-Salem when I first got here. I was so homesick, I could die.

Andy Griffith, class of 1949

went to Mr. Lanier to see if I could get my tuition deferred. He wrote down a man's name and told me to go over to see him in Raleigh. The man's name was W. Rea Taylor '14, and he got me talking right off about what I wanted to do with my life. He couldn't really understand how a man with a major in music could make a living, but he told me the state of North Carolina had a program for indigent students with physical disabilities and that they would help me out with my tuition and a few books.

I was astounded. I still am. And when I asked him how I was expected to pay back the money, all he said was: "You get a good education, get a good job, and be a good taxpayer." Well, there are a lot of things I haven't done in life. But I did get my education. I do have a good job. And I've been a wonderful taxpayer.

By then I was the dorm manager and got my room free, and I took up the laundry and got two dollars a week for that. I had some other jobs and got a little money singing here and there, and with the help the state of North Carolina gave me, I made it. But I'll tell you right now, if it had not been for that help from the state of North Carolina I would never have graduated from the University of North Carolina and I would not have achieved the success and found the happiness that I have found in my life. I will always be grateful for that.[3]

ooooo

Excerpts from Three Letters of Allard Lowenstein in Chapel Hill

Letter from Al Lowenstein to a Friend
July 2, 1945

This place is truly as swell a place as you'll find anywhere! . . . My Dorm room is one of the worst, but that's cause Navy, ROTC, Marines, Pre-Flight etc., have taken over the newer facilities. I picked myself a roommate . . . & by chance, he's swell. If not *all* I hoped for in a Roomie, he's still a wonderful person—& maybe *I'm* not all *he* hoped for. . . .

Chapel Hill girls are swell. The U.N.C. ones are all Juniors-Seniors, but seem nice. . . .

I've had some bad moments, but things seem on the upswing. . . .

The amazing amount of Freedom (with a capital "F") that we get here is a tremendous help & boon. Believe it or not, I'm going to end up in love with U.N.C. . . . . "Making the best of things" those first days is paying off dividends . . . but I *do* miss everybody & *pant* for mail.

Letter from Al Lowenstein to a Friend
MAY 6, 1946

As for UNC's "inviting Negroes," unfortunately it just ain't so. State laws forbids interracial educ[at]ion, for one thing; and for another, the student body here, even were it able to make the decision all on its own, would not vote to admit colored students, though an increasing minority would. . . .

Last fall . . . the Dialectic Senate, oldest college debating society in America, voted in favor of bills abolishing Jim Crow laws and providing for the admission of colored students to the University. These "laws" of course have no effect on anything, except as weathervanes.

Letter from Al Lowenstein
to the Editors of Life Magazine
OCTOBER 25, 1948

In Chapel Hill we are not a proud lot, so it's perfectly all right with us if *Life* (October 25th) chooses to continue doing write-ups on relatively obscure universities like those dozen in California, while ignoring the oldest State university in the Western Hemisphere—a university which, incidentally, happens to have the most beautiful campus, the best football team, and the most advanced student government in the Nation (to say nothing of its academic distinctions, which maybe wouldn't photograph well). But when, in the very same issue (page 45) *Life* dwells upon photographs of assorted personages who happen to be officials of various Pottawattomie-like institutions, while failing to so much [as] identify one of the greatest men of our times and the greatest university president in the world today, Frank Porter Graham—well, a rebellious yelp would seem in order. . . .

As I say, it's not that we're proud, generous though we are in our willingness to let the rest of the Nation know of our good fortune here at the University of North Carolina.[4]

ooooo

Charlie "Choo Choo" Justice Reflects on His Football Career at the University

There've been a lot of stories about how I was recruited and how much I got. Actually I favored Duke all along. Then I got an interest in South Carolina because of Mr. Earight [Rex Enright], the coach. But my older brother, Jack, told me if I left the state of North Carolina, he'd never have anything to do with me again. "That means the only place I can go is Chapel Hill," I said. "That's where you belong," he said.

Now the scholarship, I didn't have it. My wife did. I went on the GI Bill of Rights. As soon as they told me my wife could attend school on my football scholarship, I signed up. She wasn't much of a football player. But she cheered hard.

. . . He [UNC head football coach Carl Snavely] treated us all alike. Every man on the team. There were times when he would eat me alive. Told me I was faking poorly, that I wanted to see where the play went more than I wanted to fake. He was right. He told me how to train, what to eat, how to play. He was a great coach, a great man, and when we all saw him last at a team reunion he was almost eighty but he wouldn't let any of us help him in or out of cars or anything. . . .

I was never fast. I could fake and I learned to move my feet, to shuffle, to fake, but I was never a fast runner. There were other things, though, things that the good Lord gave me that I learned to use. . . . When I was playing football, I could see almost the whole field, everything around me. I could see players coming toward me from almost anywhere. I could see them in time to move and fake and get away. . . .

You can't forget the tough games, the toughest ones. I remember the ones with Duke and Tennessee. They were always tough. One of our roughest was against Tennessee in Knoxville. I lost three shirts, two pairs of pants, and a pair of shoes. When I got back in Chapel Hill that night I couldn't believe what had happened to me. I was battered and bruised, black and blue all over until the bruises starting running together, making my whole body a purple mass.

Doc White took me straight to the field house and put me in the whirlpool. Then he put me on the training table under heat lamps and soaked me with alcohol towels. I finally went to sleep and he stayed with me all night, changing the towels every hour until eight o'clock the next morning.

I never dressed out that week, didn't put on a uniform until the next Saturday when we played again.

I learned it's the man on the third and fourth team that makes you a good college player. These are the men you scrimmage against all week. They know they'll never make it in a game. Hardly ever. They know they're not going to play Saturday so they play hard all week. They make you play your best.[5]

Tests

*A*s the "hot" war in Korea melded into the Cold War, the 1950s served as a time of introspection and tests for the university and its students. Ever anxious to explore new boundaries of campus freedom, students often tested the limits of the administration and the trustees. In a speech delivered at the twenty-fifth anniversary of the Zeta Beta Tau fraternity on the Chapel Hill campus, Gordon Gray, the president of the consolidated University of North Carolina, warned listeners that student criticism of the university must be based in fact and leveled in a responsible manner.

One of the sternest tests for students and school alike came at the onset of the decade with the desegregation of the formerly all-white law school. In 1951, Harvey E. Beech, J. Kenneth Lee, James Lassiter, Floyd McKissick, and James Walker enrolled as the first black law students. In an interview conducted forty-five years after he began his law studies, Beech recalled the challenges that he and his fellow black students faced as they broke the color barrier on the campus.

Then, in 1955, federal court decisions mandated the desegregation of undergraduate studies at the university. Thrust into the national spotlight were the institution and especially the three young men—John Brandon, Leroy Frasier, and Ralph Frasier—who came from nearby Durham to enroll as the university's first black undergraduates. The pressure on the trio of students to succeed was great, as evidenced by a letter from a family friend to Leroy Frasier shortly after his arrival in Chapel Hill in September.

Desegregation was a slow, steady process on the campus. By the end of the decade, the black enrollment included twenty-three in undergraduate schools, sixty-nine in graduate schools, and more than thirty in professional schools. Thirteen years later, Richard Epps of Wilmington, North Carolina, would be elected the first black to serve as student body president.

The highly regarded men's basketball program was severely tested in the second half of the decade. In 1957, the Tar Heels bested every team that challenged them en route to a thrilling triple-overtime victory over the University of Kansas and its tall star, Wilt Chamberlain, in the national championship game.

At the conclusion of the memorable season, Frank McGuire, the legendary head basketball coach, went looking for a new assistant coach for the program. He recalled,

> I was sitting around in a room one night with Bob Spear (the Air Force coach) and Ben Carnevale (Navy). Bob said to me if I wanted to hire someone who was young and aggressive I should hire his assistant, this guy Smith. I told him if the kid wanted the job, he had it. Dean came to Chapel Hill, and I hired him right away.
>
> I went to Bill Aycock (then chancellor at UNC) and said I wanted to hire an assistant for $7,500.00. He said he didn't think we could pay that much. But we worked it out. I hired [Smith] as a recruiter. He hadn't done much coaching up to then. He was always chomping at the bit, he could never do enough. I had the recruiting contacts in New York and I knew just what I wanted to do in practice each day. Dean always wanted more work. He always had ideas. I told people then that some day I'd be proud to say I was the one who brought him to Chapel Hill. That's the way I start my speeches now. I brag about it.[1]

But neither a national championship nor the arrival of Dean Smith, the man who would lead Carolina basketball to even greater glory, could

I hitchhiked down here from Elgin, Illinois, and the driver dropped me off right on Franklin Street. The first thing I saw was Vance Hall, and I thought, "Any college good enough to name a building after cousin Zeb Vance is good enough for me."

Ben Jones III, class of 1950

prevent the trouble that was brewing for the program. Concern over the ever-increasing prominence of college athletics and the weak academic requirements for players caused grumbling on the campus. As the 1957 team was fighting its way through the undefeated season, the *Daily Tar Heel* published a stern editorial on February 16 wherein it applauded the university for its clean athletic programs but urged action to strengthen the academic standards for student-athletes.

Little did the student newspaper or the administration know, but recruiting violations in basketball would soon result in the first and only athletic probation for the sport at the university. In May 1957, several months after the *Daily Tar Heel* editorial, Chancellor William B. Aycock warned alumni in Washington, D.C., that there must be no double standard in college athletics.

At the same time, even the brightest students at the university sometimes questioned themselves about their college choice. Illustrative of this common test of all freshmen is the story of Norton F. Tenille, Jr., a Morehead Scholar and future Rhodes Scholar who came to Chapel Hill in 1958. He offered an account of his anxious moments on the campus in a reunion speech for the class of 1962.

ooooo

President Gordon Gray Asserts That Responsibility Is an Integral Component of Student Freedom

If a student speaks out, through a student publication or otherwise, in criticism of the administration or trustees, one limiting factor should be that the criticism be based on a knowledge of and correct understanding of the facts and not based on gossip or hearsay or assumption.

The other limitation that I would suggest as a part of the student responsibility is that what he says always [should be] circumscribed by good taste and good manners. I am glad that Chancellor House earlier pointed out that we mustn't overlook good manners in this community of the University of which we are all a part.

We in the administration will continue to assert the right of students to express their opinions when frequently very frank, [though] the administration may disagree with the views which may be expressed. I think that

... the allegation that students are not allowed to speak on this campus perhaps is made [only] by those who don't see the *Daily Tar Heel*.

... Parents have the right to believe that their sons and daughters are coming to an institution that still has a heart and spirit and that they will learn how to be responsible, useful citizens. The trustees have the right to believe that we are, in the administration, just and fair. The people of the State have the right to look to this great institution for service, as Chancellor House has said, in helping bring about a happier and more contented citizenship, a healthier and wiser and more prosperous people.[2]

ooooo

Oral History Interview of Harvey E. Beech on Integrating the Law School

Thurgood Marshall and some others came down [to North Carolina Central College] and asked if I would go to Chapel Hill. And Kenneth Lee, who was my roommate. And we said yes.

I had all A's and B's at Central. But I didn't have all A's and B's at Carolina. I had probably one C at Central. And Kenneth also. Maybe, one or two ... But at Carolina, I had to cut the mustard to get some A's. And I put on a special effort there in constitutional law, one year. Because there was prejudice all over the place, and they had some visiting professors. And one of them was from Southern California, teaching con law. And there were students from New York University, Duke, everywhere. Two hundred and some students. And they had numbers, you know, when you take the exam. I guess they still do that. They gave four A's and I made one of those, and I felt like I had done something special. When I reached that, I said,

> The UNC journalism degree gave me a better grammatical background than my Ivy League partners had.
>
> Richard Jenrette (class of 1951), founder of Donaldson, Lufkin, and Jenrette

well I think I got what it takes to compete. . . .

. . . Chancellor House was chancellor then, and he—well, first thing, we went over there, they hadn't planned for us to stay, I don't think, cause nobody said anything about a dormitory. So we asked, well, where we can stay, so they got together and they said, well, they assigned us to Steele Hall, right across from the old law school, on the third, fourth floor, I believe, or third floor, up in the very top. Nobody on the whole floor but us. And we called it the buzzard's roost because that's where the buzzards roost, and the birds, and the pigeons. . . .

. . . Nobody ever told us where we could get food. We had to ask for that. And you go in [Lenoir Dining Hall]. We made a decision that we would not sit near anybody. We'd go over on the end, and to know your friends, those who might have been well-wishers, you had to go away and let them come to you. To show their intent to help, you know . . .

One day . . . Kenneth and I were coming out of Lenoir, and at the Institute of Government they would train the sheriffs and the policemen and stuff, and it had a wire, said "don't walk on the grass," and a brick walk, I think. And we see three sheriffs, deputy sheriffs with their guns on, standing broadside in front of us, with their arms close to each other, as if to say, "niggers, don't come this way." . . . I said, "Kenneth, you see what's in front of us?" and he said, yes. I said, "You ready to die?" He said, "Yep, if need be." And we walked within ten inches of their faces, and they parted like the waters of the Red Sea. But you had to challenge every damn thing there was, in order to remove it. . . .

And you just had to tear it down. . . . The chancellor himself tells you, "Young man, I know you didn't come over here to go to the football game. You all came to go to law school." And I didn't say anything. . . . One of the fellows said, at that time, we had three or four—"yes, that's right Mr. House." I said, "Well, wait a minute." I said, "He's speaking for himself." I said, "Mr. House, don't give me a ticket." He said, "Why?" I said, "Because if you give me a ticket, I'm going to sit any damn place I want to." . . . We went with some other students, some white students, and we sat on the fifty-yard line. . . .

The next time we went back to school, I think they had to give you a physical exam. I got in line like everybody else, and I ended up with a swimming card. Kenneth and the other two black students were in a room by themselves being examined. I just followed the line; I got a swimming card. So when I got to the dormitory, I said, "What happened to you guys?" They said, "Well, we had a special doctor to examine us." . . . I said, "I just followed the line." . . . So, about three weeks later, the President, the dean of the law school, Dean [Henry] Brandis, sent for me out of class to come to his office downstairs and said, "Mr. Beech, Chancellor House has asked me to ask you, would you return that swimming card they gave you by mistake." And I said, "What?" He said, "Now listen, I'm not asking you to do it, I'm just carrying the message, he told me to do it." I said, "What mistake was it?" He said, "I'll tell you what they said. They said they thought you were from Brazil, that's why you got the card." I said, "That's a damn shame. To be a native son."[3]

ooooo

Letter from G. W. Cox to Leroy Frasier
SEPTEMBER 1955

I have just passed along my congratulations to your daddy and mother for the success which has come your way by virtue of their determined efforts to get for you the best education which the State of North Carolina affords for its citizens. They have done a very beautiful job in cooperating with other interested friends and attorneys and the NAACP, and I am very proud of the fact that your record at the high school was . . . such that upon that record you had to be admitted to the undergraduate school at *the University of North Carolina*.

Now, just a word of admonition to you. The responsibility now shifts from your parents and friends direct to *you*. You will have to prosecute a program of putting to use all of the available facilities for pursuing your major at the University and prove beyond a doubt that . . . you are worthy and capable, and that insofar as holding up the high standards of the University over the long number of years which it has served the public, you have as much of what it takes . . . as anyone else. If you are to prove that you are the equal of your fellow Americans through your opportunity, you must make up in your mind that equality is *earned* and not conferred.

Your pictures have been in the papers—not just the Durham papers, but they will find themselves in papers all over the world. Let that go to your heart and not to your head—in fact, forget about that if you can and be *yourself*. This is good advice and it will help you a whole lot if you will follow it.

You have my interest and I shall be observing you with sincerity and earnestness in your pursuit of the fulfillment of this great opportunity which has been bestowed upon you.

Good luck, best wishes, and more power to you![4]

ooooo

A Request by the Daily Tar Heel for More Stringent Academic Requirements for Athletes

Not the players, not the coaches, nor the taxpayers are to blame for what the *Daily Tar Heel* feels is the rotten[n]ess of present-day college athletics.

At most places it is the administration of the colleges and universities. For the administrations are the bodies which can make athletic policy and can enforce it. They are the bodies which send representatives to national conventions, to conferences, to associations.

At Carolina, our athletic policy appears to be far above the national level. For this we are proud. We are proud of the men who made it that way—primarily, Chancellor Robert House and former Presidents Frank Graham and Gordon Gray.

We are also proud of the men who keep it that way—primarily, Athletics Director C. P. Erikson and Coaches Jim Tatum, Frank McGuire and others.

What we ask is that the University administration raise its standards even higher than they are now. We feel the University should make academic requirements even higher for prospective athletes and those already enrolled. The grants-in-aid program should be even more selective.

The administration is the only body which can do this.

> When I was here there was only one University of North Carolina and if you'll pardon me for saying so, President Spangler, there will never be more than one in my heart and it's right here in Chapel Hill.
>
> Roger Mudd, class of 1953

The University, headed by its chancellor, can effect a gradual revolution in the running of collegiate sports.

The revolution should emphasize putting sports more into the hands of the students, insuring that athletes also be real students and taking the money pressure off the big sports.

A university, and this University, takes part in the recruiting program, in the grants-in-aid program and in all the other programs simply because it is in competition with all the other universities and colleges in the nation—everybody else does it.

But the University of North Carolina, because of the respect people have for it, because it has reasonably strong leaders and because its skirts are reasonably clean so far, can be the leader in a gradual revolution.[5]

ooooo

Excerpt from Speech of Chancellor Aycock on Academic Standards for University Athletics

I am not disturbed that alumni groups have a strong interest in athletics because I believe that the interest manifested by most alumni in intercollegiate athletics is but a symbol of a deeper interest in the totality of the programs, hopes and aspirations of the whole institution.

I believe that those alumni whose affection for the University both begins and ends with intercollegiate athletics are few in number. Unfortunately, there are some among those few who seem to entertain a misguided notion that in athletics the means are not too important if the end result is victory on the scoreboard. In those institutions, including ours, which have undertaken an extensive intercollegiate athletic program, it is not realistic in my judgment to try to separate athletics and education. They cannot be separated any more than other student activities in the University can be separated from education. A grant-in-aid program enables students with athletic ability to secure a college education. It is only on this basis that a University can justify such a program. Since the University is involved in the awarding of scholarships, it is very essential that grants-in-aid be administered in accordance with the letter and spirit of the rules and regulations. Further, a student who is an athlete should not be treated differently from a student who is not an athlete. There must be no double standard.

Moreover, no program in the University, including athletics, should be conducted in such a manner as to lower either moral or academic standards. He, who would insist on practices which nibble at or dilute the integrity and educational standards of this institution, is no friend of athletics of this institution. The two are not to be separated because, in matters fundamental, athletics and the University must rise or fall together. I regard this to be of such importance that I shall in the days to come frequently discuss the administration of our athletic programs with our alumni groups.[6]

ooooo

Misgivings of Norton F. Tenille, Jr., a Freshman Morehead Scholar

George V. Taylor was my freshman adviser. I was miserably unhappy in my first semester in that soft, golden melancholy fall of 1958, so I called home and told my mother that I was miserably unhappy, and that I had made a terrible mistake; and that I should have gone to Harvard. So my mother gets on the phone with George V. Taylor and drives down from Winston-Salem to Chapel Hill, and I am summoned in for a high-level conference with my mother and George V. Taylor. I don't know which of the two I found more frightening.

As I recall the meeting, Professor Taylor began by establishing the facts. He asked whether it was true that I was miserably unhappy at Chapel Hill and wanted to go to Harvard. I acknowledged, with a mixture of shame and relief and defiance that I was, preparing myself for the inevitable lecture that was to come, about how an education is what a man or a woman makes of it, and that . . . one could get as good an education at Chapel Hill as anywhere else, if he really wanted to.

But I received no lecture from George V. Taylor. He simply stated in his blunt, no-nonsense fashion that, if I wanted to go to Harvard, he would do anything he could to help me.

This was devastating! I felt like that form of Oriental martial art where the fighter is trained to take advantage of the momentum of his opponent's body. There I was, rushing straight at George V. Taylor with all my unhappiness, and he makes a simple move and I go sailing off into space with the force of my own momentum.

When I finally came to earth, I picked myself up, dusted myself off, thought about the matter for awhile, and concluded that I probably *could* get as good an education at Chapel Hill as anywhere else. My mother returned to Winston-Salem. George V. Taylor returned to the French Revolution. And I got on with the business of growing up.

As a footnote, I will add that I later spent a year as a graduate student at Harvard. It was very nice, and everyone was highly intelligent, and witty, and urbane. But I didn't learn any more that year than I learned in any of the years I spent at Chapel Hill. And I didn't have nearly as much fun in the process.[7]

1960
–
1969

Controversies from the Left and the Right

One of the cornerstones of the university is its freedom in all aspects of its life and being. Cherished and closely guarded, the free university was foremost in the mind of Chancellor William B. Aycock when he addressed alumni at a luncheon in Chapel Hill on June 6, 1960: "We must not—we cannot—allow our precious heritage—a free university—to be infringed upon [by] an individual or group from whatever position or by whatever disposition. We shall not sit idly by and permit this to occur. My plea to you is that in the spirit of our fathers, all of us in the University family join hands with each other and with all those who hold freedom dear to guarantee that this great instrument of democracy—the oldest of our state universities—shall not be molded to suit the notions of any single person or social group. This, my fellow Tar Heels, is the most important issue facing the University."[1]

For the remainder of the decade, Aycock and his successor, J. Carlyle Sitterson, were confronted with a series of controversies with the issue of freedom at their very vortex. From the right, the state legislature imposed "An Act to Regulate Visiting Speakers" on the university in 1963. Commonly known as "the Speaker Ban Act," the legislation attracted national attention, the university community openly denouncing it as a direct violation of the free speech and academic freedom so long nurtured and enjoyed.

Chancellor Aycock led a determined effort to repeal the onerous statute. In September 1965, he made an impassioned speech against it at a legislative study commission hearing in Raleigh. In the meantime, Aycock's Chapel Hill campus put the hated law to the test. Prohibited speakers such as Frank Wilkinson and Herbert Aptheker addressed students from the Franklin Street sidewalk, separated from the campus only by its historic stone wall.

A federal court subsequently overturned the Speaker Ban Law in 1968, but when black activist Stokely Carmichael spoke on the Chapel Hill campus and at other state universities in the wake of the court decision, Jesse Helms aired an editorial on WRAL-TV in Raleigh questioning the maturity of the students and administrators at the university and advocating that the state legislature redraft the law.

Another crisis concurrent with the Speaker Ban controversy challenged Chancellor Aycock and the entire university community. As 1963 neared a close, the effort to desegregate the restaurants and other public establishments in Chapel Hill grew in intensity. A small group of students and professors joined community activists and church leaders in sit-ins at segregated facilities that December. Some students and faculty members were arrested during the demonstrations. One of the arrested students was Karen Parker, a native of Winston-Salem who had enrolled as the first black female undergraduate at Chapel Hill earlier in 1963. Her diary entry of December 18 offers insight into her arrest. Not until the federal Civil Rights Act was enacted in June 1964 did the controversy end.

Desegregation of the men's basketball program came about in 1966 when Charlie Scott, a future All-American, Olympian, and professional basketball star, accepted an athletic scholarship to play for Coach Dean Smith. Dan Pollitt, a noted professor of constitutional law at the university's law school and a civil-rights activist, recalled the effort to bring a black athlete to Chapel Hill.

J. Carlyle Sitterson, who succeeded Aycock as chancellor in 1966,

> Chapel Hill is so smug and self-righteous and so proud of the past that it has not really kept pace with the current situation. It has been so willing to live on the moral capital of men like Odum and Graham that it is now fearfully close to being morally bankrupt.
>
> David McReynolds, *Village Voice,* 1963

faced a crisis involving the Black Student Movement and its support for the university's cafeteria workers, who were low-paid and predominantly black. At a time when the campus food services were struggling from low patronage due to poor menus and less-than-attractive facilities, a strike would be devastating. On behalf of the workers, the Black Student Movement submitted a list of twenty-three demands to Chancellor Sitterson in December 1968. The cover letter attached to their demands summarized their grievances.

In an attempt to ameliorate the controversy, the chancellor corresponded and met with leaders of the Black Student Movement. Sitterson's written reply to the demands and his statement on February 19, 1969, offer insight into his cautious handling of the volatile matter.

When negotiations broke down, more than one hundred workers went on strike. Supporters of the strike inflamed tensions in Lenoir Hall, the only campus dining facility to remain open, by inhibiting student patrons from enjoying prompt service through a series of stall-ins.

Concerned about the threat to the safety and security of the campus, William C. Friday, president of the Consolidated University of North Carolina, issued a statement warning that laws prohibiting the obstruction of university buildings would be enforced. A subsequent campus incident on March 3 resulted in overturned tables and chairs in Lenoir, and on March 13, members of the Black Student Movement holed up in Manning Hall. Eight days later, the controversy came to a peaceful conclusion when Governor Robert Scott conferred with three strike leaders and their attorneys to reach a wage adjustment for the food service workers.

At the height of the tension, Robert S. Cilley, Jr., a sophomore, took time from his studies to offer his support and encouragement to the embattled chancellor.

Throughout the decade, students faced a less momentous controversy that had lingered on the campus for many years—the requirement that they pass a swimming test in order to graduate. In 1969, an honor student in philosophy was unable to graduate with his class because he failed the

> Our position on racial matters is the position a great university must take. Every student here is a first-class student. We don't admit any other kind.
>
> Chancellor Paul F. Sharp, 1964

swimming test at the end of the spring semester of his senior year. That student was none other than Michael Hooker (class of 1969), who would return to the university in the last decade of the century as its chancellor. His reflection on the incident at the close of his undergraduate days provides a humorous look at the test that caused consternation for many.

Students in the sixties witnessed and participated in the numerous controversies that swirled about the campus and the nation. Looking back on his experiences, Hal Tarleton, class of 1971, offered a colorful description of that turbulent period in the history of the university.

ooooo

Excerpt from Opposition Statement Made by William B. Aycock to the Speaker Ban Law Study Commission
SEPTEMBER 8, 1965

My first knowledge of the Speaker Ban Law came to me over the telephone from my wife who happened to hear a report about it while listening to the radio. It was surprising to learn that a law affecting vitally the University would be passed without an opportunity for someone responsible for its administration to be heard. The surprising feature was not how quickly this law was passed but the lack of study of its provisions and the effects thereof on higher education.

I hasten to say, however, that it has always been my view that the University has a duty to obey all laws. Consequently, immediate steps were taken to comply with the Speaker Ban Law. Its proponents continue to assert that this law is a simple one to enforce. But to one charged with the responsibility of its enforcement it is extremely vague in almost every particular. It bristles with ambiguities. . . .

The time has come to appraise realistically some of the assertions made by the proponents of the Speaker Ban Law. First, they contend their objective is to protect college and university students from subversive influences which might result from an appearance on the campus by the forbidden speakers. Yet, they hasten to say that the freedom o[f] the institution has not really been taken away because the speakers can be heard anywhere but on the campuses. On the other hand, there are repeated assertions that the purpose of the law is to relieve the taxpayers of providing a public

> Meanwhile, some of the arrogant students at Chapel Hill continue to strut and threaten. It will suit us just as well if they continue to act like [the] jackals that they have proved themselves to be. If nothing else, they may serve as useful reminders to an apprehensive public that discipline is not in overabundance on our campuses.
>
> Jesse Helms, WRAL-TV
> "Viewpoint," 1966

facility for the forbidden speakers. But this is of course true only in a very limited sense inasmuch as all public facilities are available to the forbidden speakers *except* those on the campuses of state supported institutions. If the purpose of the law is to fight communism and subversion, it is at most, a feeble gesture. . . .

We can fight subversion without sacrificing a fundamental principle of our freedom for what . . . is, in reality, false security. North Carolina has come a long way short on cash but long on freedom. The Speaker Ban Law is a mistake. On previous occasions, I have said that this law was passed by friends, not enemies of the University. It was motivated by love in an endeavor to protect students in state institutions from communism. But this love is overly protective. It is a mighty blow against freedom. It will take much time and great effort to upgrade the economic status of our people, but little effort and no money will be required to restore to North Carolina its high place among those people in the world who believe in freedom. In keeping with the highest traditions of this State this law should be acknowledged to be a mistake. This mistake should be corrected by outright repeal as soon as possible.[2]

ooooo

Excerpt of "Viewpoint" Editorial by Jesse Helms on WRAL-TV
NOVEMBER 26, 1968

The appearances of Stokely Carmichael last week on the campuses of several North Carolina colleges and universities, including ones owned and financed by taxpayers, served the useful purpose of emphasizing the worthy intentions of the 1963 General Assembly which enacted the original communist speaker ban law. The appearances of this highly-publicized advocate of violence also suppl[ied] a measurement of the responsibility—or the lack of it—of college administrators who loudly condemned the 1963 legislature for what was claimed to be an invasion of "academic freedom."

. . . There were many declarations, during the months that the Speaker Ban Law was under assault, that college students of today are "too mature to be deceived"—that they are able to "see through" a phony rabble-rouser. Let the record show, if reports are accurate, that there were 5,000 on hand for Stokely Carmichael's speech at Chapel Hill, that he was given a standing ovation when he entered the auditorium, and that his advocacies of violence and anarchy were interrupted with applause on numerous occasions.

If this is what the educators call a mature "search for the truth," then maybe it's time for the educators to be called upon for some definition of "maturity" and "truth."

And, finally, the recently-elected men and women who will serve in the 1969 General Assembly ought to obtain a copy of the federal court decision that declared the much-battered 1963 Speaker Ban Law unconstitutional. . . . The court merely found fault with the *language* of the 1963 law which was admittedly drawn in haste and which contained a lack of sophistication of draftsmanship which can easily be improved under circumstances of more time and less pressure.

. . . The Carmichael episode indicated that the college authorities may lack the backbone to do what they ought to do. If this is so, the state legislature has not only the authority but the duty to step in.[3]

ooooo

Every North Carolina citizen should be proud of our University, and also the other universities and colleges in North Carolina, but when they begin to use academic freedom as an excuse to entertain a bunch of God-denying liars to try to find out what the truth is, somebody has already been brain-washed, and it ain't altogether students either.

Chub Seawell, attorney and
television commentator, 1966

Excerpt from the
Diary of Karen Parker
DECEMBER 18, 1963

This is the first time in over a week I've had time to write. We are now in a peak of tension over racial demonstrations here. There has been no violence.

On Saturday, the 14th, I decided to go to jail. It was no fun at all. There were 3 of us—James Foushee, a Negro[,] and Rosemary Ezra[,] a Jew. We went to Leo's [a restaurant on Franklin Street], were arrested, and hauled to jail. The police were nice except for the one who dragged me into the car. He was even mean afterwards.

I was cracking up in there. I like to be arou[nd] people. Rosemary and I didn't know each other that well.

Dean [Katherine] Carmichael and Dean Long came down there. Long bailed me out with CORE's [Congress of Racial Equality's] consent.

I've been getting pressure from here and there. Carmichael didn't like it and told me so. However I don't think much of her opinion on anything.

My housemother didn't understand but she was kind. She was more upset because my roommate, Jo, was in jail and decided to stay there.[4]

ooooo

Law Professor Dan Pollitt
Describes How the University
Recruited Charlie Scott

We decided we needed some black athletes. And that might draw more people. So we went to see Frank McGuire, who was the coach of the basketball team, and asked him, "Why don't you recruit a black player?" And

> I couldn't help but notice that those who argued for the Speaker Ban Law were themselves expressing a love for this university. It was only that they were misguided.
>
> Vermont Royster

he said, "I'd love to. There's a guy in New York." I forget his name [Lew Alcindor/Kareem Abdul-Jabbar], but he played in the NBA for 20 years.

He said, "See if you can help me." So [we] all wrote to this guy, and he went to UCLA, and I forget the name, but you name some all-time great basketball player. And Frank McGuire said, "Yeah, I'm ready to break the color line if we can get the right guy." And then we saw the footbal[l] coach, and he said no. He had an agreement with a coach at Michigan State that he would refer all the good black football players from North Carolina to him, and the State guy would send everybody from Michigan who couldn't get into Michigan State, down to here. S[o] he said I have this agreement. So he was not cooperative. . . . But Frank McGuire was very cooperative, and he asked us to help him.

And then when Dean Smith took over, he broke the color bar, and he got a guy named Charlie Scott, and he asked our help, he asked me to go with him—down to the southern part of the state where Charlie was going to prep school, and to watch a game and have dinner with the headmaster, and talk to Charlie. Cause I was the NAACP guy. And that's how we broke the color bar.[5]

ooooo

Demands Presented by the Black Student Movement to Chancellor J. Carlyle Sitterson
December 11, 1968

The Demands:

The Black Student Movement has found that UNC is guilty of denying equal educational opportunities to minority group members of the local community, the State of North Carolina and the nation at large. This prestig[i]ous institution of higher learning has maintained and intends to perpetuate educational inequality through its selective admissions procedures.

In addition, the University has been totally unconcerned and unresponsive to the needs of the Black Community and the working conditions and relations of the Black non-academic workers. Not only has the University been blatantly unresponsive, but also has taken full advantage of the

Black non-academic workers and has discriminated against Blacks in hiring and promotions. It has sought to pay the least allowable wages—and whenever possible, even to reduce these minimum wages. The BSM sees this as the most violent form of oppression and denial of human dignity.

Past negotiations between Black Student groups and the administration for the purpose of instituting positive change have resulted in token, symbolic acts which do not meet the educational needs of the currently enrolled or systematically rejected minority group members.

Administrative officials have presented false information, inconsistent reports and have completely misrepresented a supposedly nondiscriminatory university policy.

And, in recognizing that the cultural tools of white America are basically limited and inadequate for dealing intelligently and creatively with Afro-Americans, the BSM had earlier reached the decision that something had to be done immediately. . . . Thus, the BSM is *stomping down* and *demanding* that the University of North Carolina at Chapel Hill *immediately* revise its operational policies as outlined below, and that it not be limited by these demands, but that it use its initiative to make additions to these demands and only additions, "not changes," in these demands.[6]

ooooo

Excerpt of the Reply of Chancellor Sitterson

It has always been my belief that matters involving the University community should be freely and frankly discussed. For this reason, I would like to express my regret that when a group of black students first visited me in my office they declined my invitation to sit down and discuss any matters that were on their minds. The statement that I am now making is in an effort to respond to specific demands in the interest of promoting free and frank discussion.

The University of North Carolina makes every effort to consider on their merits all matters that are brought to its attention, including those contained in these "demands." This emphatically means that the University intends to be responsive to the educational needs of all the people including all races, colors, and creeds. Conversely, it should be clear that the University cannot, in policy or in practice, provide unique treatment for any single race, color, or creed. To do so would be a step backward, and the University should set its sights upon a better future. The University must always view the needs and hopes of a man with a humane spirit and a compassionate heart; but in determining the best means of achieving desirable goals, the University must always be guided by reason and knowledge.[7]

ooooo

Statement by Chancellor Sitterson
FEBRUARY 19, 1969

The Black Student Movement is an officially recognized student organization. I have the greatest respect for their sincere and proper interest in the welfare of black students, and I share deeply in that interest. . . . It should be evident that members of the Black Student Movement, and indeed all black students of the University, have very valuable and special contributions to make in our continuing search for solutions to University problems now and in the future. This is peculiarly true of those problems which have special import for black students. I expect to consult with representatives of the black students on matters of concern to them, and I hope that in mutual trust and good will we can thus move cooperatively and productively toward significant improvements in the University's provisions to meet the legitimate needs of its black students. . . .

These are difficult times for our University, our State, and our Nation. We all share the responsibility to seek genuine improvement in the life of the University, in the lives of its students and staff, and—so far as we [m]ay—for the people of North Carolina and of the Nation. For my part, I welcome the opportunity to join others in this continuing effort.[8]

ooooo

Statement by William C. Friday,
President of the University of North Carolina
FEBRUARY 19, 1969

Today, as throughout its history, the University of North Carolina has an honored tradition as a free and open institution. The right of peaceful demonstration is respected. Student opinions and proposals are welcome, and they receive consideration. There is need for change in our society, but it must be achieved through [the] democratic process. Students and faculty members, both as individuals and through their recognized organizations on each campus, working with many concerned citizens, have sought to preserve the rights of all students and faculty members by standing for the democratic process and against intimidation, threats, and all forces that seek to harm the institutions.

The 1965 session of the General Assembly enacted General Statute 14-132.1 which sets forth the policy of the State regarding the obstructions of public buildings. . . .

The University supports the law of the State, and when violations occur on any campus, the Chancellors and I will do what is required to enforce this statute promptly. Internal disciplinary procedures will also be invoked.

The people of the State expect the University of North Carolina to stand for a free and open society based upon the respect for the law. This obligation will be met.[9]

ooooo

Letter from Robert S. Cilley, Jr., to Chancellor Sitterson
JANUARY 1969

Dear Dr. Sitterson,

This is in reference to your recent rejection of the Black Student Movement's demands, and will be brief and to the point. Since you will undoubtedly get all manner of adverse reaction to your action as soon as the

Tar Heel sees fit to announce the perfidy, I thought you should get at least a little encouragement. There are not a few of us in Chapel Hill who are quite proud of you, Dr. Sitterson, for having preserved Carolina's integrity. A request is one thing, but for some reason, the word "demand" has always rankled for me. A demand is an order backed with a threat, and for UNC to have capitulated to the BSM in this matter would have . . . validated threats as a mode of operation for the remainder of whatever future the University would have had. The threat will come, of course, whether as a boycott or a picket line or whatever, but with the University's indication that it still has the strength of will to oppose the BSM's absurd arrogance . . . , the student body as a whole will support the school I am sure. Apathy may be an old and honorable institution at UNC, but this is no Columbia, for a handful of loudmouths to hold at bay with impunity. Indeed not. Keep up the good work, Dr. Sitterson, and good luck in the coming battle.

Sincerely,

Robert S. Cilley, Jr.
Sophomore, UNC-CH[10]

ooooo

Michael Hooker Remembers the Swimming Test—When the Dog Paddle Didn't Count

Finally, I got a stronger admonishment from the dean indicating that the last day to take the test was right around the corner. I waited until the last day—in fact, I waited until just five minutes before the end of a permissible period for taking it. I showed up at the pool after everybody but the

> I want to be successful here, but I'll never be able to do what Coach Smith did.
>
> Roy Williams

instructor had left, and he seemed a little peeved that he would have to stay longer to administer my swimming test.

He told me to jump in the pool and swim four laps, demonstrating three stroke[s]. When he gave me the instruction, I knew I faced a problem. I had known how to swim since I was very young, so I knew all along that I would have no trouble passing the test. However, I learned to swim on my own without any instruction and had never really been part of an organized swimming program ... in a real swimming pool.

Since I didn't really know any formal stroke, I swam two laps as fast as I could using the only stroke I knew, the crawl, and the instructor seemed duly impressed with my effort, but he told me I still had two strokes to demonstrate and two more laps to do it in.

I turned over on my back and flailed my arms and legs enough to get from one end of the pool to the other. And that seemed to satisfy the instructor's definition of a stroke, but by then, I had truly exhausted my repertoire. I rolled back over on my front and started dog paddling. He blew his whistle and informed me that the dog paddle was not a stroke (to this day I don't know why) and that I had flunked the test. He seemed to take a special delight in telling me that I had flunked.

That meant not graduating with my class. I was required to take beginning swimming in summer school. In those days (summer of 1969) the University operated a Head Start program during the summer. A number of [participants] didn't know how to swim, so the class consisted mostly of a bunch of students who didn't know how to swim, many of whom were truly to[o] afraid of the water, and me.

The instructor didn't know what to do with me, since I knew how to swim, so he had me play in the deep end of the pool during class while he worked with the students who were truly beginning swimmers. That went on for the whole summer, and I never learned any strokes. Of course, I passed, so I thereby passed my swimming test (you could satisfy the swimming requirement by passing beginning swimming).

To this day, I don't know any more swimming strokes than I did [when] I failed my test.[11]

ooooo

Hal Tarleton Reflects on the Controversies of the Sixties

My four years at Carolina were a time of upheaval and turmoil. At my first football game, the guys wore three-piece suits and the women wore wool suits. But my senior year, we were wearing T-shirts and patched jeans. The weekly anti-war vigil was already going on when I arrived.

I stood on the lawn of the president's house and watched classmates burn their draft cards on the porch. The night after Kent State, I marched with thousands of others to the chancellor's residence (which I had never seen before) to demand an end to classes.

Martin Luther King was assassinated near the end of my freshman year. As a senior, I heard Dion sing "Abraham, Martin, and John," at Duke.

I stood two feet from Jane Fonda the afternoon she came to campus to protest the Vietnam War and promote the Black Panther Party. Her hair was cropped into the shag cut she wore in *Klute* and she wore a tight turtleneck sweater without a bra. I stared.

I sat with six or eight students in a dormitory room at Avery the night the first draft lottery was conducted. My birthday came up number 29.

All of these memories I'll carry with me forever. And one more thing: the freshman I met at a dormitory party my senior year. Of all the things I gained from a UNC education, she, my wife of 28 years (Ginny Tarleton '74) is the best.[12]

1970
–
1979

The Endless Quest for Freedom, Support, and Excellence

*I*n a decade when the United States celebrated two hundred years of independence, the watchwords of the university were freedom, support, and excellence. The rights of college students emerged as a hot-button issue in the spring of 1970 when campus unrest occasioned by the war in Southeast Asia proliferated in every part of the country, including Chapel Hill. On May 4, 1970, National Guardsmen opened fire on students at Kent State University, killing four and wounding nine, amid a protest of the American invasion of Cambodia. In Chapel Hill, the words, "On strike, shut it down!" filled the air as more than two thousand students marched on South Building in an immediate response to the tragedy on the Ohio campus. Several days later, more than four thousand striking students filled the downtown streets of Chapel Hill in a parade to protest the blatant assault on student freedom through deadly force.

The protestors made their way to the lawn of Hill Hall to listen to a speech by Tommy Bello, who had been elected student body president less than two months earlier. Bello, a future Rhodes Scholar, sought to encourage students to participate in the campus strike in a peaceful, nonviolent manner. He later described the moment at Polk Place: "I stepped up to the microphone feeling emotionally unable to give the speech I knew I had to give. As if sensing my emotional situation, the crowd gave a very encouraging, a very spiritually boosting, and a very sustained applause. From them, and not vice versa, I received the spirit to give what is still to me the best speech I ever uttered."[1]

In the days that followed, a sympathetic faculty agreed to allow students to bypass their final examinations. In his remarks at the commencement exercises, Charles Ingram, the president of the senior class, stressed the importance of freedom to the university.

At the onset of the decade, the university broke a barrier when Dr. Blyden Jackson began his work as a tenured member of the English Department. Jackson was the first black professor at a traditionally white university in the Southeast. Soon thereafter, Jackson's wife, Roberta, was appointed as a tenured member of the Education Department. Twenty-two years later, the admissions building at the university was named in honor of the groundbreaking couple. Blyden Jackson described his early experiences on the campus in an interview after his retirement from his final post at the university—associate dean of the graduate school.

Gladys Hall Coates, a faithful friend of the university since coming to Chapel Hill with her husband, Albert, in 1928, offered a speech to the University Woman's Club in 1973 wherein she paid tribute to the loyalty of women and chronicled their quest to gain equality at the nation's oldest public university:

> Women have indeed a great heritage and tradition here at the University of North Carolina. As they were among the first to come to the aid of the infant University and help breathe into it the breath of life, so it was a woman [Cornelia Phillips Spencer] who was largely responsible for its rebirth in 1875. During all those years, though never admitted as students, women loved the University and helped in its building. Today they are participants in the rich life of this campus.
>
> The year 1973 marks the 75th anniversary of the first woman to be graduated here. I hope, and I believe, that it will mark the beginning of even greater things for the University, and that women will continue to justify the hope expressed by the trustees on their admission in 1897— that they will honor the University as the University has honored them, and that hand in hand they will march on to still greater achievements in the future.[2]

Just a year before Coates gave her speech, Title IX, an amendment to the Higher Education Act, became law. As a result, the university was required to admit women under the same standards as men. By 1977, women surpassed men in undergraduate enrollment for the first time on the Chapel Hill campus. Nonetheless, the battle to eliminate inequality based on sex was far from over. Frances Hogan, the school's first director of women's athletics, fought a gallant struggle throughout the decade to gain support for the sports programs for women. In a retrospective interview, she offered a glimpse of the difficult state of affairs facing the women's athletics program in the seventies.

In 1975, Terry Sanford, a graduate of the university who served as North Carolina's governor and as a United States senator, responded to critics who sought to level legislative funding among all state-supported institutions, admonishing, "We must now protect and upgrade this University, and not allow it to be just another campus, but the flagship of the proud fleet of all the institutions of higher education in our State system. It would be a drastic mistake to reduce support of the University in order to seek some mistaken goal of avowed equality."[3]

As the national bicentennial approached, Chancellor Ferebee Taylor offered an assessment of America's first state university. Speaking at an alumni luncheon, he pronounced the Chapel Hill school one of the great universities in the United States. At the same time, he challenged the university community to continue its relentless quest for excellence.

During the national bicentennial year, President William C. Friday examined the reasons why the Chapel Hill campus commanded such loyalty in its students and alumni. In his University Day speech in 1976, he observed,

> I kept asking myself why thousands of alumni who have worked and have studied here, who have walked these paths with the dogs and squirrels and have watched the seasons come and go as these glorious years hurry by—why do we feel so intensely loyal to this place?
>
> I believe the answer lies in the fact that each was given a unique hu-

> I have experienced an immense exhilaration of spirit every day since I first saw Chapel Hill in September 1912, rode through the red dust of then Franklin Street bordered by a forest, walked on the gravel of the then campus paths, got a grit in my shoe, and got Chapel Hill in my soul.
>
> Robert Burton House, 1972

Hark the Sound of Tar Heel Voices

man experience here. The University at Chapel Hill, and especially its faculty members, really cared about us. We came from Lincolnton and Laurinburg, from Cherokee and Currituck and from other states and other lands. Possibly we were lonely and frightened or too timid to ask or too self-centered or arrogant; many of us were needy and disadvantaged and some of us were the first members of our families to have the opportunity to study at Chapel Hill.

When we came we were not treated as an object of state subsidy. Rather this University reached out and embraced us. Its great teachers and scholars opened new worlds and guided us in self-realization. And they became our friends who nourished our sense of excitement and wonder and our desire to learn. We were made to feel at home in Chapel Hill.[4]

Toward the close of the decade, Vermont Royster gave an address wherein he attributed the outstanding national reputation of the university to the loyalty of the people of North Carolina. He described the unusual love affair that has long existed between the citizenry and the university: "Among the people there was, you see, an ambivalent attitude toward Chapel Hill. On the one hand, they wondered—and I suppose not unnaturally—what their children were being exposed to in this strange place. On the other hand, they loved their University and were proud of it. They had no intention of abandoning it."[5]

The university's quest for excellence did not end with academics. Coach Dean Smith recruited superior student-athletes to Chapel Hill. In 1974, the university landed one of the greatest college basketball players in history. At the team's annual banquet four years later, Phil Ford delivered a fanciful, tongue-in-cheek account of his recruitment into the Carolina family.

ooooo

Excerpt from the Speech of Tommy Bello
MAY 6, 1970

In standing here before you this afternoon, I cannot help but look back on this year and recall the Moratorium activities of October fifteenth and that day of hope. I can remember November fifteenth in Washington with the *Hair* cast in front of me, looking over a sea of people dancing and singing, "Let the Sun Shine In." Indeed, for that one day the sun of human communion and mutual understanding did shine in. Yet, since that day up to the [Kent State] murders of this past week, I have come to realize in my innocence that things are really not getting better, that we shall not overcome, and that unless we act, this country will destroy itself.

The evidence is obvious. By sending troops into Cambodia, Nixon's administration has admitted that it has learned nothing from the hundreds of thousands of dead in Vietnam. By resuming the bombing of the North, Nixon has shown that rather than seeking "to bring us together," he seeks to polarize this country as never before.

At Kent State University, we have relived the horrors of My Lai. Today these students—Jeffrey G. Miller, Allison Krause, Sandy Scheuer, and William K. Schroeder—lie dead, the tragic victims of Nixon's latest move "to bring us together." I am bitterly disgusted and horrified at the atrocities committed at Kent State and in Southeast Asia. We will not forget Kent State. We will never forget what Nixon is doing to America and to Asia. . . .

Over 300 universities are now on strike. I am on strike and am urging strike, not to shut down this university, but to express my commitment to whatever I can do to end the political careers of these insensitive, insecure, and blatantly inadequate individuals who hope to gain at the expense of lives in Cambodia or Kent State. . . . Instead of burning ROTC buildings, we will beat these men at their game of politics.

And even more than this, we go on strike to open up a new university; to create a free university. This meeting is not the culmination of our efforts; rather, let it be the beginning of an educational system built not on class attendance or grades, but as evidenced by this meeting today, one built on the principles of free exchange of ideas, open expression of opinion, and learning through personal interaction and involvement. We strike to establish a university that will espouse what this society so desperately needs: Mutual love, respect, and understanding.

Today we peacefully and responsibly commemorate the deaths of our fellow students at Kent State. Tomorrow we begin with the professors and educators also on strike to establish constructive educational alternatives. We will fast, we will pray, we will vigil. We will talk to the citizens of Chapel Hill and North Carolina. We will go to Raleigh. We will go to Washington and show Nixon what power is—not the power of guns and bayonets, but the power of people and their votes.[6]

ooooo

Excerpt of Remarks by Charles Ingram at Commencement Exercises
JUNE 1, 1970

Some days ago I read in the newspapers that David Eisenhower, President Nixon's son-in-law, did not plan to attend his graduation exercises. He stated that he did not feel enough attachment to his University to go. I am reminded of a statement by Zeb Vance, North Carolina's beloved Civil War governor and later Senator. He said: "A man should love his home if for nothing else but because it is his, and shelters him; he should love his wife if for no other reason than because she is his wife; he should love his state because it is his . . . ; he should love his country right or wrong because in its destiny are involved the welfare of the state, community, home, wife, children, self. But if you have no other reason for defending it, say you do so because it is your country."

My friends, I would indeed be foolish to stand here before you and tell you that you should love this University simply because you have studied here, because it is yours, because you are University men and women. But we are very fortunate. We can love and praise this school not only because it is ours but because it is a great institution, well-known and respected within the educational circles of the world; because it has been and must continue to be a great beacon of freedom, shining forth for all to benefit from its light and glory.[7]

ooooo

Dr. Blyden Jackson Discusses His Experiences As the University's First Tenured Black Professor

I didn't encounter any great wave [of] anti-Negro racism when I got here. I benefited from the fact that there were just nice people in the English department who [were] actually bending over backwards, it seemed to me, to be sure that I knew I was welcome in their department. The man that was the head of the department at the time, Carroll Horris, was also a Michigan Ph.D. And a very fine chap and politically a liberal. There was no problem there. The chancellor when I came here was a man who certainly was anxious for me to get along, and that was Carlyle Sitterson. . . . We were living in adjoining houses, and sometimes we walked home together, not that often but sometimes. And we talked. But I had a conversation in his office once, and I don't know whether he'd want me to tell it, but the subject of the black faculty did come up in that conversation. And I could quickly see, I thought, that he did have some concern less . . . I should suppose that he was at all lukewarm in his attempt to expand the number of Negroes here. See, we didn't have any, except for my wife and myself. We didn't have anybody. So he said something to me that I already knew. That at schools like UNC if professors, and especially the full professors, were not committed to a program, that program was in trouble.

The head of the school might make all sorts of pronouncements and exert himself in all sorts of ways, but universities like Carolina are actually run—and maybe I shouldn't say this so openly—by the full professors. If you can't persuade them, if you're in the history department, for example, and you can't persuade your full professors in that department to do a certain thing, you are up a creek without a paddle. . . . What we had at Chapel Hill was a situation in which there was still left enough of what someone would call the "Old Tradition" to impede the recruitment of black faculty. It would not be an open thing.[8]

ooooo

Frances Hogan Describes the Struggles of the Women's Athletics Program

When I started as Director of Intercollegiate Athletics, I was paid . . . Well, first of all, no women coaches were paid until '73, '74. And it didn't matter what you were coaching, you were paid one thousand dollars. So, if you did tennis, a thousand. Basketball, a thousand, and so on. It didn't matter the length of your season or how long you worked or who did what. You were paid the same amount. And I was paid three thousand dollars as Director of Intercollegiate Athletics for Women. And I gave up my vacations, worked all summer on handbooks and stuff. . . . The P.E. Department still didn't have a lot of money to hire coaches. . . .

One of the things you never saw was publicity on women's athletics. You just didn't hear about female athletes. And yet, we had excellent athletes. . . . I can remember Laura Dupont who won the National Collegiate Championship in tennis in 1970. It was called the USTA Women's Collegiate Tennis Tournament. Laura was an exceptionally good player, and I [felt] she had a chance to win. The P.E. Department could not finance Laura's trip to the nationals, held at the University of New Mexico. I made up my mind to go to [Director of Athletics] Homer Rice. I didn't know him at all. This was before I was made director of Women's Intercollegiate Athletics. But he said, "Well, is she any good?" And I said, "Well, I think she can win." "Well, I think we can arrange it." So, I thought, "Gosh, that was pretty easy." So, in a meek way I said, "Well, Mr. Rice, do you think I can go with her?" "I think we can arrange that." And that was all that was said and I went. . . .

. . . I even got a man who came through here selling equipment to send some tennis dresses for Laura to use. I wanted her to look nice. So anyway, Laura was given some outfits. . . . [It was] hot as hades and no trees in sight. When Laura started her final match, she lost her first three games, without a point. All of a sudden I realized the singles net posts were in the wrong positions. I ran down the bleachers and went over to the tournament director and pointed it out. They stopped the match and corrected the net posts. . . .

All of a sudden, she started winning and she won the whole thing. And when they announced the "University of North Carolina at Chapel Hill, Laura Dupont," and they went out with this big silver bowl full of roses[, t]ears were just running down my face. You know, I just couldn't believe she had done it.

And what a struggle we'd had to get there. So, I thought, "Well, when we get back, they'll really have this written up." Do you know the P.E. Department was so mad, the chairman was, that he would hardly speak to me because I had gone over his head. Before I left for New Mexico, I went over to see Jack Williams in sports information. I left all the information about Laura and where we were going to be. When I returned, there had not been one word in the papers. And I went in there and Mr. Williams said, "Well, I must have lost the information," and he kept going underneath papers on his desk, and he found the material I had left. He had no idea of writing anything.[9]

ooooo

Excerpt of Speech by Terry Sanford in 1975

This University at Chapel Hill has been a great research university for a century, and continues to be recognized nationally for its excellence. The excitement of new intellectual discoveries here should not relegate other institutions to a lesser role, but a different role—both in a quest for excellence. We need to have excellence everywhere in our system, but it is at the graduate level that the creative genius must be unloosed, the basic research pursued, and the humane leadership nurtured. It deserves an added degree of support that the General Assembly must not ignore.

It deserves also to invade the turf of the private colleges, and to seek private gifts that permit it to lift itself to the pinnacle of the state system of graduate education. There may be those in private education who do not agree with me, but they have failed to evaluate fully the total needs of society and North Carolina. For the University at Chapel Hill to rank with the best in the world is a recognition that in turn serves the best interests of every segment of education on every campus of the state system, every private college, every first grade. We must constantly strive to make Chapel Hill "something special." John Motley Morehead understood that. Private money attracts some of the best students in the nation to Chapel Hill. Private money endowed the best professorships at Chapel Hill. A great university must insist on extraordinary support from its legislature, but it must gain the crucial margin from the gifts of its friends.[10]

ooooo

Speech of Chancellor Ferebee Taylor on the Status of the University
MAY 6, 1976

As early as 1922, the University at Chapel Hill attained membership in the Association of American Universities and, even now, is the only State-supported institution in North Carolina holding such membership. In the entire Southeast, only two other state-supported universities—the University of Virginia and the University of Maryland at College Park—have attained membership in this prestigious Association.

In a recent national rating of professional schools, our Schools of Dentistry and Public Health were ranked among the best in the country. In the latest evaluation of doctoral programs by the American Council on Education, this institution had a substantially larger number of programs rated in the top categories than any other state-supported institution in the Southeast.

In the most recent year for which comparative data are available, the University at Chapel Hill ranked 22nd among all American universities (public and private) in the level of federal funding attracted to support research activities and training programs. Only two other institutions in North Carolina were ranked among the top 100 universities in this respect: Duke University[,] 27th; and North Carolina State University, ranked 77th.

This year we published an Alumni Directory containing the names of more than 137,000 persons whose lives have been touched and influenced by the spirit of this institution. Included are more than half of the State's governors elected since the University graduated its first class. Also included are countless numbers of prominent statesmen, authors, teachers, scientists, businessmen, doctors, lawyers, journalists, artists, and others who have served this State—and served it well—since the 18th century.

Just as these facts need to be known and understood by our citizens, there is a central truth about the University that needs to be remembered by all connected with the institution. This central truth is that the University at Chapel Hill was built by the people of this State, it belongs to the people of this State, and it exists to serve the people of this State.

I have spoken of those indicators that mark this institution as one of the great universities of America. National distinction is important, and we must strive to preserve and enhance it. But, in the final analysis, distinction will be ours only to the extent that we are true to our mission. Only if this institution walks hand in hand with the people it exists to serve, will this University and this State—together—attain the bright promise of the future.[11]

ᴏᴏᴏᴏᴏ

Excerpt of Address by Vermont Royster to the Order of the Tar Heel 100 in 1978

I also remind you that throughout its long history, and despite all the controversies that have swirled around Chapel Hill, the people of this State have never ceased to support [the university] and defend it, no matter how much they were disturbed by it. . . .

Now that I have lost that brashness of youth, I must confess that I listen with an understanding ear to my colleagues who complain that the people of the state "do not understand us." (We cannot even get the highway department to build us a decent road from Raleigh to Chapel Hill!)

But I also ask my colleagues, when they are crossing the campus, to look about them at all those classrooms, at all those dormitories, at that magnificent library, at the huge medical complex, at the new performing arts theatre. I remind them that all these things were paid for by the taxes self-imposed by the people of the state.

I also remind them how much we owe to those who have come here and gone out into the state, the South and world and who have tried to return to this University some measure of what it gave them.

I also think that places an obligation upon us, upon us here in the administration and the faculty—upon you out there among the people of the state. Our obligation is to keep the University a place of learning, for free inquiry among ideas, even for ferment, that the young may be richer when they leave than when they came.[12]

ooooo

Phil Ford Describes
How He Was Recruited to Play Basketball

The first person I met from Carolina was [assistant] coach [Bill] Guthridge. I remember he drove a Carolina Blue Monte Carlo to see me . . . [after] he drove a Carolina Blue Cadillac to see Walter [Davis]. I guess he thought since I was just a country boy from Rocky Mount, I wouldn't know the difference.

. . . My parents hadn't gotten home from school yet, so we went in and started watching TV. I was expecting coach to tell me how great I was, like all the other recruiters, and how much I'd play. But coach just sat there, and I just sat there. He sat there for a little longer. I cut my eyes over to coach and he would just be staring at the TV. . . . Once you get to know coach Guthridge, he's super.

[Assistant] Coach [Eddie] Fogler got so close to my family that I actually thought he was my brother one time. He had a room in our home that he stayed in every night.

To tell you a story about how my parents never told me where to go to school, one night coach Fogler and [N.C. State assistant] coach [Eddie] Biedenbach spent the night in my room. Coach Fogler, being the gentleman that he is, said to my Momma, "Mrs. Ford, if there's not enough room, I'll be glad to leave." Coach Biedenbach was standing out in the hall at the

> I enjoyed coming to Carolina so much and being able to play basketball under Coach Smith. I love the place and everything about it, and if I can help somebody else to get the same opportunity that I had to come to Carolina and play basketball and get a good education, then I want to do it.
>
> Phil Ford, class of 1978

time, and Momma pointed to him and said, "If anyone's gonna leave, it's gonna be him."

Coach Fogler and I got real close. I used to call him Eddie then, but after I signed Momma started making me call him coach.

Another story about my Momma not telling me where to go to school. [One afternoon, Norm Sloan, head basketball coach at N.C. State, and assistant coach Biedenbach were waiting at the Ford home when Phil came in]. I went into the kitchen. I was thirsty, and on the table there wasn't anything to eat. I looked on the stove, there wasn't anything. I looked in the oven, there wasn't anything. So I went out and we got to talkin'. We were sitting in the living room when coach Sloan asked if we could turn down the TV a little. Daddy went to turn it down, and Momma said, "Turn that TV back up!"

The very next night, coach [Dean] Smith , coach Guthridge, and coach Fogler were waiting when I got home. I went into the kitchen, and I thought it was Thanksgiving. We ate and ate and ate. And after we got through eating, Momma grabbed [Phil's sister] Jackie's hand and said, "C'mon baby, let's go in the other room and let the men talk."

She never told me where to go to school, but after that night the next August I was here.[13]

Hark the Sound of Tar Heel Voices

1980
—
1989

In Recognition of Greatness

Before he died in 1989, Albert Coates, the beloved son of Carolina who founded the far-famed Institute of Government in Chapel Hill, said, "The whole life of North Carolina has been favored by men and women going out from the University of North Carolina." Indeed, throughout the eighties, the state and the world at large gained a greater appreciation for the vital role that the Chapel Hill school and its graduates had played in molding the American republic.

The school was consistently ranked among the nation's top twenty universities, public and private, throughout the decade. As it celebrated its 192nd birthday, President William Friday acknowledged its special qualities:

> The University of North Carolina is a special place. For most of us, it was a place of self-realization and personal development and we hold precious and dear memories of those very happy years. We learned, we grew, and later we understood that we must give back to society the best within us to improve the well-being of those less fortunate about us. Here we also learned that respect for the dignity and worth of each individual and the protection of the rights and freedoms all citizens possess are fundamental to a democratic society and essential to our own being. We learned to be useful and responsible people and we began to understand the profound truth that sustains life and that is that love—one for

another—is indeed the greatest Commandment of all. And through this personal commitment of love, service and caring, under a Divine Providence, lies our real hope for peace among all men and women the world over.

This is the spirit of [the] Chapel Hill I know.[1]

When William S. Powell (class of 1940), one of the university's most beloved professors and historians, announced in the spring of 1985 that he was going into half-time instruction, a firestorm arose over the future of the teaching of North Carolina history at the flagship institution of the university system. Enrollment in North Carolina history courses at Chapel Hill dropped from six hundred in the spring semester of 1973 to thirty-nine in the fall semester of 1985. At a subsequent North Caroliniana Society Banquet honoring Powell, known far and wide as "Mr. North Carolina History," Dr. H. G. Jones, the former state archivist, former curator of the North Carolina Collection, and renowned historian, questioned the university's commitment to the teaching of the state's history: "Ten years from now, how many legislators will have taken a course in North Carolina history on this campus?" William Friday, the featured speaker of the evening, offered a passionate appeal for "a continuation of emphasis upon the study of North Carolina history here at Chapel Hill." He warned, "We cannot allow Bill Powell to be the last of the long line of influential state historians."[2]

> What we learned at Chapel Hill was not chemistry and economics and mathematics. Those were the instruments of learning. We learned, we absorbed, with Frank Porter Graham as our master teacher, that solid tradition, those hopes of this university born of the beginnings of a new nation, values this great university continues to nourish—freedom and liberty and tolerance, the search for truth, and defense of dignity, courage to arrive freely at convictions, and the personal courage to stand for those hopes and truths.
>
> Terry Sanford,
> 1987

In subsequent interviews, Powell, Jones, and Dr. Harry L. Watson, then a professor of history at the university and currently the director of the Center for the Study of the American South on the Chapel Hill campus, offered their opinions on the controversy.

Some of the enduring fame enjoyed by the university was the result of its willingness to not only seek and train the best and the brightest from within North Carolina but to attract outside talent from the entire nation and the world.

Dr. William E. Leuchtenburg, the distinguished New York professor and presidential scholar who came to Chapel Hill as William Rand Kenan, Jr., Professor of History in 1982, paid tribute to the cosmopolitan atmosphere of the university when he delivered the commencement address in 1984.

This mixture of homegrown and imported talent had meshed over the decades to lift the university to its place of prominence in the last quarter of the twentieth century. Charles Kuralt, the native son who ventured forth from Chapel Hill to become a household name throughout the United States, applauded this unique blend of talent with stirring words at the commencement in 1985.

Sounding a similar strain, Chancellor Christopher C. Fordham III proclaimed the university as one of the most distinguished on the face of the earth in a 1983 speech to alumni. At the conclusion of his address, the chancellor tempered his laudatory words with a challenge for the years ahead:

> The latter part of the 20th century, however, finds us in worldwide and national recession, with the state of North Carolina's economy reflecting that recession. While public interest in education and higher education may not have waned, the state's capacity to support and sustain all of its commitments, especially those large ones made in the last decade or so, is suspect. It seems altogether likely that excruciating choices will have to be made.
>
> Will one of those choices be to let slide or let fade this preeminent flower of the state, this harbinger of the future of North Carolina's youth, this testimony to our citizens' wisdom, vision and forbearance for almost 200 years? Or will our state, through the urging of her citizens, find a way to sustain her great University in quality and in magnetism, to serve future generations and to lead the way to redevelopment of the state's and nation's economy? The choices will be difficult, but they simply must be made. Let all University alumni help with those choices.[3]

One of the most recognized symbols of the university's excellence in athletics is its living mascot, Rameses. Throughout the eighties, Rameses XIV and his successor, Rameses XV, provided color for the school's football contests. Bob Hogan, whose family has tended the mascot since Rameses I was introduced, provided an interesting account of the university's pet in 1980.

Not long after C. D. Spangler, Jr., assumed the presidency of the University of North Carolina in 1987, he noted a definite improvement on the Chapel Hill campus since his student days. In an interview in the spring of

1987, Spangler compared the quality of the food and the student body in the fifties and the eighties.

ooooo

William S. Powell, Dr. H. G. Jones, and Dr. Harry L. Watson on the Future of Teaching North Carolina History at the University

William S. Powell:

I could detect a decline in student interest in North Carolina history shortly after it was no longer taught in the public schools. That was about 1972, I believe, and the young people who started coming here in the late 1970s had never had any exposure to the subject at all. Enrollment in my classes dropped about that time.

Now they are teaching [North Carolina history] again in the schools, and of course Dr. Jones had a lot to do with that, and I will hope that interest will start to grow again and we will start to see enrollments go up.

The one thing I've tried to do in 22 years of teaching North Carolina history is to rub my enthusiasm for North Carolina . . . off on my students, to make them proud to be North Carolinians, and to try to make them understand why North Carolina is like it is today—good and bad. . . .

I would want my successor to be someone who knows North Carolina history from having lived here and grown up a part of us. It shouldn't be somebody from somewhere else who just wrote a dissertation on some North Carolina subject. He or she may know everything there is to know about that particular subject, but I want somebody who knows the whole sweep of North Carolina, the people and places as well.

> Here at Chapel Hill, everything is built around the libraries—they are our most important assets.
>
> Christopher Fordham, 1987

Dr. H. G. Jones:

I'm not convinced that the current leaders of the department of history are as committed to the teaching of North Carolina history as they say they are. The state motto is *Esse Quam Videri*—"To be rather than to seem." What does this mean? It means substance, not show. Don't tell me how strong your commitment is, show me....

Two presidents of the university—first David L. Swain . . . and Kemp P. Battle . . . made North Carolina history their consuming interest, and started a tradition that has continued from J. G. De Roulhac Hamilton, Robert D. W. Connor, Albert R. Newsome, Hugh T. Lefler, and on through to William S. Powell.

. . . That's why the position left vacant by Bill's retirement is so important. It wouldn't surprise me if they did, and I hope they won't[,] fill it with someone who['s] done a dissertation in some phase of North Carolina history but who knows nothing about the state otherwise.

And whoever is chosen can't just talk to other historians, or to other education people, or even students. They must be willing to carry on the tradition of taking the history of this state to the people. They should know the people of North Carolina and feel at home among them, at every level. The average people—those are the ones that history must understand and try to reach.

Dr. Harry L. Watson:

I have to wonder if some people have stopped to think about the implications of some of the statements they have been making.

I've been here nine years and I've taught the classes. I've written two books and numerous articles on the subject. When anybody asks me to go out in the state, I'm there.

Since I'm going to keep on doing those things, and since the department has committed itself in bringing in someone else to join me, I'm a little surprised that anyone would question our commitment to North Carolina history....

The message I'd like to tell alumni is a positive one. North Carolina history is changing, just as the profession itself has changed in the last 15 or 20 years. We're interested in the old questions, but we're asking some new ones, too....

It may not look like the same North Carolina history, and it may even make some people uncomfortable. But it's the same state, and we're motivated by the same affection for it. It's simply wrong to say that because our way is different it's somehow an abandonment of the subject.[4]

ooooo

Excerpt from the Commencement Address of Dr. William E. Leuchtenburg in 1984

For a long time now, this university has appeared to be perched precariously on the edge of paradox. An institution supported by the citizens of this commonwealth for education of their own young people, it draws much of its faculty, and not a few of its students, from beyond its borders. A university that bears the name of a single state, it encourages an outlook that is not parochial but cosmopolitan. Yet, there is not truly paradox here, for in ranging so widely, the university has benefited both state and nation. Nearly 150 years ago, a federal guide observed that this university had become "the center of an aristocracy of intelligence that in half a century has transformed the state" and when President Kennedy spoke in this stadium in the fall of 1961, he noted there was an ancient tradition "that the graduate of this university is a man of his nation as well as a man of his time." And now he would say as well, a woman of her nation as well as a woman of her time.

However, the paradox is apparent rather than real only because many who have come here have valued the traditions of this state and have made themselves members of a community that has welcomed them so generously. After Proff Koch founded the Carolina Playmakers, no one any longer thought of him as a migrant from North Dakota, but as a man who nurtured the talents of Paul Green and Thomas Wolfe, writers acutely sensitive to the folkways and history of their native state, just as no one today any longer thinks of Dean Smith as a Jayhawker but as a Tar Heel born and a Tar Heel bred.

If someone who has not yet been here long enough to speak for anyone may be permitted a single appeal this morning, it is to urge those of you who are graduating today who come from other states, other lands, to continue to bear in mind the debt that all of us owe to the people of this

> The way we look at athletics at the University of North Carolina is, we are the front porch for the university. We are what people see. We are a very public part of the university. The primary mission of this university is the pursuit and development of the academic potential for the students that come to this place and we're just a part of that climate.
>
> Anson Dorrance,
> UNC women's soccer coach

state. In his own Class Day address as president of the senior class, Frank Graham said, "If we leave our university with the determination to serve her nothing will become us like the leaving." For what John Gardner once observed about a nation is no less true of a great university. "A nation," he declared, "is never finished. You cannot build it and leave it standing like the phar[ao]hs did with the pyramids. It has to be built and then rebuilt. It has to be recreated in each generation by believing and caring men and women."[5]

ooooo

Excerpt from the Commencement Address of Charles Kuralt
MAY 12, 1985

Think of our state. From time to time, it has sent scoundrels to represent us in Washington, but always, always here at home, the saving minority has returned us to reason, compassion and decency. And the headquarters of this impulse for good has always been Chapel Hill.

What if there had been no Edwin Alderman to say, "I have an ideal for this University. My desire would have it a place where there is always a breath of freedom in the air." What if there had been no Horace Williams to use that freedom to outrage and educate? What if there had been no Frank Graham, who knew that this old campus on the hill was a fortress against pettiness and cruelty and injustice and ignorance in our state—who *declared* it a fortress: "a stronghold of learning" in his words, "and an outpost of light and liberty among all frontiers of mankind." And what if there had

been no William C. Friday, who came along just in time, with a wise understanding of this tradition, and who, nobly, has kept the light burning, and
made it burn brighter?

What would North Carolina have been without this great faculty, inspirational to us in every generation, and adding, with each graduating class,
a handful of new members to the conspiracy of good people, to the saving
minority of those who care?

My own father is one of those who came to Chapel Hill . . . and found
his conscience here . . . and left to care and serve until this day, so I came to
know one of them early. And recognized others as I met Bill Geer and Paul
Green and Phillips Russell and Walter Spearman and Terry Sanford and
Jim Wallace and Tom Wicker and Al Lowenstein and Joel Fleishman and
John Sanders and many other men and women I could tell you about. You
could tell me about others still. . . .

The University knows that ignorance will have its innings, but will always lose in the ninth.[6]

ooooo

Speech to Alumni by
Chancellor Christopher C. Fordham III
FEBRUARY 1983

As the most recent studies published by the National Academy Press
show, "good old Carolina" is not just "good old Carolina." It is clearly one
of the nation's and world's distinguished academic institutions, and it is essential that alumni and citizens of the state understand the measure of what
they have so as to sustain, nurture and protect it for future generations.

The new studies show unequivocally that from the Potomac to the
Cape of Good Hope, the University at Chapel Hill has the outstanding academic faculty; from the Atlantic to Austin, Texas, and to the West Coast,
the faculty is unmatched.

How did this come about, and when did it come about? The University, like other national universities in this country, began an important move toward distinguished scholarship in the early part of the 20th century. As the century advanced, that move gathered momentum, especially as the nation placed more resources into research. By the second half of the 20th century the University had flowered into one of the nation[']s premiere research universities, in the breadth and scope of its programs and activities, as well as in terms of their quality.

The data in the new studies, "An Assessment of Research-Doctorate Programs in the United States: The Mathematical and Physical Sciences" and "An Assessment of Research-Doctorate Programs in the United States: Humanities," each of which attest to the University's premier ranking in the Southeast and to its very solid, near-the-top national rankings, give salient testimony to what people of the state have built in Chapel Hill over a period of 200 years.[7]

ooooo

Bob Hogan's Account of the Life and Activities of Rameses XIV

When you think of UNC, you think of Rameses. This is what they chose 60-some years ago. And I think he's a pretty neat mascot when you get him fixed up. . . .

We thoroughly wash him at the beginning of the season, because that coat will pick up anything—and he loves to rub against things. He doesn't mind being washed, except that he doesn't like getting water in his face. The rest of the year we just brush him real good. That usually keeps him presentable.

He rubs his horns against anything he can, and we have to wait until Friday to paint them. It's a matter of holding him by one horn while you paint the other. We have to keep him tied up Friday and Saturday so he doesn't ruin the paint job. . . .

I was driving up I-85 near the North Carolina line about 2 A.M. [returning from UNC's victory over Michigan in the Gator Bowl on December 28, 1979] when I heard this loud bang and the trailer started wobbling. I thought I had a flat. I pulled over, and Rameses was just tired of it all. He was backing up as far as he could and ramming the side of the trailer trying to get out. I had to tie him. . . .

It's usually only when Carolina is on the road that we have to worry about someone taking the ram. When they're playing in Kenan the students at the other schools don't usually consider trying it. . . .

One year the boys at State College [N.C. State] got him and took him over to the textile department and had him dyed red. That was the worst. Usually when they do something to his coat it's no problem, because his Carolina blanket will cover most of anything. . . .

The Duke boys are pretty brash. They don't seem to have as much respect for property when they try to steal the ram. They'll leave gates open and things like that. . . .

One time they came at night and my son got out in the woods and yelled, "Here's the ram!" He led them into the woods to an area behind my dad's farm that I'd have trouble finding my way out of. The next morning we went to milk the cows at 5:30 like we always do, and Duke students were still coming out of the woods.[8]

ooooo

C. D. Spangler, Jr., Compares the Quality of the Food and the Student Body in the 1950s and 1980s

As a freshman student here, I lived in Alexander dorm, and I ate at Lenoir Hall. That was in 1950.

At the end of that year, I felt I didn't want to eat at Lenoir Hall anymore.

If you will recall, it had been built by the Navy in World War II. It didn't have any warmth to it, it was sort of cold, and the food didn't exactly appeal.

When I came back as president, someone said, "Have you tried Lenoir Hall?" and the thought went through my mind[,] "Yes, in 1950." I wasn't inclined to go back there.

However, almost every week I eat in Lenoir Hall. It has been redecorated, and the food is prepared by a private operator. It has excellent food [and] I suspect the best salad bar in the state. I have the opportunity to sit at tables with students and faculty members, and it is a real delight.

I think that just as Lenoir Hall is a better place to eat now than it was in 1950, that those students who are eating there now are also as bright, if not brighter, than we were when we were there. They are more deeply involved in their studies than I recall my generation being, and yet they still maintain a good spirit about them.[9]

1990

−

1999

Two Hundred Sweet Years

s the Carolina blue skies of a lovely autumn afternoon yielded to the golden hues of sunset on October 12, 1993, the massive crowd assembled in Kenan Memorial Stadium sat in anticipation of the beginning of the celebration of the bicentennial of public higher education in the New World. Finally, at seven o'clock, a voice familiar to Tar Heels the world over resonated through the stands as Woody Durham, the longtime sportscaster for Carolina football and basketball, proclaimed, "Ladies and gentlemen, welcome to University Day 1993, the Bicentennial Celebration of the University of North Carolina at Chapel Hill. North Carolina celebrates many firsts . . . the first state university, the first state art museum, and the first state-supported symphony in the nation."

Durham's voice gave way to the North Carolina Symphony as it performed the special *Bicentennial Commemorative Suite*. After the symphony concluded the final notes of "Hark the Sound," the face of one of America's most-respected journalists appeared on giant screens throughout the venue. In his deep baritone, Walter Cronkite declared, "Tomorrow the University enters its third century. Bright and hard-working young men and women of all races, many from poor families, will go back to class to take advantage of opportunities that are all but nonexistent in too much of the rest of the world. I congratulate the University of North Carolina on its past accomplishments and wish it well in the future. And that's the way it is ... October 12, 1993!"[1]

Thus began the grand convocation to commemorate the two hundredth birthday of the university. Among the dignitaries gracing the dais were Charles Kuralt, William C. Friday, and President William J. Clinton. James B. Hunt, Jr., then governor of North Carolina, was there also. In his speech to the crowd estimated in excess of fifty thousand, Hunt, a graduate of the university's law school, extolled the ideals of freedom, service, and opportunity that had bound all generations of the university family as one.

A number of the nation's presidents, from James K. Polk to John F. Kennedy, had spoken on the Chapel Hill campus over the years. On October 12, 1993, President Bill Clinton joined the list, and if ever an American president were upstaged, albeit unintentionally, by another speaker, it occurred in Chapel Hill that autumn night when one of the university's own, Charles Kuralt, majestically proclaimed the words that will bring pride and inspiration to Carolina faithful for countless years to come.

Ironically, the university community was almost deprived of Kuralt's address. On October 11, Kuralt notified bicentennial officials that he would be unable to honor his speaking commitment because his elderly father, who lived in the far northern corner of North Carolina, had been hospitalized by a stroke. Kuralt explained that the lengthy round-trip to Chapel Hill by automobile would keep him away from his father for too long a period. Upon receiving the news, C. D. Spangler, the Charlotte business executive who was then serving as president of the consolidated university, offered a solution: "I'll make my personal plane available for him if he wants to come up just for the evening." Spangler's airplane delivered the award-winning journalist to Chapel Hill on the afternoon of October 12, and Kuralt proceeded to draw the largest ovation of the entire night with his timeless words.[2]

Unquestionably, the nineties were dominated by the celebration of that unique milestone in the history of public education in the Americas. The commemoration offered a special opportunity for supporters far and wide to reflect upon the university's storied past. That the campus, the student body, and all of Chapel Hill had changed dramatically over more than twenty decades was undeniable, yet students—and their elders—of the modern era were seized by the same playful nature as their predecessors. A 1991 exchange of letters between Raleigh business executive Jim Hughes (class of 1970) and H. G. Jones, the acclaimed historian who was then the curator of the university's North Carolina Collection, was proof that, in any age, boys will be boys.

Following the celebration, the university embarked upon its third century of service. In 1995, Michael Hooker, who would die of cancer four short years later at the age of fifty-three, was named chancellor. Young and energetic, Hooker had become the first person in his family to earn a college degree when he graduated from the university in 1969. At his installation on University Day in 1995, he delivered an eloquent address on the essence and mission of the university.

During the bicentennial decade, the university's football team enjoyed its greatest success since the Choo Choo Justice era. Masterminding the team's rise to national prominence was Mack Brown, the head coach who began his ten-year career at the university with identical records of one win and ten losses. But over the next eight seasons, each of his teams had a winning record. During Brown's final six years in Chapel Hill, the Tar Heels competed in postseason bowl games every season. In an interview after the team's close loss to the University of Texas in the 1994 Sun Bowl, Brown expressed his desire to position the North Carolina team to compete with the nation's Alabamas and Texases on an annual basis. In Brown's last two seasons in Chapel Hill, his teams finished tenth and sixth, respectively, in the final national polls, ranking higher than both Alabama and Texas both years. On December 4, 1997, Brown announced that he was leaving to accept a new coaching position—ironically, at the University of Texas.

One of the most memorable campus controversies of the decade oc-

> After 200 years, we can read again the words on the University's seal—"Light and Liberty." We can say that the University of North Carolina has lived by those two short noble words. And that in all the American story, there is no place quite like this.
>
> Charles Kuralt

Hark the Sound of Tar Heel Voices

curred in 1996 with the unveiling of a redesigned ram logo, the primary trademark of the university. The new logo, produced by a New York designer at a cost of thirty-seven thousand dollars, was distinctly different from the original, which featured a colorful, cocky, upright ram with human characteristics. Sporting a more natural look, the new ram design prompted a flood of calls to retailers from disgruntled alumni, many of whom stated their preference for the original logo. Two letters among the many written to the *Alumni Review* shortly after the new logo was introduced reveal the disdain of many graduates for the redesigned ram. In the aftermath of the controversy, the university has continued to use both logos.

ooooo

Excerpt from Speech of Governor James B. Hunt, Jr., at the Bicentennial Observance on University Day
OCTOBER 12, 1993

We are all here today to affirm the principles that gave birth and growth to America's first public university. We believe now, as the University founders did 200 years ago, that a society grows freer and stronger when opportunity is spread widely among its citizens, and we believe now, as we did 200 years ago, that a public university can do more than any other public institution to encourage opportunity and freedom and democracy. In fact, the founding of our University and the founding of our country's democracy are parallel strands of history. In 1776, when the authors of the North Carolina Constitution called for a public university, members of the Continental Congress signed the Declaration of Independence. In 1789, when the North Carolina General Assembly passed the University charter, the North Carolina State Convention voted to ratify the U.S. Constitution. In 1791, when the North Carolina General Assembly extended a building loan to the new University, the United States formally ratified the Bill of Rights. And in 1793, here in North Carolina, there was born a University of the people to challenge, to protect and to guide the government of the people. And our legislature re-enacted that action on this campus today.

For the last 200 years, Carolina has rewarded the vision of its founders by broadening opportunity and encouraging debate on the public issues

> What's different about UNC is the quality of education.
> When it comes to recruiting very rarely do we have to
> contact a player before she contacts us.
>
> Karen Shelton,
> UNC field hockey coach, 1995

of the day. Debate that has overflowed the libraries and lecture halls, and brought genuine improvement in the lives of our people.

So while we gather here today to honor those visionary founders of Carolina, we must not hold them too much in awe. We must not imagine their responsibilities any greater or their capabilities any broader than our own. We too must be agents of change. We too must strive to offer the next great ideas that will light a new torch of liberty. . . .

Today then, let us celebrate this public university and give thanks for it. May it continue to bring opportunity to all of our citizens and our State, and may that opportunity bring us closer to the society of freedom and justice to which we are called by our conscience and by the founders of this great University of North Carolina.[3]

ooooo

Excerpt from Speech of Charles Kuralt at the Bicentennial Observance

In trying to define its [the university's] spirit, I find my thoughts wandering back always to Frank Porter Graham. My own family's experience of the University may be much like your family's experience. My father, who is with us tonight from a hospital bed in Elizabeth City, came to Chapel Hill by train in those hard depression years carrying little money and much hope for the future. He hired a man with a mule and wagon to transport his trunk from Carrboro station to the campus, and soon became aware of the dominative professor who was known even then as Dr. Frank. This professor scurried everywhere, seemingly always late for an appointment. It didn't take long for my father to understand that Dr. Frank was, in fact, always late because of his habit of stopping to talk with everybody he met, grasping new students by the arm and inquiring about their hometowns,

Hark the Sound of Tar Heel Voices

their ancestors, their ambitions and their general welfare.

I say this for those who were not acquainted with Frank Porter Graham. He was a saint. Those who knew him well will not have to be told. He was one of the greatest Americans of the middle years of the 20th century, no doubt, and the most remarkable human being I ever came across.

I believe the church requires of miracles, however, before elevation to sainthood. Frank Graham performed miracles too. In the midst of that great depression of the 1930s, he took the leadership of a poor university in a desperately poor state and transformed it by tact, diplomacy, iron persistence and steady strength of character into a model of public higher education and a light for the nation. If building a great University when and where he did it wasn't a miracle, then miracles don't exist. . . .

Hundreds of people he knew were swept up in his great weight. Some of them are on this platform. Bill Friday, first among all of course . . .

I think of Terry Sanford, John Sanders, Al Lowenstein, Tom Wicker, Jim Wallace, Joel Fleishman, Tom Lambeth, Eli Evans, John Eli [Ehle], author of a forthcoming book on Dr. Frank, and many more I did not know but have heard of. All men and women whose lives were touched and changed in this place, and who went on thus touched and changed to lead politics, to head up corporations, to direct great universities and foundations and to write and think and serve their state and nation.

Frank Graham had no children. We are all his children. And so in time I came here, as my father had done before, and my brother Wallace after, and here we found something in the air. A kind of generosity, a certain tolerance, a disposition toward freedom of action and inquiry that has made of Chapel Hill, for thousands of us, a moral center of the world. This was the atmosphere that Frank Porter Graham created and left behind. The liberating and liberalizing air of Chapel Hill, breathed deeply by Bill Friday all those years. And now in the care of Dick Spangler and Paul Hardin, and of the teachers and students of the present day, it is the air that we breathe here tonight. And so on and on we might hope through the life of the University that is yet to be lived.[4]

> I have always had a view of finishing my career in Chapel Hill. The University may get tired of me as chancellor before I get tired of being chancellor.
>
> Michael Hooker, 1995

Exchange of Letters between Jim Hughes and Dr. H. G. Jones in early 1991

Dear H. G.,

I hope 1991 is the start of the turnaround for the [Carolina] Inn and a flood of new contributions to the North Carolina Collection.

A long time ago, back when I was a young hell-raiser at the Phi Gam House, a couple of us took some rocking chairs off the front porch of the Inn. They were fine chairs and they burned quite nicely, as I recall.

Back then, I did not know the connection between John Sprunt Hill's will and the North Carolina Collection. [The will bequeathed the Carolina Inn to the university, any profits to go toward funding the collection.] Now I do. So I'm sending you a check for $100 this year and expect to do the same the next year and the next year and the year after, until those damn chairs are paid for.

Best wishes to all you folks at the North Carolina Collection!

Sincerely,
Jim Hughes

Dear Jim,

I love guilty consciences. They make people do the damndest things. Such as turning a scrooge into a tender-hearted Samaritan.

Now, I don't want to sound like I approve of juvenile stealing and burning chairs from the portico of the hallowed Carolina Inn, but the Lord works in mysterious ways, and if the memory of that episode has turned the stone-cold PR man's heart into a believer in the North Carolina Collection, then you have made a good start toward the penance that will eventually remove the burden that formerly weighed upon your shoulders.

As your priest, I feel obligated to ask for a definition of the word "some" (as in "some rocking chairs.") You see, "some" can mean a few (four or five) or many (two dozen). Your conscience will be relieved only when your crime has been fully paid for. Let us estimate that "some" really meant a half dozen. The next question is how much did they cost? But good chairs increase in value as they adjust to human form and acquire an aura of importance from the distinguished men and women who sit in them. So the chairs that you burned were not just chairs that could be replaced with another set like them[,] . . . having been sat in by the great and near-great (and perhaps by some bums from Phi Gam House); they were irreplaceable chairs—seats of distinction, in which great ideas and great plans were born (and borne).

Perhaps you get the point, Jim: We are grateful for your confession and your start on the road to penance, but be careful that that business heart of yours does not calculate too fast. You aren't atoning for "some rocking chairs," you're atoning for those rocking chairs, at today's Israel Sack prices! Welcome to lifetime membership in the Friends of the North Carolina Collection!

I would share this information with the management of the Carolina Inn, but I'm afraid they'd throw a fit and claim your contribution to help cover their 1990 deficit. We haven't received a cent from the Inn this year, and I'll be damned if they're going to get your conscience-ridden hundred-dollar check.

Sincerely your[s],
H. G. Jones[5]

ooooo

Excerpt from Installation Address of Chancellor Michael Hooker
OCTOBER 12, 1995

I have spoken of this University and its duty to the people of this state—the duty prescribed by North Carolina's Constitution. But we should deceive ourselves if we thought it possible that an institution concerned with all the great thoughts, all the enlivening discoveries, all the pioneering quests for knowledge, all the aspects of science, all the beauties of art and music and imagination, an institution whose task embraces the study of everything about humankind and our universe—we should deceive ourselves if we thought such an institution could have its effect only within this state. We are, in fact, an institution of national and international significance and meaning. Chapel Hill, having begun as a crossroads in the heart of this state, has become a crossroads of the world. I think of the music of Johann Sebastian Bach, composed in towns in 18th century Germany, largely unknown for a century after his death until Mendelssohn conducted his great choral works and championed his music: Bach, who ever since has spoken to the whole world and shed grace upon the human spirit in every clime. The University of North Carolina is like that. Like Bach, it has a local place. Like Bach's, its work is now everywhere esteemed. And, like Bach's, the work of the University enlivens the human spirit. Its faculty and its graduates moderate life, not only in North Carolina, but around the globe. Its destiny is to be free, to follow truth, and to shed light.[6]

ooooo

Comments of Head Football Coach Mack Brown after Sun Bowl Loss to the University of Texas in 1994

The thing we want to do is go where North Carolina's never been, and that's to be in the Top 10 on a consistent basis. But when there's only 10 spots out of 107 teams, it's a tough neighborhood to get in. When you're playing the Alabamas and Texases, you've got to beat those people to take that step. We're proud to be here, and proud of the way our team competed. We've got to do some work, get some things shored up before we take the next step. . . .

If you're going to move up from somewhere between 30 and 10, you've got to do something else. You've got to take another step. Expanding the

> What I wish for today's students and their future children is that they, too, may fall in love with this university—a love serious enough to support it and enlarge it, a love deep enough to survive the predictable lovers' quarrels.
>
> Doris Betts,
> author and UNC faculty member

Hark the Sound of Tar Heel Voices

stadium will lend more of a big-time atmosphere. It will help recruiting nationally. It's something we need. It's time.

You get to a point after seven years that you want to step back, evaluate where you are, what you've accomplished, what your goals are. Obviously, Oklahoma has won national championships. I sure wouldn't stay here if I didn't think we could do the same thing.[7]

ooooo

Letters of Lee S. Nixon and Stephen Schneider to the Alumni Review *in Response to the University's Redesigned Logo*

The purpose of this letter is to comment on the new Carolina "ram."

This new logo must be the result of some sort of fraternity prank by an alumnus of N.C. State. For proof, I submit the following:

1. If you take away the "horn," the remaining animal favors a wolf.

2. If you take away the "animal," the remaining favors tractor tires.

The ram being integrated with the interlocking "NC" distorts that there is indeed an "NC" in the logo. It looks like it could also be "XC."

There is an age-old saying that simply states "If it ain't broke then don't fix it." Grammatically, it is horrendous; however, its meaning is profound.

Here in Greenville, the people at ECU [East Carolina University] liked our mascot ram so very much, they simply removed the fur, added a jacket [and] a pirate head and painted it purple and gold.

A few years ago, the people at Coca-Cola made a huge mistake with the new Coke. It was only a matter of days before Coca-Cola Classic hit the shelves.

Where is our Rameses Classic?

Lee S. Nixon '82
Greenville, NC

Over the weekend I was told by my sister (UNC Nursing School class of 1997) that UNC had an ugly new logo. I couldn't believe it (and I am not an "older alumni"). Then on Monday my copy of the *Carolina Alumni Review* came, and lo and behold there was a picture of the monstrosity.

The University paid $37,000 for this piece of junk, at a time when the libraries are canceling journal subscriptions and tuition is rising? You couldn't even find a Tar Heel to do the redesign, but you had to get some Yankee to do it?

Aside from hating change to begin [with], I dislike the new logo because it totally obscures the "N." Unless you are familiar with the original emblem, it is very hard to tell it is an interlocking "N" and "C." The addition of the "Carolina Tar Heels" isn't a bad touch, but the redesigned Ram[e]ses looks awful. Who approved this new design?

I hope the old logo will be available because I refuse to buy anything with this new logo on it, and I hope other Tar Heels will boycott it as well!

Stephen Schneider '94[8]

Lux Libertas

*E*mblazoned on the great seal of the university is the motto *Lux Libertas*. These two simple Latin words, meaning light and liberty, render a fitting description of the mission of the institution that has set the standard for all public universities in the United States. Upon the dawn of the twenty-first century, it earned the singular honor of becoming the only public university in the nation to educate students and graduate classes in four different centuries. That it has been able to survive every war, every economic crisis, and every political and social change in American history since the Revolutionary War era is testimony to its unwavering commitment to be and remain the university of the people.

Aside from the lessons learned in some of the world's finest libraries and laboratories and in classrooms led by some of the most outstanding scholars in academia, generation after generation of Chapel Hill students have learned intangible lessons about the importance of freedom, tolerance, diversity, and the dignity of every human being. In 2001, Stuart Scott, the popular star of the ESPN cable network, returned to Chapel Hill to deliver the commencement address at his alma mater. His speech, laced with humor, acknowledged the value of the lessons of tolerance and diversity taught at the university.

Early in the new millennium, the university was beset by a number of attacks because of its commitment to diversity. As part of its required summer reading program for incoming freshmen in 2002, the university selected a work that offered selections from the holy book of Islam, as carefully translated and annotated by its author, Michael Sells. Fundamentalist Christian organizations joined with various taxpayers, students, and politicians to assail the choice of compulsory reading material. Unyielding in its determination to remain a source of light and liberty to the state, the university weathered the storm. In a speech entitled "A Tempest in a Textbook: Academic Freedom and the Qur'an Controversy," delivered in the Murrow Room at the National Press Club, Chancellor James Moeser praised the university for its steadfast adherence to the long-established principles of academic freedom and tolerance.

To ensure that the university would be the nation's leading public institution of higher learning in the new millennium, the Carolina First Campaign was initiated in 2000. Its goal of raising two billion dollars by December 31, 2007, was exceeded almost one year ahead of time. When the campaign was introduced to the public, Gene Nichol, then the dean of the law school, stressed its importance for the nation's oldest public university in a rousing speech: "A couple of years ago I was on a panel at Georgetown with a friend who was then the dean of the law school at the University of Virginia. During the course of the discussions, he explained that he was in charge 'of a school that has a quasi relationship with a university that has a quasi relationship with the state of Virginia.' In other words, he said, 'We're a private school and the quicker we can become completely private, the better we'll like it.' I replied, only half in jest, that this was 'yet one more piece of evidence that if Thomas Jefferson were alive today, he'd be a Tar Heel.' "[1]

But to achieve the avowed purpose of the Carolina First Campaign— to keep the Chapel Hill campus the place of light and liberty for the people of North Carolina—more than money would be needed. Erskine Bowles, the president of the consolidated university and the former chief of staff for

President Bill Clinton, infused a new spirit into the quest when he delivered the University Day address at his alma mater in 2006:

> Yes, Carolina defines quality, and nobody can give you that kind of reputation. You have to earn it. I love the fact that on every national ranking of educational value, Chapel Hill ranks right up there at or near the top—and for good reason. We earned it. But we who love Chapel Hill and we who work for this great university—we have a big job to do. We have a real responsibility, not just to maintain our well-deserved, well-earned reputation for quality and value—but to improve upon it, and to improve upon it so that we are unquestionably again the best public university in America. I don't want to hear excuses about why Berkeley or Michigan—or, for God's sake—Virginia rank ahead of us. The chancellor behind me knows that I am a zero-excuses guy. As Chancellor Moeser said not long ago in his "State of the University" address, "We must never—this University must never—be content with the status quo. Good enough is never good enough. Not for an institution that aspires to be America's leading public university."[2]

ooooo

Excerpt of Commencement Speech by Stuart Scott at Kenan Stadium
MAY 20, 2001

I am blessed to have gone to school here for four years. You are all blessed for the same reason. And you won't realize the depth of it until later on in life, and that's natural. All of us who have gone to school here, we know there is something very special about this place—the tradition, the campus, the social life, the academic life. That's why those kids down Highway 15-501 love to playa hate on us, don't they? Jealousy is an ugly emotion, isn't it?

> You can't be a bigger North Carolina basketball fan than Roy Williams.
>
> Roy Williams

Oh, by the way. Speaking of Duke, did you all hear the news? It's really good. Shane Battier has been granted special permission by the NCAA to go back to Duke and play college basketball as long as he likes. It's called ambassador status. And it's cool—no, it's good news for Duke 'cause you know they're no good in the NBA anyway. They're also gonna let Shane call his own fouls. One NCAA official said, "Our referees do their very best to help Shane out, but as everybody can see, especially from the February 1st game with North Carolina, they do occasionally inhibit his game. . . ."

Back to reality. Back to us. There is something that's a unique shared bond that all of us here at Carolina have. And in my business, I run into a whole lot of Tar Heel alums basically because, you know, we dominate the rosters of the NBA, NFL, Major League Baseball, soccer, track and field. We're all over the place. And every time we see one another, it's always the same thing: "Yo, what up, Tar Heel." We all do it. Well, all of us except Rasheed Wallace. I saw 'Sheed. I said, "Yo, what up, Tar Heel." He just stared at me. I had no other choice, man. I had to "T" him up twice and throw him out of the game.

Rasheed is different, and you know what? That's cool, that's OK. It is the beauty and it's one of the best things we learn here about Carolina. Diversity is special. And you all have probably had more diversity here than you will as you move forward. I know all of you want to do more than just get a job, go to grad school. I know you want to make a difference. Keep this in mind as you do that: Remember the walks of life that you've seen here, all the colors, races, religions, athletes, academic nuts, hippies, fraternity boys, sorority girls, different sexual make-ups. Understand whatever is different from you is just that—it's just different.[3]

ooooo

Excerpt from Speech of Chancellor James Moeser to the National Press Club in Washington, D.C.

AUGUST 27, 2002

For the past four years, as part of an effort to enrich the intellectual climate at Chapel Hill, we have asked all new freshmen and transfer students to take part in a summer reading program. They read an assigned book before they come to campus. Then, the day before classes begin, they attend small discussion sessions about the book. Our goal is to create an early expectation among students that they will think critically and discuss different points of view throughout their time at UNC.

This year, we evidently did the unthinkable. . . . We selected *Approaching the Qur'an: The Early Revelations*, by Michael Sells, a professor of religion at Haverford College. . . .

It is precisely in times like these in our history that it is important to reaffirm a university's role in addressing controversial subjects.

One of the many newspaper headlines said it best: "The University's summer reading program is about ideas, not indoctrination[.]" The role of the university is to educate, not to advocate. But an idea—especially an idea about religion, or an even more combustible mixture, religion and politics—is dangerous only when we don't have the critical thinking to examine it. . . .

The University of North Carolina has long been credited with taking the sons and daughters of mill hands and farmers and preparing them to be leaders. This is our proud legacy. Ferrel Guillory, who heads UNC's Program on Southern Politics, Media and Public Life, . . . points to John Egerton's book, *Speak Now Against the Day*, which is an account of the South in the 1930's, 40's, and 50's. Egerton says in this book, "The single most glowing exception to broad-based mediocrity in the Southern academic

> The people of Carolina have always found ways to do the remarkable, the right, the just thing. That is a characteristic that will forever mark this University.
>
> Chancellor James Moeser, 2003

world was the University of North Carolina at Chapel Hill. The University acquired a level of independence and quality that kept it in the front rank of public and private schools in the region."

. . . Today, at Chapel Hill we still have students from very small towns, but we also have students from very sophisticated big-city schools in North Carolina, from the District of Columbia, from the other 49 states and 100 countries. But wherever they hail from, our students all come to Chapel Hill to learn about themselves and the world in an atmosphere of open, free and rigorous inquiry.

That atmosphere has served our students and the state of North Carolina exceedingly well. A leading public university fearlessly tackles subjects that make all of us a little uncomfortable. . . . The only way we'll find answers to the really big issues facing our state, our nation, and our world is to create an environment of unfettered inquiry in which our students learn to think critically, ask tough questions and come to their own conclusions. . . .

. . . Throughout this controversy, a few of our critics have lumped UNC-Chapel Hill with the likes of Harvard and Berkeley.

That's the kind of guilt by association that I can embrace.[4]

ooooo

Excerpt from Speech of Gene Nichol Entitled, "On Being Great and Public: Or, Why I Work at Carolina"

When we speak at Carolina of striving to be the nation's leading public university, we believe that the term "public" relates to something more than ancestral pedigree—more than the happenstance of a university's founding.

> Silent Sam fires his musket every time a virgin passes by.
>
> Oft-repeated campus legend

The charge of a public university—its "public" mission—must mean something special, something distinctive. After all, private higher education had been the norm at the time William Richardson Davie opened our doors at New Hope Chapel Hill. Surely Carolina was meant to serve a need not then being met. And today, private higher education dominates the elite quarters of the American academy. Public higher education is not designed to be just a cheaper, mass-produced copy of its private counterparts. . . .

The University of North Carolina is hardly a perfect institution. But, in my judgment, we do have a near-perfect mission. We exist in order to secure a platform upon which to stand for the citizens of this state. We were created to assure that the daughters and sons of North Carolina—whether they are born high or low, black or white, rich or poor, rural or urban—have access to the best education and opportunity that the world has to offer. Carolina thrives, in Frank Porter Graham's words, in order to "savor and preserve . . . for even the poorest youth . . . the intellectual and spiritual resources of mankind."

So commitments to access and equality lie at the heart of the University of North Carolina's public mission. . . . If the bulk of modern higher education principally provides opportunity and expertise to the already-blessed, the University of North Carolina was literally created to pursue a different, more ennobling path. Our aspirations require it. Our constitution ratifies it.

And the echoes of our most inspiring leaders demand it. If, in a search for resources or prestige, we ever lose our grip on that mandate—the mandate of affordable, accessible, extraordinary education—the University of North Carolina will no longer truly exist. We would abandon a mission as clear as it is sacred. Virginia, Michigan and Texas may go another way. But not North Carolina.[5]

ooooo

Excerpt from Speech
of Erskine Bowles on University Day
OCTOBER 12, 2006

For you see, I just plain love Chapel Hill. It's true. I love this University to the very core. I am a Tar Heel born. I am a Tar Heel bred, and, by God, when I die I'll be as Tar Heel dead as you can be, and I hope to dickens I get lucky enough to be buried right here in my beloved Chapel Hill.

Serving as the 16th president of the University of North Carolina is by far—nothing else is even close—it's by far the single greatest honor I can imagine being given. Because I love what this University stands for and, particularly, what this campus stands for. It is proudly a public university and it is—this campus is—a university of the people. . . .

That's why in this new job of mine that I love I have to work as hard as I possibly can to hold down the cost of a college education and to do all I can to make sure that everyone that we accept into any of our universities graduates with a diploma that means something. A diploma at Chapel Hill has always, always meant something! I love the fact that a Chapel Hill degree means quality. It stands for excellence. But I agree whole-heartedly with Chancellor Moeser that Chapel Hill must again become the number-one public university in America.[6]

Notes

The following abbreviations are used in the notes:

NCC North Carolina Collection, Wilson Library, UNC
SHC Southern Historical Collection, Wilson Library, UNC

Introduction

1. *North Carolina Journal*, Oct. 30, 1793.
2. Allan Nevins, ed., *Polk: The Diary of a President, 1845–1849.*
3. Phillips Russell, *The Woman Who Rang the Bell: The Story of Cornelia Phillips Spencer*, 103.
4. Lucy Phillips Russell, "She Saw the University Open Its Doors Again," *Raleigh News & Observer*, Nov. 18, 1956.
5. Louis Round Wilson, *The University of North Carolina, 1900–1930* (hereafter cited as *University*), 37.
6. Ibid., 191–92.
7. Frank Porter Graham, "Commencement Talk," *Alumni Review* (May 1943).
8. "Remarks by the President at University of North Carolina, October 12, 1993," Office of the Press Secretary, the White House.

1792–1799: The Infant University

1. Blackwell P. Robinson, *William R. Davie*, 232.
2. *North Carolina Journal*, Sept. 25, 1793.
3. *North Carolina Journal*, Oct. 30, 1793.
4. *North Carolina Journal*, Feb. 25, 1795.
5. *North Carolina Journal*, June 22, 1795.
6. R. D. W. Connor et al., *A Documentary History of the University of North Carolina, 1776–1799*, vol. 2, 347–49.
7. Pettigrew Family Papers, file no. 592, SHC.
8. Ibid.
9. Ibid.

1800–1809: The New University Enters a New Century

1. Kemp Plummer Battle, *History of the University of North Carolina* (hereafter cited as *History*), vol. 1, 203.
2. University Papers, no. 40005, University Archives, UNC.
3. *University of North Carolina Magazine* 9 (June 1860).
4. University Papers, no. 40005, University Archives, UNC.
5. Ibid.

1810–1819: Challenges for the Young University

1. General Faculty and Faculty Council Records, no. 40106, University Archives, UNC.
2. Iveson Lewis Brookes Papers, no. 3249, SHC.
3. *Raleigh Minerva*, Oct. 18, 1816.
4. University Papers, no. 40005, University Archives, UNC.

1820–1829: The University As a Home Away from Home

1. Battle, *History*, vol. 2, 358–59.
2. Leander Hughes Papers, no. 1691, SHC.
3. Rufus Reid Papers, no. 2712, SHC.
4. Polk and Yeatman Family Papers, no. 606, SHC.
5. "Letter of Elisha Mitchell to the Parents, December 9, 1824," call no. Vcp 378, NCC.

1830–1839: Ups and Downs and in Between

1. Wilson and Hairston Papers, no. 4134, SHC.
2. "Poem by George M. Horton, September 1838," call no. VC 071 R16r, NCC.
3. University Papers, no. 40005, University Archives, UNC.
4. Pettigrew Family Papers, no. 592, SHC.
5. University Miscellaneous Papers (1802–1976), no. 3129, SHC.
6. John Francis Speight Papers, no. 3914, SHC.

1840–1849: Students, Students, Students

1. Pettigrew Family Papers, no. 592, SHC.
2. Ibid.
3. "Desultory Reflections—No. II. The College Campus," *North Carolina University Magazine* 1, no. 4 (June 1844).
4. *Chapel Hill Weekly*, Dec. 5, 1947.
5. University Papers, no. 40005, University Archives, UNC.

1850–1859: The Calm before the Storm

1. *North Carolina University Magazine* 9 (Sept. 1859): 108.
2. Clement Dowd, *Life of Zebulon B. Vance*, 22.
3. Daniel W. Barefoot, *Let Us Die Like Brave Men: Behind the Dying Words of Confederate Warriors*, 109.
4. Gustavus A. Henry Papers, no. 1431, SHC.
5. Dowd, *Life of Zebulon B. Vance*, 18–19.
6. Charles Lee Smith, *The History of Education in North Carolina*, 77.
7. Burgwyn Family Papers, no. 1687, SHC.
8. Ibid.

1860–1869: Promise Turns to Despair

1. *University of North Carolina Magazine* 9 (1860): 571–72.
2. Circular, May 1, 1861, University Papers, University Archives, UNC.
3. Julien Dwight Martin Papers, no. 3639-Z, SHC.
4. Jonathan Jacocks Papers, no. 372, SHC.
5. Henry Armand London Papers, no. 868-Z, SHC.
6. C. B. Mallett Papers, no. 3165, SHC.
7. Ruffin Thomson Papers, no. 3315, SHC.
8. *The Sentinel*, Apr. 6, 1869.

1870–1879: From the Ruins

1. Zebulon Baird Vance, *Sketches of North Carolina*, 57–58.

2. Records of the Board of Trustees of the University of North Carolina, no. 40001, University Archives, UNC.
3. Cornelia Phillips Spencer Papers, no. 683, SHC.
4. Ibid.
5. Ibid.
6. Battle, *History*, vol. 2, 583–86.
7. Henry William Faison Papers, no. 3789, SHC.

1880–1889: The "Frosh" Life

1. Kenan Family Papers, no. 4225, SHC.
2. Archibald Henderson, *The Campus of the First State University* (hereafter cited as *Campus*), 246.
3. L. A. Southern Papers, personal collection of Samuel O. Southern, Raleigh, N.C.
4. *Alumni Review* 62 (Nov. 1973).
5. Miscellaneous Personal Papers, University Archives, UNC.
6. Battle, *History*, vol. 2, 347.
7. Ibid., 348–49.
8. Ibid., 513–14.

1890–1899: The Centennial Campus Spirit

1. Daniel W. Barefoot, *General Robert F. Hoke: Lee's Modest Warrior*, 333.
2. William Starr Myers Papers, no. 3260, SHC.
3. Battle, *History*, vol. 2, 477.
4. John Worth McAlister Papers, no. 4321, SHC.
5. Henderson, *Campus*, 348–49.
6. *Alumni Review* 31 (Dec. 1942): 95–97.
7. William Starr Myers Papers, no. 3260, SHC.

1900–1909: Vision for the Twentieth Century

1. Battle, *History*, vol. 2, 588.
2. Ibid., 591–92.
3. Ibid., 623.

4. *Tar Heel*, Dec. 5, 1901.
5. Battle, *History*, vol. 2, 587–88.
6. "Letter from Francis P. Venable, Louis R. Wilson, and J. G. De Roulhac Hamilton to the Alumni and Friends of the University, September 25, 1909," Clipping File 1976–1989, NCC.
7. Battle, *History*, vol. 2, 644.
8. Ibid., 644–46.
9. *Yackety Yack* (1909).

1910–1919: Of Students and Their Teachers

1. *Carolina Quarterly* 52, no. 3 (Summer 2000).
2. Ibid.
3. *Chapel Hill Weekly*, Oct. 21, 1970.
4. Horace Williams Philosophical Society, *Horace Williams: Individualist, Teacher, Philosopher*.
5. *Alumni Review* 64 (Nov. 1975): eight-page supplement between pages 12 and 13.
6. "Drama in the South," University of North Carolina Clipping Service, vol. 4, 1015, NCC.
7. *Chapel Hill Weekly*, Oct. 21, 1970.

1920–1929: Tar Heels at Work and at Play

1. *Chapel Hill Newspaper*, Dec. 1, 1972.
2. Ibid.
3. *Raleigh News & Observer*, Dec. 16, 1956; *Chapel Hill Newspaper*, Sept. 8, 1974.
4. *Alumni Review* 79 (Winter 1990): 23–24.
5. *Tar Heel*, Jan. 28, 1925.
6. *Tar Heel*, Feb. 12, 1927.

1930–1939: A Benevolent University Family

1. Wilson, *University*, 593.
2. "Janitor Gives an Intimate View of Early College Life," unidentified

newspaper clipping, University of North Carolina Clipping File, vol. 10, 3178, NCC.

3. *Chapel Hill Weekly*, Nov. 27, 1931.
4. *Tar Heel Topics* (Summer 1935), NCC.
5. *Alumni Review* 24 (Feb. 1936): 143.
6. *Alumni Review* 67 (Sept. 1979): 16.
7. *Alumni Review* 65 (Sept. 1976): 8–11.

1940–1949: Fame in War and in Peace

1. *Chapel Hill Newspaper*, Oct. 13, 1985.
2. University of North Carolina Clipping File, vol. 15, 4649, NCC.
3. "Remembering Carolina," *UNC Tar Heel Alumnus* (Sept. 1983).
4. Allard Kenneth Lowenstein Papers, no. 4340, SHC.
5. *Chapel Hill Weekly*, Nov. 12, 1968; *Durham Morning Herald*, July 22, 1973.

1950–1959: Tests

1. *Raleigh News & Observer*, May 3, 1983; *Washington Post*, May 4, 1981.
2. *Raleigh News & Observer*, Feb. 20, 1952.
3. Oral history interview with Harvey E. Beech, Sept. 25, 1996, interview J-0075, Southern Oral History Program Collection no. 4007, SHC.
4. Leroy Benjamin Frasier Papers, no. 4375, SHC.
5. *Daily Tar Heel*, Feb. 16, 1957.
6. William Brantley Aycock, *Speeches and Statements of William Brantley Aycock: 1957–1989* (hereafter cited as *Speeches*), 18.
7. *Alumni Review* 76 (Fall 1987): 65–66.

1960–1969: Controversies from the Left and the Right

1. Aycock, *Speeches*, 94.
2. Ibid., 363–64.
3. Promotional transcript of a "Viewpoint" editorial from Jesse Helms of WRAL-TV, Nov. 26, 1968, call no. C384.5 H48v, NCC.
4. Karen L. Parker Diary, file no. 5275z, SHC.

5. Oral history interview with Daniel H. Pollitt, Feb. 22, 2001, interview K-0215, Southern Oral History Program Collection no. 4007, SHC.

6. "Reply by Chancellor Sitterson to a Set of Demands Presented to Him by the Black Student Movement," call no. Cb 378 UC 372, NCC.

7. Ibid.

8. University of North Carolina Clipping File, vol. 3, 721, NCC.

9. Ibid., 722.

10. Records of the Office of Chancellor—J. Carlyle Sitterson, series no. 40020, University Archives, UNC.

11. *Alumni Review* 87 (July–Aug. 1998).

12. *Alumni Review* 88 (Nov.–Dec. 1999).

1970–1979: The Endless Quest for Freedom, Support, and Excellence

1. Thomas M. Bello, "The Student Strike at the University of North Carolina at Chapel Hill" (hereafter referred to as "The Student Strike"), 60–61, NCC.

2. *Alumni Review* 62 (Nov. 1973).

3. *Alumni Review* 64 (Sept. 1975): 13.

4. *Alumni Review* 65 (Nov. 1976): 11.

5. *Alumni Review* 67 (Sept. 1978): 16.

6. Bello, "The Student Strike," 61–63.

7. Charles Ingram, "Remarks Made at Commencement, June 1, 1970," NCC.

8. Oral history interview with Blyden Jackson, June 27, 1991, interview L-0051, Southern Oral History Program Collection no. 4007, SHC.

9. Oral history interview with Frances Hogan, May 23, 1991, and June 3, 1991, interview L-0044, Southern Oral History Program Collection no. 4007, SHC.

10. *Alumni Review* 64 (Spring 1975): 13–14.

11. *Chapel Hill Newspaper*, May 12, 1976.

12. *Alumni Review* 67 (Sept. 1978): 16–17.

13. *Durham Morning Herald*, Apr. 28, 1978.

1980–1989: In Recognition of Greatness

1. *Chapel Hill Newspaper*, Oct. 13, 1985.

2. *Raleigh News & Observer*, Aug. 3, 1986.

3. *Alumni Review* 71 (Feb. 1983): 27.

4. *Raleigh News & Observer*, Aug. 3, 1986.

5. *Alumni Review* 72 (Summer 1984): 19.

6. "Commencement Address of Charles Kuralt, May 12, 1985," call no. Fcp 378 UKb, NCC.

7. *Alumni Review* 71 (Feb. 1983): 27.

8. *Carolina Blue*, Oct. 18, 1980.

9. *Alumni Review* 75 (Spring 1987): 8.

1990–1999: Two Hundred Sweet Years

1. Stephen J. Tepper, *The Chronicles of the Bicentennial Observance*, 78.

2. Ibid., 83–84.

3. Ibid., 127–28.

4. Ibid., 219–20.

5. *Alumni Review* 81 (Spring 1991): 6.

6. *University Gazette*, Oct. 18, 1995.

7. *Alumni Review* 84, no. 2 (March–Apr. 1995).

8. *Alumni Review* 85, no. 2 (March–Apr. 1996).

2000 and Beyond: *Lux Libertas*

1. "On Being Great and Public: Or, Why I Work at Carolina," Office of University Development, UNC.

2. "Address by UNC President Erskine Bowles, October 12, 2006," University News Services, UNC.

3. "Stuart Scott Speech, May 20, 2001," University News Services, UNC.

4. "A Tempest in a Textbook: Academic Freedom and the Qur'an Controversy, August 27, 2002," University News Services, UNC.

5. "On Being Great and Public: Or, Why I Work at Carolina," Office of University Development, UNC.

6. "Address by UNC President Erskine Bowles, October 12, 2006," University News Services, UNC.

Bibliography

Allcott, John V. *The Campus at Chapel Hill: Two Hundred Years of Architecture*. Chapel Hill: Chapel Hill Historical Society, 1986.

Ashby, Warren. *Frank Porter Graham: A Southern Liberal*. Winston-Salem, N.C.: John F. Blair, Publisher, 1980.

Aycock, William B. "A Brief History of the Name: The University of North Carolina at Chapel Hill." *Carolina Alumni Review* 80 (Fall 1991): 76–81.

Aycock, William Brantley. *Selected Speeches and Statements of William Brantley Aycock: 1957–1989*. Chapel Hill: Colonial Press, 1989.

Barefoot, Daniel W. *Let Us Die Like Brave Men: Behind the Dying Words of Confederate Warriors*. Winston-Salem, N.C.: John F. Blair, Publisher, 2005.

———. *Robert F. Hoke: Lee's Modest Warrior*. Winston-Salem, N.C.: John F. Blair, Publisher, 1996.

Barrett, John G. *Sherman's March Through the Carolinas*. Chapel Hill: University of North Carolina Press, 1956.

Barrier, Henry Smith. *On Carolina's Gridiron: A History of Football at the University of North Carolina*. Durham, N.C.: Seeman Printery, 1937.

Battle, Kemp Plummer. "An Address on the History of the Buildings of the University of North Carolina." *University Magazine* 3 (1883): 71–89.

———. "David Lowry Swain." *North Carolina Journal of Education* 3 (Sept. 1899): 27–30.

———. "Hinton James: The First Student of the University of North Carolina." *North Carolina University Magazine* 7 (1887–88): 1–6.

———. *History of the University of North Carolina*. 2 vols. Raleigh: Edwards and Broughton, 1907–12.

———. *Memories of an Old-Time Tar Heel*. Edited by William James Battle. Chapel Hill: University of North Carolina Press, 1945.

———. "The Opening of the University, January 15, 1795." *North Carolina University Magazine* 15 (1897–98): 22–28.

———. "Recollections of the University of North Carolina of 1844." *North Carolina University Magazine* 13 (1893–94): 289–318.

———. "Struggle and Story of the Re-Birth of the University." *North Carolina University Magazine* 17 (1899–1900): 303–21.

———. "War Clouds over the Campus, '61, '98, '17." *University of North Carolina Magazine* 35 (1917–18): 104–5.

Bello, Thomas M. "The Student Strike at the University of North Carolina at Chapel Hill (May 1970): An Eyewitness Historical Memoir." Honors thesis, UNC, 1971. North Carolina Collection, Wilson Library, UNC.

Bishop, Don. "Tom Wolfe as a Student." *Carolina Magazine* (March 1942): 28–29, 35, 47–48.

Bursey, Maurice J. *Francis Preston Venable of the University of North Carolina.* Chapel Hill: Chapel Hill Historical Society, 1989.

Caldwell, Joseph. *Autobiography and Biography of Rev. Joseph Caldwell.* Chapel Hill: J. B. Neathery, 1860.

Chamberlain, Hope Summerell. *Old Days in Chapel Hill: Being the Life and Letters of Cornelia Phillips Spencer.* Chapel Hill: University of North Carolina Press, 1926.

Coates, Albert. *Edward Kidder Graham, Harry Woodburn Chase, Frank Porter Graham: Three Men in the Transition of the University of North Carolina at Chapel Hill from a Small College to a Great University.* Chapel Hill: privately published, 1988.

———. "Tom Wolfe As I Remember Him: A Very Personal Recollection." *Alumni Review* 64 (Nov. 1975): eight-page supplement between pages 12 and 13.

———. "The University in War Time." *University of North Carolina Magazine* 35 (1917–18): 106–11.

———. *What the University of North Carolina Means to Me: A Report to the Chancellors and Presidents and to the People with Whom I Have Lived and Worked from 1914 to 1969.* Richmond, Va.: William Byrd Press, 1969.

———. "William Brantley Aycock." *Alumni Review* 45 (1956–57): xix–xxi. Reprinted from *Popular Government.*

———. "William Clyde Friday." *Alumni Review* 45 (1956–57): iii–v. Reprinted from *Popular Government.*

Coates, Gladys Hall. *Fifty Years with Albert Coates.* Chapel Hill: University of North Carolina Press, 1980.

Cobb, Collier. "Mrs. Cornelia Phillips Spencer." *University of North Carolina Magazine* 25 (1907–8): 261–69.

Coffin, James P. "Chapel Hill at the Close of the Civil War." *North Carolina University Magazine* 18 (1900–1901): 272–75.

Coker, W. C. "Our Campus." *University of North Carolina Magazine* 33 (1915–16): 173–76.

Connor, R. D. W. "Connor Address Is Brief University History." *Alumni Review* 35 (1946–47).

———. "The Historic University, 1795–1945." *Alumni Review* 29 (1940–41): 264–66.

———. "Morehead Is Illustrious in State History." *Alumni Review* 14 (1925–26): 41–42.

Connor, R. D. W., Louis R. Wilson, and Hugh T. Lefler. *A Documentary History of the University of North Carolina, 1776–1799.* 2 vols. Chapel Hill: University of North Carolina Press, 1953.

Coulter, E. Merton. "Early Life and Regulations at the University of North Carolina." *University of North Carolina Magazine* 29 (Feb. 1912): 9–13.

Creecy, R. B. "University Days Seventy Years Ago." *University of North Carolina Magazine* 20 (1902–3): 89–96.

Donald, David Herbert. *Look Homeward: A Life of Thomas Wolfe.* Boston: Little, Brown, 1987.

Dowd, Clement. *Life of Zebulon B. Vance.* Charlotte, N.C.: Observer Printing and Publishing House, 1897.

Duls, Henry D. "History of Baseball at Carolina: Thirty Years of Intercollegiate Baseball, 1892 through 1922." *Carolina Magazine* 40 (May–June 1923): 3–5.

Eaton, Clement. "Edwin A. Alderman: Liberal of the New South." *North Carolina Historical Review* 23 (1946): 206–21.

Emken, Judy. "Cornelia Phillips Spencer: An Influential Nineteenth Century Woman." Honors thesis, UNC, 1980. North Carolina Collection, Wilson Library, UNC.

Fimrite, Ron. "A Long Locomotive for Choo-Choo." *Alumni Review* 61 (Nov. 1973): 20–22. Reprinted from *Sports Illustrated.*

Flagler, Bunky. "The Happy Transition from Editor Royster to Professor Royster." *Alumni Review* 62 (Jan. 1974): 10–13.

Floren, Gillian Dae. "Speaking Freely: UNC-CH Administrators Respond to Freedom of Expression, 1963–1970." Master's thesis, UNC, 1989. North Carolina Collection, Wilson Library, UNC.

Fordham, Christopher C. *University of North Carolina at Chapel Hill: The First State University.* New York: Newcomen Society of the United States, 1985.

Friday, William Clyde. "Why Are Carolina Alumni So Loyal?" *Alumni Review* 65 (Nov. 1976): 10–11.

Gass, W. Conrad. "Kemp Plummer Battle and the Development of Historical Instruction at the University of North Carolina." *North Carolina Historical Review* 45 (1968): 122.

Giduz, Roland. "Bill Friday Recalls Dr. Frank." *Alumni Review* 65 (Nov. 1976): 14–17.

————. " 'The Great Event' Is Revealed by 'Dr. Frank.' " *Alumni Review* 65 (Sept. 1966): 8–11.

————. "How Did It Look?: The Campus in 1818." *Alumni Review* 64 (May 1976): 9–12.

Graham, Edward K. "Address to Welcome the War Classes at the Commencement of 1911." *University of North Carolina Magazine* 29 (Oct. 1911): 10–12.

Graham, Frank P. "Evolution, the University and the People." *Alumni Review* 13 (1924–25): 205–7.

————. "A Football Ramble." *University of North Carolina Magazine* 32 (1914–15): 48–53.

Gullick, J. G. "Francis P. Venable." *Carolina Magazine* 39 (March 1922): 24–26.

Gunter, Timothy Lee. "No Reds in Blue Heaven: A Discourse on the Passage, Amendment, and Repeal of the North Carolina Communist Speaker Ban Law." Honors thesis, UNC. North Carolina Collection, Wilson Library, UNC.

Hamilton, J. G. De Roulhac. "The Return of the War Classes." *University of North Carolina Magazine* 29 (Oct. 1911): 16–24.

Henderson, Archibald. *The Campus of the First State University.* Chapel Hill: University of North Carolina Press, 1949.

————. "Fifty Years at the University." *The State* 12 (June 24, 1944): 7.

————. "The Heritage of the University of North Carolina Man." *University of North Carolina Magazine* 26 (May 1909): 3–12.

————. "The Laying of the Cornerstone." *The State* 36 (Feb. 4, 1950): 18.

Hill, G. Maurice. " 'Dr. Frank' Held Them in the Palm of His Hand," *Alumni Review* 64 (May 1976): 4–8.

Hooper, William. "Fifty Years Since." *North Carolina University Magazine* 9 (1859–60): 577–611.

Horace Williams Philosophical Society. *Horace Williams: Individualist, Teacher, Philosopher.* Chapel Hill: Horace Williams Philosophical Society, 1970.

Horner, William E. "Episodes in the Career of James K. Polk: A Man Whose Watchwords Were Duty and Diligence." *New Carolina Magazine* 38 (March 1921): 18–23.

House, Robert B. *The Light That Shines: Chapel Hill, 1912–1916.* Chapel Hill: University of North Carolina Press, 1964.

Huggins, Leonard Victor. *Anecdotes.* Edited by Roland Giduz. Chapel Hill: privately published, 1981.

Hughes, James P. "A Tribute to Frank Porter Graham." *Alumni Review* 76 (Winter 1987): 15–17.

Hutchinson, Glenn. "Carolina Goes to War: A Lesson from Campus History, 1915–1919." *Carolina Magazine* 67 (Dec. 1937): 3–7.

Ivey, Pete. "President Friday Already Has Shown Vigorous Leadership." *Alumni Review* 45 (1956–57): 147.

Jackson, Blyden. "George Moses Horton, North Carolinian." *North Carolina Historical Review* 53 (1976): 140–47.

Jones, Anne. "Mr. Bennett's University." *Alumni Review* 59 (May 1971): 26–27.

Jones, H. G. "Preserving North Carolina's Literary Heritage." *Popular Government* 55 (Winter 1990): 20–28.

Joyce, Bob. "Reds on Campus: The Speaker Ban Controversy." *Carolina Alumni Review* 72 (Spring 1984): 4–11, 25.

Kennedy, Richard S. *The Window of Memory: The Literary Career of Thomas Wolfe.* Chapel Hill: University of North Carolina Press, 1962.

Kitchin, Reed. "The *Tar Heel.*" *Carolina Magazine* 41 (May 1924): 29–36.

———. "The *Yackety Yack.*" *Carolina Magazine* 41 (June 1924): 22–29.

Koch, Frederick H. "Twenty-five Years at Chapel Hill." *National Theatre Conference Bulletin* 6 (June 1944): 13–24.

Kuralt, Charles. "From a Village of Scholars on a Hill." *Alumni Review* 74 (Winter 1986): 21–22.

Lauder, Val. "Thinking of You: The Living Legacy of Kay Kyser '27." *Alumni Review* 79 (Winter 1990): 22–29.

Leigh, Daniel. "Adventures of Rameses." *The State* 50 (Nov. 1982): 14–16.

Lewis, McDaniel. "Early Athletics." *University of North Carolina Magazine* 31 (1913–14): 358–64.

Lewis, Richard H. "Athletics in the University, Muscular and Vocal, Forty Years Ago." *North Carolina University Magazine* 14 (1894–95): 98–100.

Link, Arthur Stanley. "A History of the Buildings at the University of North Carolina." Honors thesis, UNC, 1941. North Carolina Collection, Wilson Library, UNC.

Madry, Robert W. "The University Celebrates." *The State* 11 (Oct. 23, 1943): 6–7.

Malone, Dumas. *Edwin A. Alderman: A Biography.* New York: Doubleday, Doran, and Company, 1940.

Mangnum, Charles S. "Recalls Football's Genesis at Chapel Hill." *Alumni Review* 23 (1934–35): 54, 62.

————. "Those Were the Days When." *Alumni Review* 23 (1934–35): 148–49.

Manning, John. "The University and State History." *North Carolina University Magazine* 9 (1899–90): 131–33.

Martin, Carolyn Patricia. "The North Carolina Collection in the University of North Carolina." Master's thesis, UNC. North Carolina Collection, Wilson Library, UNC.

Matson, Robert. "The Morehead Legacy: A History of 'Uncle Mot's' Contributions to UNC-CH, the State, and the Nation." *Alumni Review* 77 (Spring 1988): 16–23.

Maultsby, R. C. "On the Gridiron." *Carolina Magazine* 40 (May–June 1923): 8–11.

McAlister, A. W. "Recalls Old Days in Chapel Hill." *Alumni Review* 20 (1931–32): 281–82.

Moser, Artus M. "Old Days at the University." *New Carolina Magazine* 38 (March 1921): 40–42.

————. "The School Days of Zebulon Baird Vance." *Carolina Magazine* 39 (Nov. 1, 1921): 6–8.

Moss, William D. "Henry Horace Williams and His Message." *Carolina Magazine* 40 (Feb. 1923): 17–21.

Neal, Louise. "The Immortal 'Proff.'" *The State* 15 (Nov. 15, 1947): 11.

Nevins, Allan, ed. *Polk: The Diary of a President, 1845–1849*. New York: Longmans, Green & Company, 1952.

Nowell, Elizabeth. *Thomas Wolfe: A Biography*. Garden City, N.Y.: Doubleday, 1960.

O'Callaghan, Erin. "For Whom the Governor Tolls." *The State* 58 (Oct. 1990): 29–30.

Parker, Roy, Jr. "Bob House: Credentials of Excellence." *Alumni Review* (Fall 1987): 69.

Pearson, T. G. "The Dialectic Literary Society." *North Carolina University Magazine* 16 (1898–99): 85–89.

Pollitt, Daniel H. "Campus Censorship: Statute Barring Speakers from State Educational Institutions." *North Carolina Law Review* 42 (1963–64): 179–99.

Powell, William S. *The First State University: A Pictorial History of the University of North Carolina*. Chapel Hill: University of North Carolina Press, 1972.

————. "University Days of the Past." *Alumni Review* 64 (Nov. 1975): 8–9.

Pugh, J. F. "The History of the Library of North Carolina." *University of*

North Carolina Magazine 31 (1913–14): 207–13.

Robinson, Blackwell P. *William R. Davie.* Chapel Hill: University of North Carolina Press, 1957.

Royster, Vermont. "Change and Controversy in Chapel Hill." *Alumni Review* 67 (Sept. 1978): 16–17.

Russell, Phillips. *These Old Stone Walls.* Chapel Hill: University of North Carolina Press, 1972.

———. *The Woman Who Rang the Bell: The Story of Cornelia Phillips Spencer.* Chapel Hill: University of North Carolina Press, 1949.

Sanders, J. Maryon. "Chase Decade Marks Eminent Achievement." *Alumni Review* 18 (1929–30): 156–58.

Sanders, John. "Albert Coates: Institution Builder." *North Carolina Law Review* 67 (Apr. 1989): 747–48.

Sanders, John L., ed. "The Journal of Ruffin Wirt Tomlinson, the University of North Carolina, 1841–1842." *North Carolina Historical Review* 30 (1953): 86–114, 233–60.

Schumann, Marguerite. *The First State University: A Walking Guide.* Chapel Hill: University of North Carolina Press, 1972.

Sellers, Charles Grier, Jr. "Jim Polk Goes to Chapel Hill." *North Carolina Historical Review* 29 (1952): 189–203.

Smith, Charles Lee. *The History of Education in North Carolina.* Washington, D.C.: Government Printing Office, 1888.

Smylie, Jonathan. "Carolina Now Has 14 Pulitzer Winners." *Alumni Review* 70 (June 1982): 4–8.

Snider, Jane. "Women at Carolina: From 'The Petticoat Invasion' to Coed Dorms." *Alumni Review* 59 (May 1971): 18–20.

Snider, William D. *Light on the Hill: A History of the University of North Carolina at Chapel Hill.* Chapel Hill: University of North Carolina Press, 1992.

Spearman, Walter. *The Carolina Playmakers: The First Fifty Years.* Chapel Hill: University of North Carolina Press, 1970.

Spencer, Cornelia Phillips. "Dr. Joseph Caldwell: A Study." *North Carolina University Magazine* 12 (1892–93): 45–55.

———. "Old Days in Chapel Hill." *University Monthly* 3 (1883–84): 289–93, 326–29, 394–98; *University Monthly* 4 (1884–85): 15, 22.

———. *Selected Papers of Cornelia Phillips Spencer.* Edited by Louis R. Wilson. Chapel Hill: University of North Carolina Press, 1953.

Stahr, Alden. "Thomas Wolfe at Chapel Hill." *Carolina Magazine* 61 (Apr. 10, 1932): 1–8.

Stancill, Jane. "It Was Wartime." *Alumni Review* 76 (Fall 1987): 43–46.

Stephens, Florence W. "Getting Next to a Great Man Is an Easy Proposition." *Alumni Review* 15 (1926–27): 119, 140.

Stone, Richard G. "The Graham Plan of 1935: An Aborted Crusade to Deemphasize College Athletics." *North Carolina Historical Review* 64 (July 1987): 274–93.

Sumner, Jim L. "The North Carolina Inter-Collegiate Foot-Ball Association: The Beginnings of College Football in North Carolina." *North Carolina Historical Review* 65 (1988): 263–86.

Tennille, Norton F., Jr. "Things That Never Happened." *Alumni Review* (Fall 1987): 65–68.

Tepper, Stephen J. *The Chronicles of the Bicentennial Observance.* Chapel Hill: University of North Carolina Press, 1998.

Terry, Walter. "Solomon Pool: The Forgotten President." *Carolina Magazine* 62 (May 14, 1933): 5, 7.

Thorpe, Judith L. "A Study of the Peace Movement at the University of North Carolina at Chapel Hill Viewed within the Context of the Nation, 1964–1971." Master's thesis, UNC. North Carolina Collection, Wilson Library, UNC.

Tilley, Greta. "The Man As President: It's Not a Simple Thing." *Alumni Review* 74 (Winter 1986): 23–25.

Tomberlin, B. M. "William Richardson Davie." Master's thesis, UNC. North Carolina Collection, Wilson Library, UNC.

Turnbull, Andrew. *Thomas Wolfe.* New York: Scribner's, 1967.

Vance, Zebulon B. "The Life and Character of Hon. David L. Swain." *University Magazine* 1 (1878): 73–93.

Vance, Zebulon Baird. *Sketches of North Carolina.* Norfolk, Va.: Norfolk Landmark, 1875.

Vickers, James. "The Hill Family Legacy." *Alumni Review* 75 (Spring 1987): 25–29.

Waddell, Alfred M. *The Ante-Bellum University: Oration Delivered at the Celebration of the Centennial of the University of North Carolina, June 5th, 1895.* Wilmington, N.C.: Jackson & Bell, 1895.

Wagstaff, Henry M. *Impressions of Men and Movements at the University of North Carolina.* Edited by Louis R. Wilson. Chapel Hill: University of North Carolina Press, 1950.

Walker, Thomas H. "Television Station Meets with Good Reception." *Alumni Review* 43 (1954–55): 98–105.

Walser, Richard. *Thomas Wolfe: Undergraduate.* Durham, N.C.: Duke University Press, 1977.

Weaver, Fred H. "The Tradition of Student Life at Chapel Hill." *Carolina*

Quarterly 5 (Spring 1953): 14–22.

Webb, W. R., Jr. "Anecdote and Reminiscence." *North Carolina University Magazine* 14 (1894–95): 267–71.

Weeks, Stephen B. "Biographical Sketches of the Confederate Dead of the University of North Carolina." *North Carolina University Magazine* 7 (1887–88): 35–40, 83–86, 109–13, 171–76, 232–36; *North Carolina University Magazine* 8 (1888–89): 27–29, 75–79, 176–79, 227–31, 271–74; *North Carolina University Magazine* 9 (1889–90): 25–28, 80–82, 140–43, 198–201, 340–45; *North Carolina University Magazine* 10 (1890–91): 102–9, 160–66.

———. "The University of North Carolina in 1805." *North Carolina University Magazine* 13 (1893–94): 328–29.

———. "The University of North Carolina in the Civil War." *University of North Carolina Magazine* 28 (Nov. 1910): 5–17.

Wicker, Tom. "The Future of the University at the End of an Era." *Alumni Review* 74 (Winter 1986): 7–19.

———. "The Legacy of Dr. Frank." *Alumni Review* 80 (Spring 1981): 8–12.

Williams, Henry Horace. *The Education of Horace Williams.* Chapel Hill: privately published, 1936.

Williams, J. Derek. " 'It Wasn't Slavery Time Anymore': Foodworkers' Strike at Chapel Hill, Spring 1969." Master's thesis, UNC. North Carolina Collection, Wilson Library, UNC.

Wilson, Louis R. "The Acquisition of the Stephen B. Weeks Collection of Caroliniana." *North Carolina Historical Review* 42 (1965): 424–29.

———. *The Chronicles of the Sesquicentennial.* Chapel Hill: University of North Carolina Press, 1947.

———. *Harry Woodburn Chase.* Chapel Hill: University of North Carolina Press, 1960.

———. *The Library of the First State University.* Chapel Hill: University of North Carolina Press, 1960.

———. *Louis Round Wilson's Historical Sketches.* Durham, N.C.: Moore Publishing Company, 1976.

———. *The University of North Carolina, 1900-1930: The Making of a Modern University.* Chapel Hill: University of North Carolina Press, 1957.

Winston, George T. "The University of To-day." *North Carolina University Magazine* 13 (1893–94): 325–28.

Winston, Robert Watson. *Horace Williams: Gadfly of Chapel Hill.* Chapel Hill: University of North Carolina Press, 1942.

Index

Pool, Solomon, 82, 87–88, 90, 91–92
Powell, William S., 5, 202, 204, 205
president's house, 14
Princeton University, 5, 32, 33, 34, 38
Program on Southern Politics, Media, and Public Life, 227
Public Health, School of, 14, 15, 197
Public Welfare, School of, 13

Radical Republicans, 8
Raleigh, 14, 21, 82, 86, 102, 147, 160, 175, 193, 198, 214
Raleigh Minerva, 39, 42
Raleigh News & Observer, 153
Raleigh Register, 53, 54
Rameses, xi, 13, 138, 140–41, 203, 222
Ramsey, John Ambrose, 37, 39–40
Randolph-Macon College, 62
Ransom, Paul J., 139, 143–44
Republican Party, 38
Return of Buck Gavin, The, 134
Revolutionary War, 3, 17
Rhodes Scholars, 166, 188
Rice, Homer, 195
Richmond College, 113
Rockingham County, 100, 103
Rocky Mount, 199
Rondthaler, Howard, 113
Rooke, Leon, 75
Roosevelt, Franklin D., 147, 152, 153
Royster, Vermont, 17, 20, 146–47, 151–52, 180, 191, 198–99
Ruark, Robert, 17
Russell, Lucy Phillips, 8
Russell, Phillips, 208

Sanders, John, 208, 217
Sanford, Terry, 190, 196–97, 202, 208, 217
Saunders Hall, 12
Saunders, William L., 97
Scheuer, Sandy, 192
Schneider, Stephen, 221–22
Schroeder, William K., 192
Scott, Charlie, 175, 181
Scott, Randolph, 17
Scott, Robert W., 176
Scott, Stuart, 223, 225–26
Seawell, Chub, 179
Sells, Michael, 224, 227

Sentinel, The, 82
Sessoms, Preston H., 81, 83–84
Sharp, Paul F., Jr., 16, 176
Shelby Daily Star, 35
Shelton, Karen, 216
Shephard, William Biddle, 38, 42–43
"Silent Sam." *See* Confederate Memorial Statue
Sinclair, Neil A., 101, 106–7
Sitterson, J. Carlyle, 16, 48, 64, 175, 176, 181, 182–83, 184–85
Sloan, Norman, 200
Smith, Dean, xi, 121, 165, 175, 181, 184, 199, 200, 206
Smith, Franklin Lafayette, 45–46, 48–49
Smith Hall, 10, 158
Smith, Sidney, 82
Snavely, Carl, 162
Sneede, William M., 25
South (Main) Building, 5, 14, 33, 149, 151, 188
Southern Historical Collection, 155
Southern, Leonard Anderson, 100, 102–4
Spaight, Richard Dobbs, 5, 22–23, 25
Spangler, C. D., Jr., 170, 203, 210–11, 213, 217
Speak Now Against the Day, 227
Speaker Ban Law, 16, 174–75, 177–78, 179
Spear, Bob, 165
Spearman, Walter, 208
Spencer, Cornelia Phillips, 7, 8, 9, 82, 88–89, 93–94, 94–95, 96, 189
Spencer Residence Hall, 12, 158
Steele Hall, 12
Sun Bowl, 214
Swain, David Lowry: as teacher at UNC, 72, 75–76, 88; assists students, 72, 74; contacted by Joshua Perry, 58–59; death of, 97; efforts to save UNC during Civil War, 7, 81, 82, 86; honored at reopening, 96; praised by Zebulon B. Vance, 76; service as UNC president, 8, 148, 205; succeeds Joseph Caldwell as president, 6, 26, 52, 55
Swain, Ella, 86
Swain Hall, 15
Swofford, Oliver, 17

Tar Heel. See Daily Tar Heel

Hark the Sound of Tar Heel Voices